New Perspectives in Typography

DATE DUE	RETURNED

LAURENCE KING

Published in 2015 by
Laurence King Publishing Ltd
361–373 City Road
London EC1V 1LR
T +44 (0)20 7841 6900
F +44 (0)20 7841 6910
email: enquiries@laurenceking.com
www.laurenceking.com

A catalogue record for this book
is available from the British Library

ISBN: 978 1 78067 306 6

Edited and designed by A2/SW/HK

Printed in China

**Edited by Scott Williams
& Henrik Kubel**

New Perspectives
in Typography

Philippe Apeloig
ARC (RCA) journal
Phil Baines
André Baldinger
Ludovic Balland
Marian Bantjes
Jonathan Barnbrook
Nick Bell Design
Jop Van Bennekom
      & Veronica Ditting
Laurent Benner
Pierre Bernard
Bibliothèque
Michael Bierut
Peter Bil'ak
Nicholas Blechman
Sara De Bondt Studio
Irma Boom Office
Erich Brechbühl
Anthony Burrill
Cartlidge Levene
Atelier Carvalho Bernau
Change is Good
Commercial Type
De Designpolitie
Dot Dot Dot magazine
Doyle Partners
Markus Dreßen/Spector
      Bureau
Atelier Dyakova
Esterson Associates
e-Types
Experimental Jetset
Farrow
Ed Fella
Frost* Design
FUEL
Till Gathmann
Gavillet & Rust
James Goggin
Graphic Thought Facility
Julia Hasting
Jonathan Hoefler &
      Tobias Frere-Jones
Hort
Thomas Huot-Marchand
Gary Hustwit
David James
      & Gareth Hague
Julia
karlssonwilker inc
Zak Kyes/Zak Group
Scott King
Alan Kitching
Joerg Koch
Kontrapunkt
Rasmus Koch Studio
L2M3
Jürg Lehni

Made Thought
Karel Martens
Pablo Martin
Peter Mendelsund
Metahaven
Niels Shoe Meulman
J. Abbott Miller
Monocle
Julian Morey
John Morgan Studio
Norm
North
Optimo
OurType
David Pearson
David Pidgeon
Playtype/e-Types
Mark Porter
Project Projects
Sagmeister Inc.
Office of Paul Sahre
Peter Saville
Paula Scher
Ralph Schraivogel
Erik Spiekermann
Spin
Astrid Stavro
Stockholm Design Lab
Studio Dumbar
Studio Frith
Suburbia
Jeremy Tankard
Thonik
Triboro
Troika
Niklaus Troxler
Richard Turley
Andreas Uebele
Value and Service
Vier5
Micha Weidmann Studio
Why Not Associates
Cornel Windlin
Martin Woodtli

New Perspectives
in Typography

Scott Williams & Henrik Kubel
A2/SW/HK

Foreword

This book is not an attempt to identify a new movement, latest trends in graphic design, or present a manifesto. Nor is it a definitive survey. But rather a 'selection' of work that we feel demonstrates an intelligent, thoughtful and, above all, inspirational use of typography. *New Perspectives in Typography* sets out to uncover some of the ideas that preoccupy contemporary designers, and hopefully offers a range of responses to the question of what applied typography might mean today.

Broadly international in scope, our selection features the work over 100 designers from more than 20 countries, and charts work produced by typographers and graphic designers during the postmillennial era, including the work of established names within graphic design, alongside the work of a generation of emerging designers. *New Perspectives in Typography* celebrates the handmade; bespoke and made-to-measure type; customized or bastardized versions of pre-existing fonts; the use of freely available typefaces in inventive ways; and how technology has impacted on contemporary design.

Across cultures there seems to be a renewed interest in all things type. A greater public awareness of typography is in part due to the access ordinary people now have to type and type selection on their personal computers and mobile devices. Following on from this trend are the efforts of designers, journalists and curators to bring the once esoteric art of typography to a broader audience.

Recent examples of this democratization include: *Helvetica*, the feature-length documentary marking the 50th anniversary of the eponymous typeface (directed by Gary Hustwit and released in 2007); the publication of *Just My Type* by Simon Garfield in 2010, and now an international bestseller; MoMA, New York's acquisition of 23 influential typefaces from the past century for their permanent collection; and the advent of the physical type shop, notably the Playtype Concept Store that opened in Copenhagen in late 2010, offering a genuine retail experience. And not to forget the numerous type pop-up stores that have quickly followed suit.

This book features type that we feel is truly ground-breaking, produced by pioneers in the field of contemporary design. Some works are distinguished by their originality, offering new perspectives on the discipline or presenting a distinct personal voice. Other featured examples are intelligent responses to a specific problem posed by a client or a keenly observed opportunity to play or subvert an established idiom. Some are simply supremely well crafted—a pejorative term a decade ago—an interest that has made a comeback during this period.

Arguably some of the examples are well known, and may be familiar to many readers, but our motivation has been to represent the work that is truly important and vital to us, irrespective of exposure or familiarity: to present seminal work produced by established practitioners as well as the work of an emerging generation of younger designers.

We are not setting out to be the arbiters of a perceived 'good taste', or to delineate good from bad, but modestly to present a selection of work we admire. To some extent our choices will inevitably reflect our own aesthetic preferences and individual sensibilities, but we have endeavoured to put our personal tastes aside in order to focus on work that has a certain conceptual rigour, and ultimately a story to tell.

It has been an honour to work with the writers Rick Poynor, Paul Shaw, Emily King, Monika Parrinder and Colin Davies, who have contributed illuminating essays that offer broader cultural and art-historical perspectives on the work we have selected. Paul Shaw has contributed a comprehensive overview of twentieth-century typographic design, chronicling the significant figures and moments that have shaped the contemporary design scene; Monika Parrinder and Colin Davies investigate 'Type Today' and the impact new technologies have had on current design practice; Emily King explores the link between graphic design and the use of typography within contemporary art; and Rick Poynor provides an insightful introduction and the contextual framework for the collection of type presented in this book. Our thanks also to Michael Evamy who researched and wrote the text for the extended captions in the Designer's section.

And finally, we also extend our thanks to Deirdre Kelly and the team at Laurence King Publishing: Laurence King (publisher), Jo Lightfoot (commissioning editor), Donald Dinwiddie (senior editor), Rosanna Lewis (copy-edit) and Angela Koo (proofread), Sue Farr (index), Rosie Martin, Rebecca Moldenhauer and Giulia Hetherington (picture research), Ida Riveros (photography) and Felicity Awdry (production).

Paul Shaw

A Typographic Legacy

A short history of twentieth-century typography is destined to be one of three things: superficial, full of gaping holes, or a droning litany of people, works and dates. A different approach is needed. The one chosen here is to single out a handful of individuals and companies who have exerted an outsized impact on it, whose influence has been either broad or long-lasting—or, in some instances, both. This is a roll-call not of the best, most exciting, most innovative or coolest typographic designers of the past 100 years, but of those whose work or ideas have reverberated the most. There are 20 individuals and 8 companies. Although most are obvious candidates, a few will be surprising.

William Morris
The multi-talented William Morris (1834–96) has had an impact on twentieth-century typography that goes far beyond the immediate sensation produced by his Kelmscott Press books in the 1890s. The private press mania he precipitated has never wholly gone away—the current boom in letterpress printers is proof of that—but it is not his central typographic legacy.

The Kelmscott Press, founded in 1891 but in the works for several years before that, established the modern notion of the well-made book, of which all elements were of the highest quality and workmanship, from its materials (paper, ink and typeface) to its design (layout, ornamentation and illustration) to its execution (printing and binding). Morris emphasized the total work of art (*Gesamtwerk*). In doing so he elevated the role of type in design to a key position as the initial building block for a page layout and, hence, for a book. The other elements—initials, ornaments and illustrations—were subsequently created to be in tonal and aesthetic harmony with it. Although Morris's medieval aesthetic has been rejected by most designers since his death, his notion of the importance of the typeface has become a central tenet of design.

Morris's first face, the Golden Type (1890), was based on the incunabula types of the fifteenth-century printers Nicholas Jenson and Jacobus Rubeus. He designed it using photographic enlargements of pages from their books, although he did not trace their letters. This was the first time that photography had been used as part of the process of type design, a practice that soon became commonplace and is still a model (albeit with scans often replacing photographs) for much contemporary font design.

Golden Type was the first instance of historicism in type design, the practice of looking to past types as the model for present ones. It spurred other private press owners to do the same—with most looking to Jenson's roman, widely viewed as the most perfect roman ever devised—and type foundries quickly followed suit. With Golden Type Morris had initiated the now common, though often divisive, idea of typeface revivals.

Jenson's roman is dark, a deliberate rebuke on Morris's part to what he saw as the feeble text type of the Victorian age. But it was not dark enough for him, so his second type, the Troy Type, was a rotunda inspired by the fifteenth-century blackletters of Peter Schoeffer, Johannes Mentelin and Günther Zainer. Initially, type foundries jumped on Morris's new fashion, but they soon realized that blackletter was not going to be a lasting craze. Instead they turned to making heavier, darker romans—dubbed 'rugged' by American Type Founders—which were quickly embraced by the emerging advertising industry. Similar rugged romans became part of the arsenal of commercial artists from Lucian Bernhard in Germany to the Beggarstaff Brothers in England to Oswald Cooper in the United States, whose lettering itself became the basis for typefaces in this vein. Morris had unwittingly inspired a new breed of bold faces, intended for text as much as for display, and helped define the face of advertising typography.

Title spread of Dante Gabriel Rossetti's
Ballads and Narrative Poems
William Morris, Kelmscott Press
1893

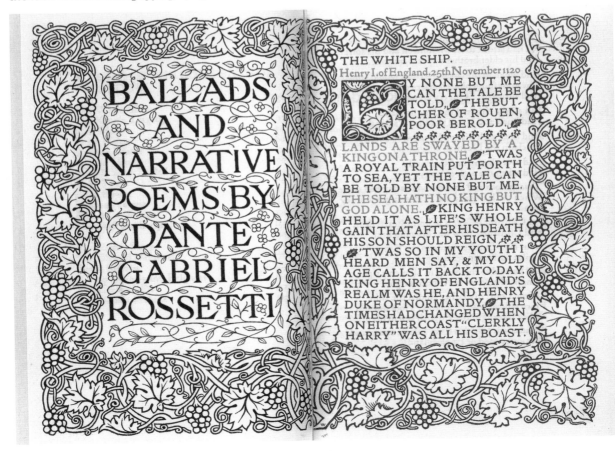

American Type Founders: Linn Boyd Benton, Morris Fuller Benton and Henry Lewis Bullen

American Type Founders (ATF) was created in 1892 through the merger of 23 type foundries, one of which was the Benton, Waldo & Co. Type Foundry of Milwaukee, part-owned by Linn Boyd Benton (1844–1932). Seven years earlier, Benton had patented a pantographic punchcutting machine, which became a cornerstone of ATF's success. More importantly, the machine (and its later adaptation as a matrix-engraving machine in about 1899) revolutionized the design of type in general. No longer was it necessary to cut punches by hand at the actual size of the type to be used. Instead, typefaces could be drawn on paper at any size as patterns for the machine, thus opening the floodgates for artists to become type designers. Typefaces were no longer the province of punchcutters with specialized sculptural skills.

Consequently, the end of the century saw type foundries, ever eager for new sources of typefaces, turning to the new breed of commercial artists for ideas. In 1900 the Rudhardsche Gießerei (later known as Gebrüder Klingspor) issued Eckmannschrift, commissioned from Jugendstil artist Otto Eckmann; and G. Peignot et Fils issued Grasset, designed by poster artist Eugène Grasset. A year later Peter Behrens created Behrensschrift for Rudhardsche, and George Auriol drew Auriol for Peignot. The naming of typefaces reflected the newfound celebrity of artists as type designers and the increased importance of names as a marketing tool.

ATF, as part of its effort to winnow and consolidate the stock of its constituent foundries, adopted the point system invented in 1877 by Nelson Hawks of Marder, Luse & Co., and established the common line, a standardized baseline for all its typefaces (with the exception of some titling and script faces). British foundries subsequently adopted the American point system and the standard line in 1902; German foundries, which already used the Didot point system, created their own common line, based on the proportions of blackletter faces, in 1905. The common line made it possible for designers to combine different typefaces easily within a line rather than line by line as in nineteenth-century broadsides.

Linn Boyd Benton's son Morris Fuller Benton (1872–1948) became head of the type design department at ATF in 1900. Under his direction—and with the advice of Henry Lewis Bullen (1857–1938), the company's general advertising manager and creator of its famed library—ATF was the first type foundry to rake through the history of printing for typefaces to revive. Between 1910 and 1928 Morris designed five revivals: Bodoni in 1910, Cloister (based on Jenson) in 1914, Baskerville Italic in 1915 (Baskerville Roman was Fry's Baskerville, licensed from Stephenson Blake), Garamond in 1919 and Bulmer in 1928.[1]

ATF was also the first type foundry to create the concept of a large type family. It marketed a series of gothics (sans serif faces) designed by Morris Benton: Franklin Gothic (1902), Alternate Gothic (1903), Monotone Gothic (1906), News Gothic and Lightline Gothic (both 1908)—as a de facto type family. At the same time it built Cheltenham, originally designed by Bertram Grosvenor Goodhue in 1896 but not completed until 1902 (with modifications by either Benton or Joseph W. Phinney of ATF's Boston branch), into the first true type family. The immediate popularity of Goodhue's face led Benton to design 19 variants of it between 1904 and 1913. The standardized point system and the advent of cohesive type families allowed typographers, especially in the realm of advertising, to create more harmonious designs.

Cover of Book of American Types
American Type Founders
1934

---
[1]
ATF Garamond was erroneously based on the work of Jean Jannon (1621).

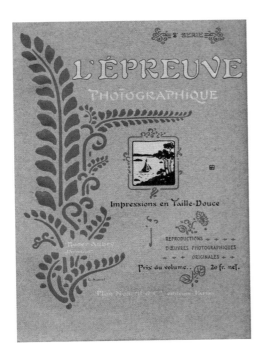

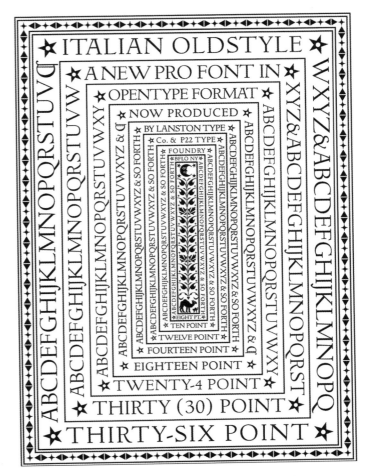

First series cover of *L'Épreuve Photographique*
George Auriol
1905

Italian Old Style specimen
Frederic W. Goudy
1924

Frederic W. Goudy

In his lifetime Frederic W. Goudy (1865–1947) was the most famous type designer in the United States and possibly the world, the one figure in the graphic design world in America known to the general populace. He owed much of his fame to his profligacy and much to his talent for self-promotion. Although the latter was often good-natured, it engendered a backlash among the typographic elite in the United States and England in his day, and a sense of embarrassment among designers since that has contributed to an unfair diminishing of his achievements.

Goudy rivalled M.F. Benton of ATF and Robert Hunter Middleton of the Ludlow Typograph Company as the most prolific type designer in the metal era. Although the precise number of faces he designed is open to dispute, his output is more impressive than either of the other two men, given that much of it was accomplished without the aid of others. Whereas Benton and Middleton worked all their lives for foundries, Goudy worked alone.[2] Early in his career Goudy relied on Robert Wiebking of the Advance Type Foundry to cut typefaces for him, but after 1926 he cut all his own faces, using the Benton punchcutting machine. He was the first independent type designer (as opposed to punchcutter). His contemporaries who are

2
Although Goudy was art director of the Lanston Monotype Machine Company from 1920 to 1939 and typographic counsel to the company from 1940 until his death in 1947, and vice president of the Continental Typefounders Association from 1925 until 1930, he was not involved in the daily operations of either company. His roles were largely symbolic. He provided publicity and good will for them while they, in return, distributed his typefaces.

Goudy's Village Letter Foundry, established in 1910, was the forerunner of the boutique type foundries of the digital era.

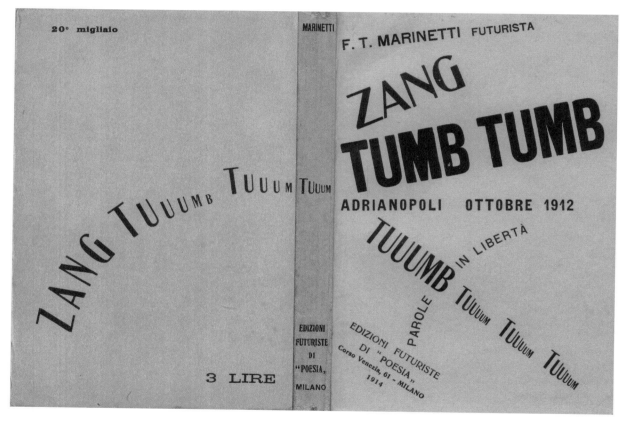

Jacket of *Zang Tumb Tumb*
Filippo Tommaso Marinetti
1914

renowned for their typefaces—Eric Gill, Paul Renner, E.R. Weiss, F.H.E. Schneidler, Bruce Rogers, W.A. Dwiggins and Oswald Cooper among them—were artists, book designers or letterers first and type designers second.

Goudy's Village Letter Foundry, established in 1910, was the forerunner of the boutique type foundries of the digital era. Before and after it was established, Goudy designed typefaces not only for foundries and composing-machine companies but also for commercial businesses, institutions and individuals, such as the Pabst Brewing Company, Scripps College and publisher Mitchell Kennerley. His reliance on custom work was unusual in its day, but is now the norm. His relentless self-promotion through books, articles, lectures, radio programmes, films and—most of all—the names of his typefaces was considered shameless by snobbish contemporaries such as Daniel Berkeley Updike and Stanley Morison, but it was essential to his success, if not to his economic survival. Crass or not, Goudy provided the model for subsequent type manufacturers from the International Typeface Corporation in the 1970s to House Industries today.

Goudy's typefaces were largely grounded in the past, whether Roman inscriptions or Renaissance printing types, but they were not revivals in the Morris, Benton or Morison manner. Rather, they were fantasies in which he spun his own interpretation from a few letters that appealed to him. They were idiosyncratic, inconsistent and sometimes downright odd, but they were also warm and personal—and several were immensely popular. They were typefaces for advertising as well as for books; and they were typefaces made for modern printing by high-speed rotary presses on wood pulp or coated paper.

Filippo Tommaso Marinetti

Filippo Tommaso Marinetti (1876–1944), the founder of Futurism, was the individual who did the most to upset conventional typography early in the twentieth century. His manifestos and poetical works had a greater impact than those of predecessors such as Lewis Carroll and Stéphane Mallarmé or contemporaries such as Guillaume Apollinaire and Wyndham Lewis.

Marinetti was not the first to break out of the so-called prison of letterpress printing, with its emphasis on horizontal lines. The Artistic Printing movement of the 1870s and 1880s had quite literally bent the rules, as it set type diagonally, on a curve and in circles and ellipses. But these pyrotechnic displays were accomplished in the service of advertising and bore no relation to the content of the text. Despite their ground-breaking use of white space, both Mallarmé's *Un Coup de dés jamais n'abolira le hasard* (*A Throw of the Dice Will Never Abolish Chance*) (published first in 1897, but not in book form until 1914) and Apollinaire's 'Il pleut' ('It's Raining') (1918) are set conventionally, achieving their sense of motion and movement through asymmetry and 'stepping' rather than through true diagonality. Apollinaire's other calligrammes—like Lewis Carroll's famed 'Mouse's Tale' from *Alice's Adventures in Wonderland* (1865)—are figurative, something Marinetti, who preferred visual analogies, condemned. Dadaist typography was chaotic and more visually exciting than the calligrammes, but it was also random and devoid of meaning. The Dadaists splashed a mix of letters in various styles, sizes and orientation across pages in a nihilistic fashion.

In contrast to these experiments, Marinetti's *parole in libertà* ('words in freedom'), as articulated in 'The Technical Manifesto of

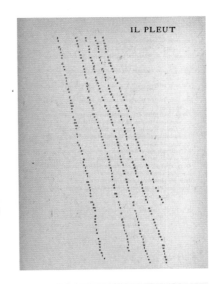

Top
'Il pleut'
Guillaume Apollinaire
1918

Bottom
Mouse's Tale
Lewis Carrol
1865

Futurist Literature' (1912) and 'Destruction of Syntax—Imagination without Strings—Words-in-Freedom' (1913), sought to destroy syntax, abolish the adjective and adverb, and inject emotion, dynamism and speed into poems. 'My revolution,' he wrote, 'is aimed at the so-called typographical harmony of the page, which is contrary to the flux and reflux, the leaps and bursts of style that run through the page. On the same page, therefore, we will use three or four colours of ink, or even twenty different typefaces if necessary. For example: italics for a series of similar or swift sensations, boldface for the violent onomatopoeias, and so on. With this typographical revolution and this multi-coloured variety in the letters I mean to redouble the expressive force of words.'

Marinetti first accomplished this goal in *Zang Tumb Tumb* (or *Zang Tumb Tumb*) (1914), a sound poem/concrete poem about the Battle of Adrianopoli of 1912, in which the words set diagonally and on a curve in a variety of typefaces and type sizes evoke the chaos and noise of war along with a wide range of moods. The text was onomatopoeic, simultaneous and multi-linear, which is why it required this radical typographic form.

More astonishing than *Zang Tumb Tuum* is 'In the evening, lying on her bed, she reread the letter from her artilleryman at the front' (1917), usually described as 'SCRABrrRrraaNNG', the large onomatopoeic word at the top representing the sound of an incoming artillery shell, from *8 Anime in una bomba—romanzo esplosivo* (1919). This collage poem, accurately described as a typographic explosion, is a visual evocation of life at the front during World War I. Marinetti could only have published it—and other non-linear examples of *parole in libertà* such as 'Après la Marne, Joffre visita le front en auto' from *Zang Tumb Tuum*—through the use of photo-engraving, a reproduction technology invented in the 1860s by John Calvin Moss that enabled artists to translate drawings, decorations, lettering and paste-ups of printed material directly into letterpress.

Photo-engraving bypassed the woodcut artist or copperplate engraver who had previously been an often necessary middleman between the artist and the print. It was a technology that not only made Marinetti's experiments possible but also transformed the profession of graphic design at the turn of the twentieth century, as commercial artists and typographers came to replace printers and compositors as the driving forces behind typographic designs; and as paste-ups and mechanicals made free-form designs more possible.

The Monotype Corporation: Frank Hinman Pierpont, Stanley Morison and Beatrice Warde

The Lanston Monotype Corporation Ltd., established in 1897 to sell the monotype machine in England, is commonly known as the Monotype Corporation to distinguish it from the original American company. From just before World War I until the 1970s it not only dominated type design and typesetting in England but also heavily influenced typography in Europe, the United States and throughout Britain's empire. Although it was not the first type company to emphasize revivals of classical historical typefaces, it created the greatest number of them and, more significantly, did more than any other firm to stress their continuing relevance in the modern world. The Monotype Corporation essentially carried the banner for traditional quality in typography, especially in books, that had been raised by William Morris into the modern world of mechanized printing and typesetting.

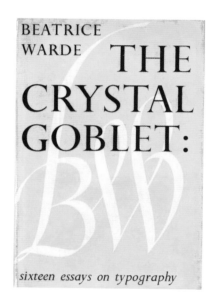

Cover of *The Crystal Goblet: sixteen essays on typography*
Beatrice Warde
1955

Gill Sans typeface specimen
Lanston Monotype Corporation Ltd.
1928

Frank Hinman Pierpont (1860–1937), manager of the Monotype Works from its establishment in 1900 until his death, oversaw the production of Imprint (1912), the first original design issued by the Monotype Corporation, and designed its second, Plantin (1913). Both were part of the revivalist wave inaugurated by William Morris. But it was the series of historical revivals carried out between the two world wars under the aegis of Stanley Morison (1889–1967), who was appointed typographical advisor to the company in 1922, that secured Monotype's reputation in this area. The first was Garamond (1922), mistakenly based, like ATF's earlier design, on the types of the seventeenth-century printer Jean Jannon rather than those of the sixteenth-century publisher Claude Garamond. The revivals that followed, however, were grounded in Morison's thorough scholarship: Poliphilus (a revival of a type by the fifteenth-century Italian Francesco Griffo) and Baskerville in 1923, Fournier in 1924, Bembo (another Griffo revival) and Centaur (Bruce Rogers's Jenson tribute, originally cut privately in 1913) in 1929, Bell in 1930, Walbaum in 1933, Van Dijck in 1935 and Ehrhardt (based on types by the seventeenth-century punchcutter Miklós Kis) in 1937. The most important of all these was Bembo, Morison's successful second attempt to revive the roman of

Cover and inside spread of
Plak (Futura specimen)
Paul Renner
1928

Francesco Griffo as a lighter, crisper alternative to the then-dominant Jenson model of an oldstyle typeface.

Morison's other great accomplishment as Monotype's typographical advisor was the addition of new type designs in the classical manner for the machine, some of them originated by the company and some adopted from outside sources. He jump-started Eric Gill's career as a type designer with Gill Sans (1928) and Perpetua (1929), added Jan van Krimpen's Lutetia (1930, but designed in 1925 for Johan Enschede en Zonen) and Spectrum (1955; Enschede 1952) and Giovanni Mardersteig's Dante (1957; Officina Bodoni 1955).

Morison's typographic legacy extends beyond his role at Monotype to encompass several other—often overlapping—positions he held, among them co-founder of *The Fleuron* (1923–30), and typographical consultant to Cambridge University Press (1925–59) and *The Times* of London (1929–60). In the last role he midwifed Times New Roman (1932), produced by Monotype for *The Times* as a new newspaper typeface but destined to have a more popular life as a book and document face (often under Linotype's stripped-down name Times Roman).

Through *The Fleuron*, as well as a blizzard of scholarly articles and books (such as *Four Centuries of Printing* [1924] and *The Typographic Book 1450–1935* [1963]), Morison led the way in establishing a classical canon of book design that linked typography and typefaces to calligraphy and inscriptions. In this endeavour he was later supported by Jan Tschichold and Mardersteig. The canon provided the foundation for the concept of invisible typography enunciated by Beatrice Warde (1900–69), Monotype's long-time publicist, in 'The Crystal Goblet' (1930) and in his own *First Principles of Typography* (1936). Warde's lecture-turned-essay is one of a handful of seminal documents of typography, the most famous and best articulated argument for typographic form to be subordinate to the content of the text. It has remained a lodestone for conservative book designers and a flashpoint for experimental typographers, as evidenced by the debates over its relevance in the 1990s.

Paul Renner

The sans serif typeface that elevated the genre from the depths of jobbing printing to the heights of fashion advertising was Futura, designed by Paul Renner (1878–1956) and released in 1927. It arose from the avant-garde search in the 1920s for a geometrically based, Platonic ideal of a sans serif typeface. But it was not the Bauhauslers Josef Albers and Herbert Bayer, nor any of the other proponents of the 'new typography' such as Kurt Schwitters and Johannes Molzahn, who solved the problem but Renner, a member of the older generation.

Renner married the proportions of classical, Trajan-esque capitals to a geometric lowercase to achieve, in its lightest weight, a pure letterform. But at its blackest Futura is a planar sans serif that has more in common with Art Deco lettering experiments of the time than avant-garde ones. Thus, the Futura family managed to straddle the two modernist camps—the ideological and the commercial—of the interwar years. This contributed to its phenomenal commercial success and its continued popularity.

Futura created a whole new category of sans serifs—geometric sans—that broke from the grots and gothics of the nineteenth century; and in this it was far more radical than the later Univers or Helvetica. It immediately spawned countless imitators as well as a number of typefaces that sought to 'improve' upon it (including Kabel, Gill Sans and Metro). Decades later it led to ITC Avant Garde Gothic, Avenir and Gotham. Futura's eternal appeal lies in its blend of idealism and sophistication, classicism and modernity.

Jan Tschichold

Jan Tschichold (1902–74) was arguably the single most important typographic figure of the twentieth century – an icon to both the modernist left and classical right of the typographic spectrum.

The young Tschichold, classically trained as a calligrapher and typographer in Leipzig, was transformed by seeing the Bauhaus exhibition in Weimar in 1923. He became a convert to *Die neue Typographie*, as Bauhausler László Moholy-Nagy called the nascent movement that sought to overturn existing typography of all stripes, whether Victorian, Art Nouveau or Arts & Crafts. Although not the originator of the new style, Tschichold quickly became its leading proponent and its most accomplished exponent. In 1925 he edited 'Elementare typographie', a special issue of *Typographische*

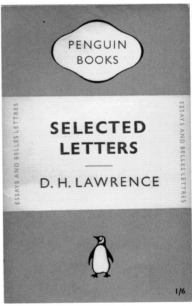

Top
Cover of *Typographische Gestaltung*
Jan Tschichold
1935

Bottom
Cover of *Selected Letters* by D.H. Lawrence
Jan Tschichold
1950

Mitteilungen, which was both the first detailed exposition of the ideas behind *Die neue Typographie* and a showcase of its leading practitioners, among them Moholy-Nagy, Herbert Bayer, El Lissitzky, Max Burchartz and Kurt Schwitters. In it he outlined ten principles of elementary typography (a term adopted from an essay of 1921 by Theo van Doesburg), which described the new typography as purposeful and having a social function. Its purpose was communication in the shortest, simplest manner; and the means of achieving that lay in organizing its internal and external parts (content and printing methods), which meant restricting its elements to the most basic ones: photography for pictures and sans serif type for text. The emphasis was on rationalism and logic.

Tschichold followed 'Elementare typographie' with *Die neue Typographie* (1928), an expanded book-length exposition of the new movement, and *Typographische Gestaltung* (*Typographical Layout*) (1935), a more nuanced and less dogmatic view of what constituted modern typography. The latter—with its cover set in a mix of script, slab serif and neoclassical types—allowed the use of other styles of type besides sans serif, and dispensed with rules and heavy bars in favour of a more sophisticated use of white space.

TM   Typographische Monatsblätter
SGM   Schweizer Graphische Mitteilungen
RSI   Revue suisse de l'Imprimerie
Nr. 5   Juni/Juin 1961, 80. Jahrgang
      Herausgegeben vom Schweizerischen Typographenbund
      zur Förderung der Berufsbildung
      Editée par la Fédération suisse des typographes
      pour l'éducation professionnelle

typographische monatsblätter

Cover of *Typographische Monatsblätter* (no. 5, June 1961)
Emil Ruder
1961

The same year, Tschichold wrote 'Vom richtigen Satz auf Mittelachse', an essay for *Typographische Monatsblätter* that admitted the value of centred typography for some forms of printing. This began his turn away from modernism, which his first admirers considered apostasy. But with his subsequent work for Penguin Books between 1947 and 1949 and his design of Sabon in 1964, Tschichold gained an entirely new group of admirers. For Penguin he designed a template for all its books with designated positions for title and author separated by a line; unified the design of the front, spine and back of all covers; established detailed rules for typesetters, encapsulated in the slim *Penguin Composition Rules* (1947); and redrew Edward Young's Penguin symbol. This work not only laid the basis for Penguin's reputation for high design quality, but also established the idea of typographic systems within the publishing industry.

In 1960 a committee of German master printers commissioned Tschichold to design a new typeface that would be not only pleasing to read and 5 per cent narrower than Stempel Garamond, but also virtually identical whether set by hand, on the Linotype or on the Monotype. Sabon, the resulting design—based on the types of Claude Garamond, Pierre Le Bé and Robert Granjon—was released in 1967 and became an instant classic.

Emil Ruder

The International Typographic Style that came to define and dominate design worldwide in the aftermath of World War II has its roots in the typography developed in Switzerland in the 1940s and 1950s, especially at the Basel Allgemeine Gewerbeschule (now part of the University of Applied Sciences Northwestern Switzerland), where Emil Ruder (1914–70) began teaching typography in 1946. Ruder was a fierce advocate of asymmetrical typography and the use of grotesque, especially Adrian Frutiger's Univers. Inspired by Kakuzo Okakura's *The Book of Tea* (1906), he saw asymmetry as allied to the simple, the natural and the highly imaginative. Asymmetry activated white space, making a design more vital. Ruder's emphasis on the positive and dynamic aspects of white space continued and extended a trend that began with Mallarmé's 'Un Coup de dés' and Apollinaire's 'Il pleut', and was refined by Tschichold in his modernist phase. Through his textbook *Typographie* (1967), Ruder's functional yet poetic conception of typography has spread beyond Basel and remained influential long after his death.

Ruder's other significant achievement is his championing not only of grotesque as the style of type most suited for contemporary typography but specifically of Univers. He and his students worked with Frutiger's typeface while it was in development, and in 1961 he designed and edited an issue of *Typographische Monatsblätter* dedicated to Univers. In his view, most sans serifs at the time, including Akzidenz-Grotesk and its successor Helvetica, were illegible and thus not functional when used in lengthy texts. Their letters lacked balance between their strokes and their inner and outer forms. Univers was the only grotesque to display this balance. Furthermore, because its family was pre-programmed, its weights and widths were harmoniously graded, thus making it economical as well as legible. Univers's perfection was important to Ruder, who believed that typography should be done from the inside out, beginning with the typeface: 'The beauty of a letter and its relationship to word and space remain at the beginning and at the centre of design.'

Univers's perfection was important to Ruder, who believed that typography should be done from the inside out, beginning with the typeface: 'The beauty of a letter and its relationship to word and space remain at the beginning and at the centre of design.'

Karl Gerstner

What sets Karl Gerstner (b. 1930) apart from his Swiss colleagues typographically is his relentless logical pursuit of the possibilities inherent in typography. Systematic design thinking underlays *Designing Programmes* (1963), his collection of essays which included an exploration of the shortcomings of Univers and a proposal for a refashioning of Akzidenz-Grotesk into a coherent type system. (The latter was eventually issued as Gerstner Program in 1967 by Berthold, but by then both Univers and Helvetica had become entrenched.) He explored the permutations possible with type in a morphological typogram programme (1968) that sought to provide designers with a streamlined method for producing variations of a wordmark, and then further explicated the variations in *Kompendium für Alphabeten* (*Compendium for Literates*) (1972). Typographic permutations characterized his identity for the Basel music shop Boîte à Musique and advertising work for the Bech Electronic Centre (1962).

Gerstner is also known for his theory of integral typography, first promulgated in 1959 and later included in *Designing Programmes*, which proposed that typography could have visual meaning beyond the content of the words it made visible. This idea is slightly but significantly different from the notion of typographic expressionism advocated by Herb Lubalin. Integral typography is not about turning type into a pictorial or illustrative image but about taking advantage of its inherent properties—form, weight, scale, etc.—to augment visually the meaning of a text. Gerstner's most memorable instance of integral typography in practice is his design for Markus Kutter's *Schiff nach Europa* ('Ship to Europe'; 1957).

Gerstner's typeface KG Privata (originally Gerstner Original 1987; then KG Vera 1997) reveals the limitations of his rational approach to letter design. Despite the decades of refinements it remains, in Richard Hollis's words, 'uninvitingly eccentric' and seemingly detached from the hard-headed typography he practised and preached in the 1950s and 1960s.

Josef Müller-Brockmann

Among those sympathetic to modern typography and design, Emil Ruder has generally been overshadowed by Zürich-based Josef Müller-Brockmann (1914–96). The latter began his career in an 'individualistic' style, but by the early 1950s he had shifted to a more 'anonymous' style, forsaking the subjectivity of illustration for the objectivity of photography. This is most evident in the series of Constructivist posters he designed for the Zürich Tonhalle between 1950 and the mid-1970s. It is these posters—in which every element is carefully considered from a geometric and mathematical point of view—that won Müller-Brockmann international fame and, in some quarters, the status of standard-bearer for Swiss design after World War II.

The rigorous architecture of Müller-Brockmann's music posters led to a deep interest in grid systems. Although grids had been employed in design before, and Allen Hurlburt's *The Grid* (1978) was published first, Müller-Brockmann became internationally known as the leading proponent of this design methodology. *Grid Systems in Graphic Design* (1981) cemented his reputation in this area. Müller-Brockmann's rationalist grid systems—and similar ones by Wim Crouwel and Massimo Vignelli—have prevailed over the more flexible, rhythmic grids employed by Ruder.

Cover of *Schiff nach Europa* by Markus Kutter
Karl Gerstner
1957

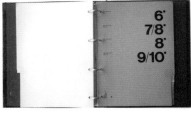

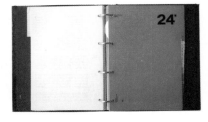

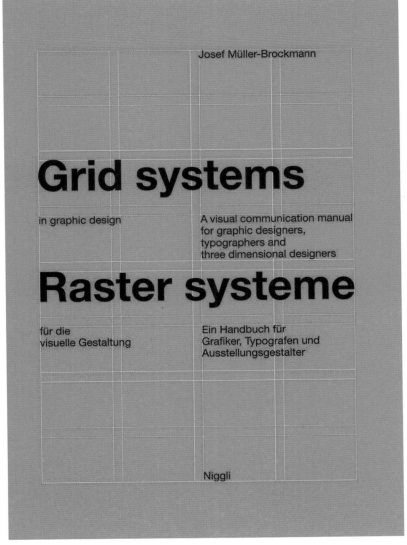

Josef Müller-Brockmann

Grid systems

in graphic design

A visual communication manual
for graphic designers,
typographers and
three dimensional designers

Raster systeme

für die
visuelle Gestaltung

Ein Handbuch für
Grafiker, Typografen und
Ausstellungsgestalter

Niggli

Left
Cover of *Grid Systems in Graphic Design*
Josef Müller-Brockmann
1981

Above
**Manual design for *Die
Neue Haas Grotesk***
Josef Müller-Brockmann
1957

Basler
Freilichtspiele
1959
19.-31. August
im
Rosenfeldpark

Giselle

Armin Hofmann

Armin Hofmann (b. 1920) is, first and foremost, a great design teacher. His influence has been strongest in the realm of education, especially via his perennially popular textbook *Graphic Design Manual* (1965), not as a typographer. Yet his posters—almost always in black and white, since he believed that colour distracted from form—have been influential. Hofmann's typography appears disarmingly straightforward, yet it is subtly crafted. For instance, the Akzidenz-Grotesk that he uses so often is tightly spaced and leaded, an indication that the letters were probably assembled by hand from galley proofs rather than printed directly from metal type (e.g. *Giselle*, 1959). In some he altered the letters subtly to make the wordmarks stronger (e.g. *Spitzen*, 1969). In others he cut the texts out of linoleum, a feature that distinguishes his work from that of Gerstner, Ruder or Müller-Brockmann (see *Das Holz als Baustoff* [1952] and *Theater Bau von der Antike bis zur Moderne* [1955]). One of Hofmann's recurring motifs is the use of enlarged initials as abstract formal shapes, a feature that gives some of his posters the look of educational assignments.

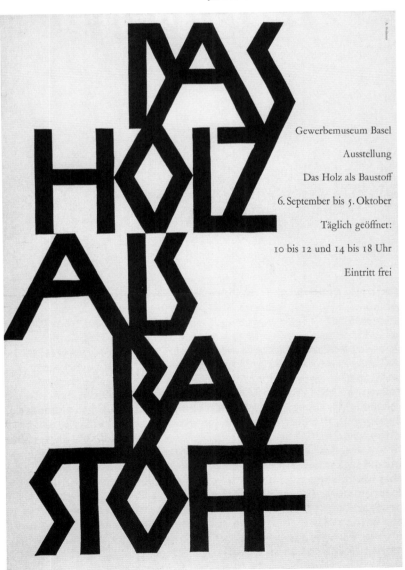

Opposite page
Giselle poster
Armin Hofmann
1959

Left
Das Holz als Baustoff poster
Armin Hofmann
1952

Programme for the Munich Olympics
Otl Aicher
1972

Otl Aicher

Although he was not the first to design a systematic identity for the Olympics, the work Otl Aicher (1922–91) did for the 1972 Munich Olympics has come to be seen as the epitome of such design. Aicher's design programme was anchored typographically by Univers, probably the best use of Adrian Frutiger's typeface outside Emil Ruder's explorations in the early 1960s.

Aicher's other notable typographic achievement is Rotis (1988), the anti-authoritarian typeface he created a few years before his untimely death. Rotis was not the first typeface to challenge the divide between serif and sans serif—Lucida and ITC Stone were already there in the 1980s—but it garnered the attention. One reason is that Rotis had four variations, rather than two or even three: serif, semi-serif, semi-sans and sans. The two intermediate faces were the most popular. They fitted in with the trend of the time towards altering existing fonts by hacking off serifs here and there, yet they were coherently designed—even if a few letters raised the hackles of more conservative designers.

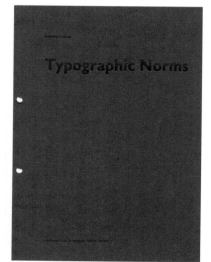

Cover and interior pages of _Typographic Norms_
Anthony Froshaug
1963

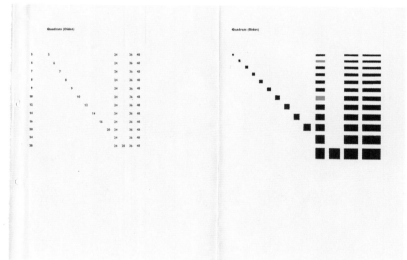

Anthony Froshaug

Along with Herbert Spencer, best remembered as the editor and designer of _Typographica_ (original series: 16 issues from 1949 to 1959; and new series: 16 issues from 1960 to 1967) and author of _The Visible Word_ (1968) and _Pioneers of Modern Typography_ (1969), Anthony Froshaug (1920–84) was the principal figure in Britain's belated discovery of modernist typography and graphic design following World War II. His modernism was derived from Jan Tschichold's _Typographische Gestaltung_ (1935), not the grid-based typography of the so-called International Typographic Style, and often relied on Gill Sans rather than any of the fashionable grotesques of the day. It was thus more poeticthan deterministic. Froshaug's output was small in quantity and generally diminutive in size, so that his influence was as much from his teaching and his writing as from his work. _Typographic Norms_ (1963), a slim visual/verbal presentation of the materials and concepts defining typography in the letterpress era, is the quintessential Froshaug work in its rigorous logic and poetic appearance. For Froshaug typography was about clarity, directness and legibility.

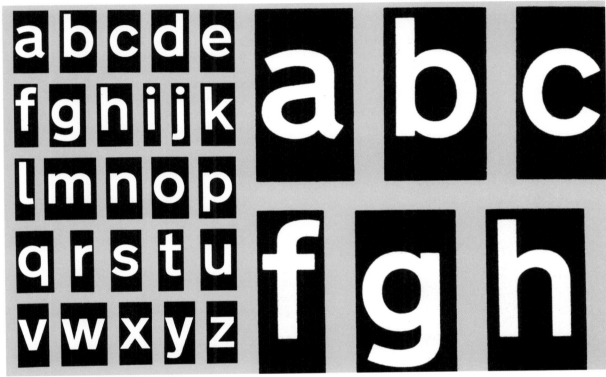

Jock Kinneir and Margaret Calvert

The new field of signage design that emerged in the early 1960s was led by Jock Kinneir (1917–94) and Margaret Calvert (b. 1936), his student turned partner. Their work for the 'new' Gatwick Airport in 1958, British motorways and roads from 1958 to 1963, and British Rail in 1965 established standards for modern, user-tested signage, and introduced the notion of custom typefaces—designed principally by Calvert—for such projects. Their signage broke new ground for Britain by being set in upper- and lowercase rather than all capitals. For both the road system and British Rail, sans serif typefaces, derived from the then-popular Akzidenz-Grotesk, were created. The former became known as Transport while the latter, part of the identity system along with Gerald Barney's 'double arrow' symbol designed at the behest of the Design Research Unit, was called the Rail Alphabet. After the 1960s, Kinneir Calvert Associates designed the signage for airports in Melbourne, Sydney and Dubai as well as the Tyne & Wear Metro system (1977). For the latter, Calvert created a slab serif typeface that was later revised for general release as Calvert (1980).

Sign system for Highways Agency, United Kingdom
Jock Kinneir and Margaret Calvert
early 1960s

**Cover of *The Anatomy of Revolution*
by Crane Brinton**
Paul Rand
1956

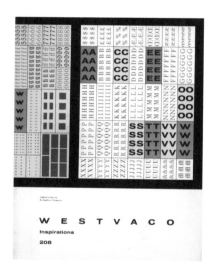

**Cover of *Westvaco Inspirations
for Printers* (no. 208)**
Bradbury Thompson
1958

Paul Rand

Paul Rand (1914–96) is not generally known for his typography, which has been overshadowed by his corporate identity work. Yet type was a key element of the best of his advertising work, and handwriting was a distinctive feature of his book-cover designs. In the 1940s, Rand—through his work for Stafford Robes, Benzedrine Sulfate, Jacqueline Cochran, *Architectural Forum*, Ohrbach's and Kaufmann's department stores, and Disney Hats— brought the avant-garde aspects of Stéphane Mallarmé's *Un Coup de dés* to mainstream advertising. The advertisements for these clients all share a similar asymmetric approach to typography, with type (often Futura or Bodoni) arranged loosely, the position of each line and its length being determined by the accompanying imagery and the surrounding white space. This was a form of modernist typography that was playful, intuitive and stylish, influenced by the modern architecture of Frank Lloyd Wright and Le Corbusier.

Many of the covers Rand produced in the 1950s for Alfred A. Knopf, Pantheon, Meridian Books, Anchor Books, Harvest Books and Vintage Books stand out because of the use of scribbled writing in place of type. This was his own un-artistic scrawl, not calligraphy, and thus freed from tradition. He considered handwriting a part of modernism since it was unavoidably contemporary. Whether Rand initiated the style or not, the use of handwriting became part of modernist American design after World War II, and is found in the work of Alex Steinweiss, Alvin Lustig, George Tscherny and Ivan Chermayeff, among others. Rand's influence even extended to English designers such as Alan Fletcher and Derek Birdsall.

Bradbury Thompson

Although Herb Lubalin gets most of the credit for the typographic expressionism that burst forth in the United States at the end of the 1950s, Bradbury Thompson (1911–95) had already been working in that vein for more than a decade as art director for *Westvaco Inspirations for Printers*, a promotional vehicle for the West Virginia Pulp and Paper Company. Thompson's notion of type as a toy was illustrated in its pages between 1939 and 1962, where he made type form the tracks of a railway and the path of a croquet ball, simulate the explosive power of a sneeze and the depth of a lake, sprinkle down like rain (with a nod to Apollinaire) and form a mask. At the same time he extensively used Futura (often in all lowercase à la Bayer) in free-form layouts like those of Paul Rand and Alexey Brodovitch. Given the magazine's wide distribution among printers, advertising agencies and design firms, it is arguable that Thompson had a bigger impact than either of those designers in shifting American typography from the Victorian to the modern.

Thompson also used the pages of *Westvaco Inspirations* to advocate for alphabetic/typographic reform. The Monalphabet (1944) and Alphabet 26 (1950) were two attempts, in the manner of Herbert Bayer's Universal Alphabet, to solve the supposed problem of a dual-case alphabet.

Herb Lubalin

Beginning in the late 1950s, the universality of the objective, rational Swiss approach to typography and design was challenged by Herb Lubalin (1918–81), who preferred typographic play to typographic order. He urged designers to experiment typographically in order to discover new ways of capturing the attention of readers and, presciently taking television into account, viewers. Lubalin's expressive typography, in which distortion and disfiguration were acceptable, stressed attention-getting over legibility. It thus threatened the Crystal Goblet theory (after Beatrice Warde's essay of that name, 1930) of invisible typography as much as it did the ordered typography of Ruder, Müller-Brockmann and Gerstner.

Lubalin was not the first to promote typographic playfulness—Bradbury Thompson had been treating type as a toy since 1944 in his designs for *Westvaco Inspirations*, and the Dadaists had certainly had their fun as far back as 1914—but he was the individual who most forcefully argued the point and then admirably demonstrated it in the work he and his colleagues did from the mid-1950s into the early 1980s. Whereas invisible typography was book-orientated, expressive typography was driven by advertising. It recognized that the modernist ideal of a universal typography for everyone and for every kind of printed matter was a chimera; that different forms of print demanded different typographies. Expressive typography was not an alternative to ordered typography or invisible typography but an additional, necessary, option.

Typographic expressionism was aided by changes in typesetting technology as photo-composition had, by the 1960s, successfully begun to challenge metal type. But more important than that was the mechanical and the ability to design on the drawing board as opposed to the bed of the press. Lubalin had achieved his early typographic designs with metal type, proofed as galleys that were cut up, retouched and recomposed—a method that was not materially affected in the following decades by the substitution of photo-typeset proofs for metal ones. It was this willingness to alter typographic letters manually—cutting off serifs, shortening strokes, joining letters, drawing swashes—that set Lubalin and his studio apart from most of the others, such as Robert Massin, who played with type in this era and those, principally David Carson, who followed in his footsteps decades later.

Lubalin's open approach to typography led to a reinvigoration of handlettering. His colleagues Tom Carnase, Ronne Bonder and Tony Di Spigna not only contributed to the modification of type but also, in the studio's downtime, drew alphabets that subsequently became the basis for typefaces from ITC, a company that Lubalin co-founded. Most notably, Carnase and Di Spigna created a new style of drawn lettering, grounded in nineteenth-century American penmanship, which they called Spencerian after the legendary penman Platt Rogers Spencer. Spencerian lettering was exuberant, decorative and hard to read—the ultimate rebuke to modernist typography. It has served as a touchstone for the new wave of letterers that has emerged in the twenty-first century, from Jessica Hische to Marian Bantjes.

International Typeface Corporation: Aaron Burns, Ed Rondthaler and Herb Lubalin

The International Typeface Corporation (ITC), founded by Aaron Burns (1922–91), Ed Rondthaler (1905–2009) and Herb Lubalin in 1970, represented a new paradigm in the type industry. The company made typefaces and nothing else. It did not manufacture typesetting machines, sell printing presses and ancillary equipment, or supply other graphic products. Burns's concept for the company was ground-breaking: it would design typefaces to be licensed to type companies that would be responsible for the ultimate manufacturing and sale of those faces. Within reason, the companies were allowed to adapt and adjust the type designs to meet the

Avant Garde Gothic typeface specimen
International Typeface Corporation (ITC)
1970

ITC transformed the type industry by severing type designs from devices. It provided a new model for remunerating type designers; and established a prototype for the marketing of type.

technical requirements of their typesetting equipment. There was no restriction on how many companies could license the faces or on the typesetting methods used. The intent of the licences was to prevent piracy of the type designs, a growing problem as the type industry shifted from metal to film and a host of new businesses—such as RCA, IBM, Singer and Wang—shouldered their way into it. To encourage type designers further to create new faces for it, ITC paid them royalties on their typefaces in addition to the usual, upfront design fee.

For the ITC system to work, advertising agencies, graphic designers and others needed to be encouraged to use its typefaces. Initially, this was done by releasing typefaces originally designed for in-house use at the Lubalin, Smith & Carnase (LSC) studio. These faces, most importantly ITC Avant Garde Gothic by Lubalin and Tom Carnase (1970), were instantly popular thanks to their association with Lubalin and the expressive typography he espoused. Quickly ITC typefaces, at the behest of Burns, took on a distinctive look characterized by a large x-height and families composed of eight members (four weights of matching romans and italics). ITC was the first company to issue standardized type families, a practice that prevailed through the 1980s.

Excluding the LSC faces, ITC adopted a two-pronged strategy of devising new typefaces in the 1970s and 1980s: first, it secured the rights to mine the American Type Founders catalogue for typefaces to revive and redesign; and second, it enticed the best European type designers of the time, many of whom were finding themselves caught between technologies, to work for it. The first approach yielded ITC Souvenir (1972), ITC Cheltenham, ITC Bookman, ITC Garamond and ITC Century (all 1975) and ITC Cushing (1981), while the second resulted in typefaces from Hermann Zapf, Aldo Novarese, Albert Boton and José Mendoza y Almeida. ITC relied on the type house Photo-Lettering, founded by Rondthaler in 1936, as its production facility and, in many instances—with Ed Benguiat, Tony Stan, Victor Caruso and Vincent Pacella on staff—its design studio as well.

ITC promoted its typefaces through the magazine *U&lc* (Upper- and lowercase), designed and edited by Lubalin. *U&lc* was significantly different from *The Monotype Recorder* and other magazines previously issued by type companies. It acted as a design magazine—with articles on advertising, graphic design, illustration, lettering, calligraphy and more—rather than a sales catalogue. It showcased its typefaces by setting all the articles in them. The content, coupled with Lubalin's design (and the fact that it was free), made *U&lc* the most popular design publication of all time.

ITC transformed the type industry by severing type designs from devices. It was instrumental in gaining widespread acceptance for the new photo-typesetting technology that had finally matured during the 1960s; provided a new model for remunerating type designers; and established a prototype for the marketing of type.

Derek Birdsall

One of those heavily influenced by Anthony Froshaug was Derek Birdsall (b. 1934), whose design work has ranged from advertising and collateral for Pirelli to magazines (such as *Nova*) to Penguin book covers to exhibition catalogues. His covers for Pelican in the early 1960s and then for the Penguin Educational Series a decade later were part of Penguin's revitalization under Germano Facetti. The Pelicans, making good use of the Romek Marber grid, vary in style, with typography only occasionally taking centre stage; but the Penguins of the 1970s are deeply influenced by what can be done to make type illustrative. Following the American example of Herb Lubalin, Birdsall replaces letters with numbers (*Inflation*) and images (*Human Ageing* and *City*).

Since 1970 Birdsall has been best known for his work as a book designer (usually under the company name Omnific), creating books marked by transparent typography in the manner of his mentor Froshaug. His most heavily praised work is *Common Worship: Services and Prayers for the Church of England* (2000), set in Gill Sans.

Alexey Brodovitch

Modern magazine design can be said to have begun with Alexey Brodovitch's tenure at *Harper's Bazaar* from 1934 to 1958. His layouts are renowned for the photographs by such luminaries as Irving Penn, Richard Avedon, Hiro, Martin Munkácsi and Lisette Model, but they are also seminal examples of typographic modernism. Brodovitch (1898–1971) introduced white space to American magazine design, not only allowing the photographs to shine but also providing room for the accompanying text to work with them. He replaced lifeless blocks of text with columns that curved in imitation of a model's torso or zigzagged in counterpoint. In Brodovitch's hands, type became an active part of the layouts.

Brodovitch can also be credited with popularizing the notion of Didones as the definitive typefaces for fashion, the typographic epitome of elegance. He used a mix of Didot, Bodoni and drawn lettering in a neoclassical vein in his cover lines, headlines and body text for *Harper's Bazaar*. In the first number of *Portfolio* (1950), the short-lived magazine he art-directed, he showcased Giambattista Bodoni's *Manuale Tipografico* (1818) and his own Didone typeface, Al-Bro—as well as the advertising work of the young Paul Rand. Al-Bro, manufactured by Photo-Lettering in 1949, is a neoclassical typeface with an Art Deco flair; it has been rediscovered in recent years by the accessories designer Kate Spade and others.

> **Brodovitch can also be credited with popularizing the notion of Didones as the definitive type-faces for fashion, the typographic epitome of elegance.**

Spread from *Portfolio* 1
Alexey Brodovitch
Winter 1950

Henryk Tomaszewski and Polish posters

In the aftermath of World War II, Polish posters gained worldwide fame for their designs, which were outside the prevailing trends in the rest of Europe and the United States where modernism struggled with traditionalism for pre-eminence. The posters—usually designed for the circus, theatre and cinema—tended to be metaphorical and symbolic rather than objective or neutral as the designers sought not only to plumb the contents of the plays and movies

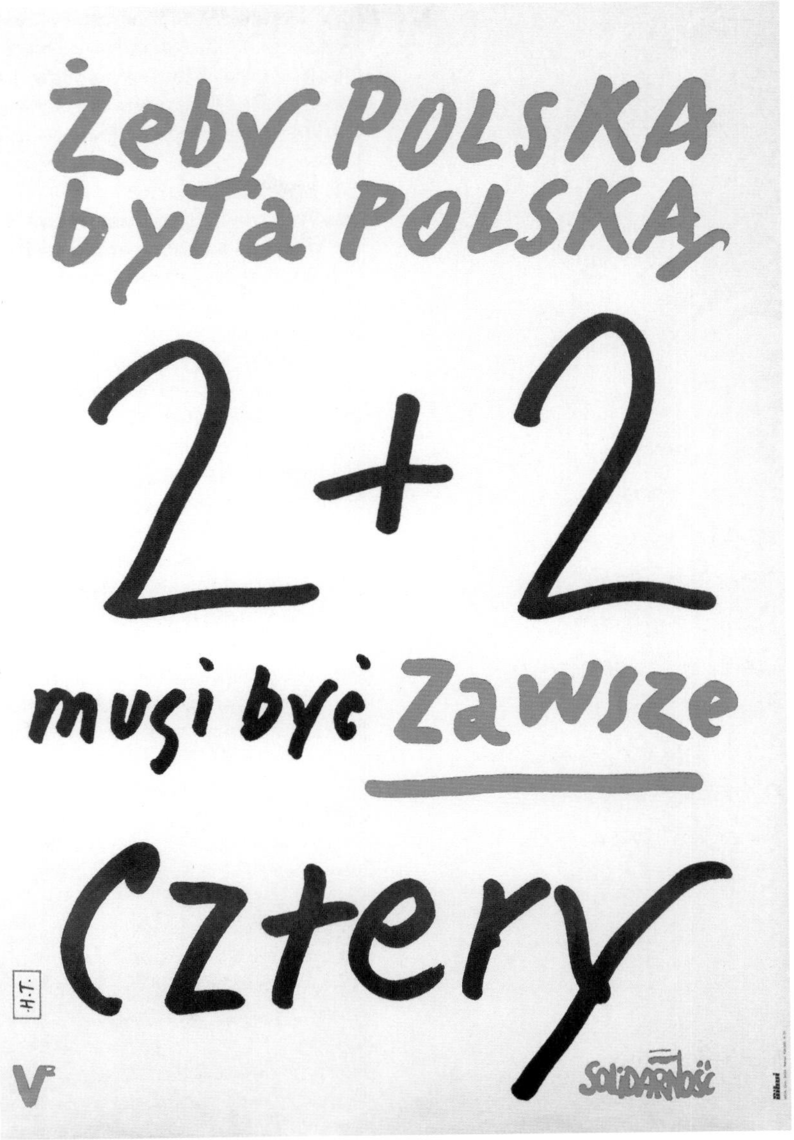

2 + 2 poster
Henryk Tomaszewski
1989

Moore poster
Henryk Tomaszewski
1989

being advertised but also to evade the censors of the Communist regime. The designs were also free of the commercial pressure exerted on posters in capitalist societies then and now. Illustration and handmade letters played a significant role for their expressive and ambiguous potential—and because they were cheaper than photography and typesetting.

Henryk Tomaszewski (1914–2005) was one of the leading figures in the development of the Polish poster, designing his first in 1947. His posters are colourful, witty and often surreal. He used handwriting, painted letters, cut and torn letters (his poster for an exhibition in 1959 of Henry Moore sculptures in this manner is a masterpiece), pictorial letters, brush-written letters and letters drawn in imitation of type (see his poster of 1948 advertising the Orson Welles film *Citizen Kane*). Although the cut and torn letters and the pictorial letters (for instance, the bowl of a P forming a mouth for a Polska Pantomima poster, 1964) reappear in his work, there is no signature style. His 'typographic' legacy, and that of his Polish cohorts—most notably Tadeusz Trepkowski (1914–54), Roman Cieslewicz (1930–96), Jan Lenica (1928–2001), Waldemar Swierzy (1931–2013) and Jan Sawka (1946–2012)—lies in the willingness to explore all manner of letters, whether handmade or typographic. When the Polish designers resorted to type, the faces were often not part of either the modernist or traditionalist repertoires (e.g. Arnold Böcklin, Cooper Black, Herold Reklame, Windsor). However, in the end, the power of the Polish posters lies in their astonishing, disturbing and sometimes mystifying illustrations, not in their letters.

The *Push Pin Graphic*:
Milton Glaser and Seymour Chwast

The other major challenge to Swiss design in the 1960s came from Push Pin Studios, founded in 1954 by Cooper Union classmates Seymour Chwast (b. 1931), Milton Glaser (b. 1929), Ed Sorel (b. 1929) and Reynold Ruffins (b. 1930). To promote themselves they created the *Push Pin Almanack*, which was succeeded by the *Monthly Graphic* in 1957, eventually renamed the *Push Pin Graphic*. The magazine became more than a vehicle for self-promotion. It served as a petri dish of experimentation and exploration where the members of the studio, all illustrators first and designers second, could try out new ideas unbound by the limitations of commercial assignments. The result was a pot-pourri of different styles, methods and structures inspired by the Renaissance, Impressionism, Victoriana, Art Nouveau, Art Deco, Expressionism, Dadaism, Surrealism and Cubism; but also by the circus, Freud, Kafka, film, the urban activist Jane Jacobs and a host of other influences.

The *Push Pin Graphic*'s emphasis on illustration—in all its varied glory—was a direct rejection of the Concrete art-infected Swiss view that images in design should be anonymous and objective. But the magazine had a typographic legacy as well. Its articles and essays were typeset in a myriad of styles that perfectly complemented the diverse imagery. Both text and imagery were not, despite the historicism, mere revivals of past styles; instead they were combined, re-imagined, reinvented and thus made fresh. Fette Fraktur— the studio's signature typeface—was combined with grotesques; Bookman coexisted with Baskerville; fat faces and 'artistic' faces such as Smoke were revived; hairline rules were used to divide columns and box in blocks of text; and dense, justified columns of type, reminiscent of nineteenth-century American newspapers, provided ballast for the often light and effervescent illustrations.

Kitchen typeface specimen
Milton Glaser
1996

Beginning with number 48 of the *Push Pin Graphic* in 1965, Glaser and Chwast created novelty lettering that formed their first foray into the designing of type. Glaser's typefaces—notably Houdini and Baby Teeth (both 1964), Baby Fat (1965), Kitchen (1976) and Hologram Shadow (1977)—tend to be three-dimensional, while Chwast's—among them Artone (1964), Blimp and Filmsense (both 1970), Monograph (1972) and Bestial Bold (1980)—are flatter and more decorative. Although none are significant historically, they embody the belief that, contrary to the assertion of Eric Gill, type can be pictorial. Push Pin Studios and the *Push Pin Graphic* specifically prefigured Postmodernism in graphic design, especially the eagerness to revive historical styles that had been shunned or derided by typographic classicists and modernists alike.

Fletcher Forbes Gill

Fletcher Forbes Gill, the forerunner of the design consultancy Pentagram, was formed in 1962 by the Englishmen Alan Fletcher (1931–2006) and Colin Forbes (b. 1928) and the American Bob Gill (b. 1931). Through Fletcher, who had studied and worked briefly in the United States, and Gill, the firm brought an American design attitude to London. What this meant was that its work was eclectic in style, focused on content and concept rather than aesthetics,

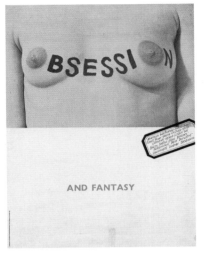

***Obsession and Fantasy* exhibition poster**
Robert Brownjohn
1963

Pirelli tyre poster
Fletcher Forbes Gill
1961

and typographically catholic. Fletcher's work was especially diverse typographically: distorted type, Pop art lettering, psychedelic type, Lubalin-esque letter substitution, collage, rebuses and word games.

Fletcher Forbes Gill and the expatriate American designer Robert Brownjohn (1925–70) (a founding partner of Brownjohn, Chermayeff & Geismar) deserve much of the credit for bringing British graphic design out of the austerity of the postwar period and into the Swinging London of the 1960s. Fletcher's playfulness was a breath of fresh air at a time when Stanley Morison, Beatrice Warde and Monotype still reigned supreme in the British type world. And Brownjohn's injection of sex into the equation—most famously in the opening credits of the James Bond films *From Russia with Love* (1963) and *Goldfinger* (1964)—further emphasized the split between the book typography of the past and the new graphic design typography. Brownjohn even titled his essay for *Typographica* in 1964 'Sex and Typography'.

Alphabet
Giacomo Franco
1596

Production shot of Naked Ladies Alphabet
Anthon Beeke
1970

Anthon Beeke

Anthon Beeke's (b. 1940) typographic work—with one notable exception—has been characterized by an emphasis on concept over style in which imagery is dominant. That imagery has often been yoked to an urge to skewer bourgeois sensibilities, inevitably by being sexually provocative (as in his notorious poster of 1981 for a performance of *Troilus and Cressida* showing a woman from behind, bent over with her buttocks trussed up and her pudenda front and centre). This is true of Beeke's famous human alphabet of 1969. Although some of its characters are witty (such as the woman curled up embryo-like to form the dot for the exclamation point and question mark), the concept is an age-old one—see Giacomo Franco's alphabet of 1596 or Horst P. Horst's 'logo' of 1940 for *Vogue*, composed of women in bikinis—that is notable principally for its nudity. The only advance Beeke has made has been to use many women, and thus avoid relying on props such as scarves to portray the letters accurately.

Adobe Systems:
Sumner Stone and Robert Slimbach

Two digital type companies were founded in 1981: Adobe Systems, by computer scientists who knew nothing about type; and Bitstream, by veterans of Mergenthaler Linotype eager to get in on the ground floor of the next major technological change in the business. Of the two, it is Adobe that has had the greater impact. Adobe's key technology, developed by its co-founders John Warnock (b. 1940) and Charles Geschke (b. 1939), was PostScript, a page description language. PostScript did for Adobe what licensing did for ITC: it severed the link between typefaces and specific machines; and it did it in a manner that was more permanent. PostScript effectively killed off or severely crippled the type companies, both those that had survived the demise of metal and the newcomers that had joined during the brief moment of photo-composition.[3] As one of the key elements in desktop publishing—along with Apple's Macintosh computer, Aldus's PageMaker layout software and the Canon Laserwriter—it contributed to the swift demise of the type houses that set the type used in paste-ups and mechanicals.

With the hiring of Sumner Stone (b. 1945) in 1984, Adobe went from being a technology company to a true type foundry. Under Stone's leadership, the company developed original typefaces, established digital font standards and led the way in educating a new generation of designers about the details involved in good typography in the classical mode. The first set of Adobe Originals released in 1989—the trio of Lithos, Trajan and Charlemagne by Carol Twombly and Adobe Garamond by Robert Slimbach (b. 1956)—proved to a doubting graphic design profession that fonts as good, if not better, than those in the heyday of metal type could be made with the new digital technology. Like the Monotype Corporation before it, Adobe led the way in creating revivals of historic designs, following Adobe Garamond with Adobe Caslon (1991) by Twombly; three sets of Adobe Wood Type (1990, 1991 and 1994) by Barbara Lind; Adobe Jenson (1994) and Adobe Garamond Premiere Pro (2004), both by Slimbach; and the historically inflected Minion (1990), Poetica (1992) and Arno (2006), also by Slimbach.

As well as reviving classical typefaces for the digital age, Adobe sought to bring back the elements of classical text typography that had been abandoned during the photo-composition era,

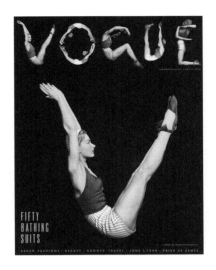

Cover of *Vogue* (8 June 1940)
Horst P. Horst
1940

3
The only survivors today are Monotype Imaging, which owns not only the old Monotype Corporation, but also Compugraphic, ITC and Linotype; and Berthold Direct Corporation, an American company that owns the original library of H. Berthold GmbH.

ITC STONE
ITC BODONI
AREPO
SILICA
STONE PRINT
BASALT
MAGMA
ꟿUNC

Stone Type typeface specimen
Stone Type Foundry
1990s–2014

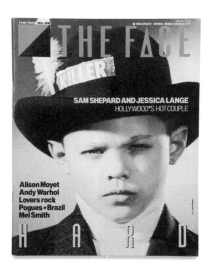

Cover of *The Face* (8 March 1985)
Neville Brody
1985

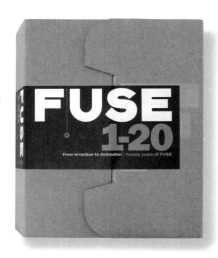

Packaging design for *FUSE*
Neville Brody
2012

and to educate users on why they matter and how to use them. Thus, Adobe Originals included expert sets—supplementary fonts that consisted of small capitals, oldstyle figures, true fractions, ligatures, swash characters and alternatives—and accompanied by thorough specimen books of a kind rarely seen before, even at the height of Monotype's influence. Through *Font & Function*, its short-lived magazine, Adobe gave proscriptive advice to users on good typography, a project it continued in more depth (and with a good dose of humour) with the publication of *Stop Stealing Sheep & Find Out How Type Works* (1995) by E.M. Ginger and Erik Spiekermann.

Neville Brody and *FUSE*

Considered by many to be the first rock-star or celebrity designer, Neville Brody's (b. 1957) design influence in the 1980s and early 1990s stretched beyond Britain to the United States, Europe and Japan. Much of that influence was typographic as Brody, in his layouts for *The Face* (1981–86) and, to a lesser extent, *Arena* (1987–90), employed typefaces of his own making. These Constructivist letterforms were systematic inventions inspired by but not copied from the interwar avant-garde experiments of Theo van Doesburg, Josef Albers, Herbert Bayer and others. Although they looked techy, they were made by hand, since retail font programmes were not yet available. Brody's typefaces revived the spirit of the heroic age of modernism—when it was vibrant, raw and messy, before being chloroformed with Helvetica and grids—in a different manner from that of others, such as Paula Scher, who simultaneously discovered the design avant-garde. Eventually, the alphabets became true typefaces, with the release first of Arcadia (done for *Arena*), Industria and Insignia by Linotype in 1990 and then of Typefaces 4, 6 and 7 by FontShop International the following year.

Brody's use of self-generated typefaces for Fetish Records and *The Face* foretold the direction much graphic design would take once drawing programmes and retail font software became available. He himself continued to design unique letters for projects and then sell them (the faces Tyson, Dome and Tokyo, for example, were derived from the poster he designed for the Mike Tyson/Tony Tubbs boxing match in 1988). Brody's outlet for these and other fonts was FontShop International, a font distributor that he co-founded with Erik and Joan Spiekermann in 1989.

In 1991 Brody, in collaboration with the design journalist Jon Wozencroft, initiated *FUSE*, a project of experimental typefaces that has, in fits and starts, now reached its 20th edition. The fonts, initially released four at a time, and commissioned from a range of newcomers to graphic design and a few old hands in the type world (Matthew Carter, Erik Spiekermann, Bruce Mau, Pierre di Sciullo, Tobias Frere-Jones, Malcolm Garrett and more), have been ostensibly dedicated to a theme, such as religion, disturbance or virtual reality. The results have been predictably unpredictable as the fonts jump from the purely formal to the highly conceptual to the utterly impractical. A few, such as Moonbase Alpha (1991) by Cornel Windlin, Lushus (1992) by Jeffery Keedy and You Can Read Me (1995) by Phil Baines, have become familiar totems of their era, but none has entered the mainstream of typographic use. And that is probably in *FUSE*'s favour, since its goal has been to provide a 'dynamic new forum for typography' that will take type out of the museum of the past.

8vo and *Octavo*

The studio 8vo, formed in 1985 by Hamish Muir (b. 1957), Simon Johnston (b. 1959) and Mark Holt (b. 1958), made its mark by producing the magazine *Octavo* a year later. *Octavo* lasted for eight issues (seven in print and one on CD-ROM) from 1986 to 1992, and was a splash of cold water amidst the Postmodernist fires then raging. It swore an allegiance to modernism, and its design, favouring layered and overlapping texts in varying sizes and weights, was as much a part of its message as its contents. *Octavo*'s layouts were lively and exciting, the antithesis of the International Typographic Style. It was an updating of Gerstner's integral typography—modernism for the computer age.

Octavo particularly resonated with designers in the United Kingdom and Europe, and in the United States, though it had to compete with the clamour over Rudy VanderLans and Zuzana Licko's *Emigre*, it also struck a chord. It led 8vo to important assignments for the Flux new music festival in Scotland and the Museum Boijmans van Beuningen (MBvB) in Rotterdam, where it put into practice the new modernism that it had espoused in the magazine. The typography for both—marked by overlapping, boxing, outlining and perspectival shifts—managed to create order from chaos. It was controlled clutter. The MBvB work relied on Futura—reinvigorating the old standby—while a special liquid grid typeface, originally called Interact but later renamed Tephra, was created for Flux.

Emigre: Rudy VanderLans and Zuzana Licko

While Adobe brought classical type design and typography to digital type, the company that made digital type exciting and fresh was Emigre, which began life as a cultural magazine before morphing into a design magazine and sprouting a related foundry. *Emigre* the magazine was founded by Rudy VanderLans (b. 1955) and Zuzana Licko (b. 1961) in 1984. Once the tabloid-size publication had shifted its emphasis to graphic design and typography with issue 10 (1988), devoted to the Cranbrook Academy of Art, it became the nexus for typographic turmoil and innovation for the next six years. (In 1994, issue 32 signalled a change towards in-depth graphic design theory and criticism, which dominated the magazine until its demise in 2005.)

It was in the pages of *Emigre* during those six years that the experimental typefaces of Licko, Max Kisman, Pierre di Sciullo, Barry Deck, Jeffery Keedy, P. Scott Makela, Miles Newlyn, Jonathan Barnbrook and Frank Heine were introduced, to the delight of a younger generation and the consternation of an older one. It was also where the battles over the legibility and beauty of the typography made with these fonts, often marked by layering and messiness, was fought. Beatrice Warde's 'Crystal Goblet' essay of 1930 was at the centre of many of the debates. Notable issues of *Emigre* with a typographic theme were no. 11, 'Ambition/Fear' (1989), on the emotions the Macintosh engendered in designers; no. 15, 'Do You Read Me?' (1990) on type; no. 18, 'Type Site' (1991), which introduced LettError's random font Beowolf; no. 23, 'Culprits' (1992), which contained Gerard Unger's essay 'Legible?'; issues 24, 'Neo-Mania' (1992), and 27, 'David Carson' (1993), which extensively documented the designer of *Beach Culture* and *Ray Gun*; and no. 30, 'Fallout' (1994), which was a lengthy response to Steven Heller's essay 'The Cult of the Ugly' in *Eye* magazine (vol. 3, no. 9, 1993).

Emigre became a foundry in 1985, first releasing Licko's typefaces but soon expanding to include those showcased in the magazine's pages, including those by students at CalArts, Cranbrook and the Royal College of Art. It became the locus for the typographic experiments of a new generation. The attitude of these designers was often summed up in the names of their faces, particularly Dead History (1990) by Makela, Arbitrary Sans (1990) by Deck, NotCaslon by Mark Andresen (1991) and Remedy [for too much Helvetica] (1991) by Heine. The fonts ranged from the bitmapped to the vernacular to the hybrid. Emigre's fonts celebrated the democratization of type design made possible by the software programmes Fontographer (1986) and Font Studio (1990). The overtly experimental phase of Emigre fonts ended in 1996 when Licko designed both Mrs Eaves and Filosofia, revivals—albeit with a twist—of classical typefaces by Baskerville and Bodoni respectively.

Tibor Kalman

Tibor Kalman (1949–99), head of M&Co., was not the first graphic designer to discover the charms of the vernacular—Ben Shahn documented vernacular lettering in the 1930s as part of his work for the Farm Security Administration and later published a tribute

neo-
mania

No. 24

Price$7.95

Cover of *Emigre* (no. 24)
Rudy VanderLans and Zuzana Licko
1992

FUCK BUSH. VOTE.

entitled *Love and Joy about Letters* (1963)—but his writings, talks and work in the 1980s spread the gospel of anti-elitism in design. His work—mainly advertisements but also stationery and an ever-changing menu board for Restaurant Florent—often deadpan and frequently slyly humorous, was as much about content as about style. The typography and imagery worked in tandem.

Kalman was not the only one to explore the vernacular in the 1980s. He was joined by Joe Duffy, Charles Spencer Anderson, John Sayles, Rick Valicenti and Art Chantry in the United States; and Piet Schreuders in Holland. Kalman criticized as nostalgia Duffy's and Anderson's use of the vernacular, seeing it as the superficial lifting of designs from the past for the purpose of styling. But they were not alone in treating the vernacular as an alternative to the empty modernism epitomized by the International Typographic Style.

From Shahn and Walker Evans on, an interest in the vernacular has often centred on lettering, whether handwritten or handmade with non-professional tools and materials such as typewriters, stencils, templates, rubberstamps, Dymo lettering devices or masking tape, sticks and routers. Type designers including Tobias Frere-Jones, LettError and House Industries have turned to vernacular lettering for inspiration, including alphabets designed for signage and other specialized printing. The result has been typefaces as diverse as Template Gothic (1990), FF Trixie (1991), Garage Gothic (1992), FF Instant Types (FF Dynamoe, FF Flightcase, FF Stamp

Three competing visions of what printed typography should be— invisible, rational and expressive— emerged during the twentieth century. The sheer diversity of such material, coupled with the ever-widening ambit of graphic design and typography, ensures that no single philosophy of typography is likely to triumph.

Gothic, FF Karton and FF Confidential; 1992), Interstate (1993), Street Van Collection (1996), Flyer Fonts and Tiki Types (both 1997) and Gotham (2000), referencing laundromat signage, manual typewriters, stencilled wooden crates, parking tickets, rave flyers and Polynesian-themed restaurants. Vernacular type is a thumb in the eye both to those championing the classic typefaces of the past and to those promoting a one-size-fits-all no-frills typeface.

Summary
The individuals and companies profiled here were chosen because they illuminate the key concepts that have driven type design and typographic design in the past century and more. These concepts are the revival of typefaces from the past, the proliferation of sans serifs, an increasing emphasis on type families, the ability to mix typefaces, the recognition of the importance of white space, the increasing reliance on grids to structure typography, and a celebration of the vernacular. Three competing visions of what printed typography should be—invisible, rational and expressive—emerged during the twentieth century. The sheer diversity of such material, coupled with the ever-widening ambit of graphic design and typography (which now takes in work for the screen), ensures that no single philosophy of typography is likely to triumph. Instead, typography in the twenty-first century, heir to the cacophonous past, is itself a jumble.

**Monika Parrinder
& Colin Davies**

Type Today and Tomorrow

At the start of every new decade, it is fashionable to hail the end of an era: the death of the author; of the book; of graphic design and typography; and, of course, of the web. But here we are in the second decade of the new millennium, and, despite calls to the contrary, typography and design are flourishing in the multi-platform worlds of digital and analogue.

Typography, arguably the backbone of most graphic design, has had to fight its corner quietly against both the wilder excesses of Postmodernism and the seemingly closed cohort of fonts available on PCs. It could be argued that Apple brought the aesthetics of typography to a wider audience, but did not extend choice.

Today, screen-based platforms are maturing. No longer must typographers struggle with the vagaries of screen resolution, as even the smallest mobile phone or other digital device can represent the most demanding of ligatures and serifs. The screen is no longer a problem to be 'solved' for the sake of readability and so on. Instead, it is part of a set of truly new creative spaces for typography to explore (while always informed by the original driving forces of analogue production in type process and design history).

A repositioning of practice

Typography—as a base unit, or pixel, of communication—has re-emerged as a crucial tool in expressing identity and anchoring meaning in the contemporary, globalized world. This is evident in much of the work featured in this book, and in the way digital type foundries are expanding the development and distribution of typefaces both globally and locally. The Indian Type Foundry, for example, has introduced Kohinoor Multiscript with versions in Latin, Bengali, Gujarati and Devanagari, among others. It is also formalizing regional languages, some of which face extinction, by opening its doors to designers of Indic scripts from India and elsewhere. From nationhood to branding and beyond: place, history and typographic aesthetics coincide.

The new typography in areas outside North America and Europe—Asia, Africa, the Middle East and elsewhere—proves the cultural essence that resides in type design. Below, we talk about the Khatt Foundation, which is an excellent example of such thinking.

Dance Writer 2 app
Valentina Scaglia
2011

> **Lots of scripts come from a similar origin. This becomes a starting point or a going-back-to point to reconsider cultural connections for future.**
>
> Huda Smitshuijzen AbiFarès

1

Monica Racic, 'Under Cover: Atelier Carvalho Bernau & Octavo Publicaties', *New Yorker*, 14 July 2011; newyorker.com/online/blogs/books/2011/07/under-cover-atelier-carvalho-bernau-octavo-publicaties.html (accessed January 2014).

Oded Ezer, meanwhile, underneath the jokes and performances inherent in much of his work, is exploring the importance of typography to the Hebrew language.

What we are describing here, in both technological and cultural terms, is an atomized design realm. In response, typographers and designers are engaging with mass- and digital production in a global context, but with bespoke typography. This creative surge, where a visual literacy is sustained between disparate projects, languages and geographic spaces, is as much about typographic skill and craft as design *chutzpah*.

The increasing number of digital type foundries creating custom typefaces is a demonstration of this. Search online for 'font' or 'type' and you are inundated with results; surf designers' web pages and you will find that many have their own foundry. Commercial Type (page 126) is one of the better known foundries, set up by Paul Barnes and Christian Schwartz. Like Lineto, set up by the Zürich-based designers Urs Lehni and Lex Trüb, type foundries often become a point of connection in a network of designers who, if not necessarily wedded in outlook, occupy an overlapping virtual space. Many use the skill and craft of typography to create cultural reflection, rather than simply fashionable visual statement, in their work.

De Zaak Nu, set up by Atelier Carvalho Bernau (page 122), meanwhile, links Holland's cultural past and today's protest movement. Born in the climate of 'cuts' and austerity measures, this is a new syndicate for art spaces and a 'podium' for debate between contemporary art and government agencies in the Netherlands. Carvalho Bernau's design inverts the logo for an earlier iteration of De Zaak, so that the simple rectangle with a diagonal, spelling out a 'Z', becomes a 'No' symbol. Illuminating the relationship between such individual projects and their broader philosophy of practice, Susana Carvalho and Kai Bernau comment: 'We believe in *modern*, not *ism*. Even if our work often comes out as sober and reduced, we consider our approach not a dogmatic attitude or a design preference, but always a reaction to the content and the ideas we give shape to.'[1]

Across the spectrum, what we see is modernism reborn (if indeed it ever died). It is modernism as an active *meme*, rather than a passive historical referent, although, of course, those abound as well. Type styles—like a cultural baton—move from hand to hand, from typographer to typographer.

Beyond Postmodern excess, beyond techno-fetish, beyond fashion, something new is going on: a renewed emphasis on the process of type and design as a site of cultural engagement. In the attention to process, via re-engagement with the bespoke, we see a repositioning of practice.

At the vanguard of this repositioning are typographers and designer/typographers. Each brings a personal twist to typography in the twenty-first century. The typographer creates, in the main, sculptural, technical forms that can be discussed in the same spatial terms that are used in the appreciation of three-dimensional arts. Designer/typographers, on the other hand, are always conscious of their creations living in an already visually populated world.

The sculptural and technical emphasis of the typographer can be seen in experiments with physical materials, 3D printing and the urban fabric. Take Cyril Cohen's research typeface Le Téocalli, which is inspired by the art of Japanese folding and games that play with form, or Yara Khoury and Melle Hammer's Kasheeda 3D font, which is based on the concept of a wide ribbon curving through space.

Alternatively, look to the inspiration of 1950s exhibition signage, which abounds in the use of typography in urban space and architecture today.

The emphasis is different for designer/typographers, who always understand their creations as design in context, be it in the physical or the digital world. The way in which typographic communication operates between these two realms is captured to useful effect in the exhibition *Becoming Istanbul* (2008–11, travelling; now online). Here, the designers Project Projects (page 242) used a composite of database, wayfinding and feedback systems to enlist the public's participation in contemplating urban issues.

The way in which typography—in common with design more generally—reflects the process of its making and responds to a world of use is made explicit in the design for the exhibition *New Simplicity* (temporary space, London, 2010) by studio Julia (page 48). Inspired by the simplicity of the 3D print production techniques of some of the furniture in the show, the designers used a single piece of communication to provide a whole set of materials. The exhibition catalogue was printed on demand and trimmed to create the signage. These signs were then placed on a wall grid at various heights to suit the audience.

Both the typographer's and the designer/typographer's approach—especially in the emerging world of gesture interfaces—can have a significant role in how we all appreciate the visual experience. The tablet computer and subsequent high-resolution devices have for the first time allowed anyone to appreciate almost forensically the potential of type; we can zoom in and out, capturing the minutest details on screen.

Kasheeda 3D font
Yara Khoury and Melle Hammer
2011

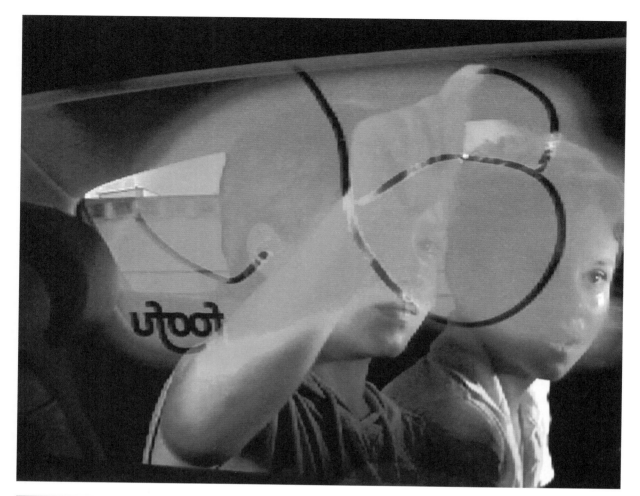

**Windows of Opportunity interactive in-car
displays, commissioned by General Motors**
Future Lab, Bezalel Academy of Art and Design, Israel

Top
Foofu finger painting app
2012

Bottom
Pond music-streaming and message-sharing app
2012

A practice of possibility

To 'find out how type works' today,[2] one also needs to be open to its expanded repertoire of hybrid, hyphenated practices: not only type-as-text but also the type-image, type-sculpture, type-animation and type-sound, and all the things still uninvented. Far from being an assault on the essence of type design, what we see here is type and design re-articulated as a practice of possibility.

Dance Writer 2, for instance, is a website and app where typing in a word and hitting ←return→ activates a white-clad figure to 'dance this'—your message—'live' on your screen. With a further click, Valentina Scaglia's animated type-performance can be emailed or shared with others on a host of platforms. Here, the typographer collaborates not only with the dancer, but also with the choreographer and code-writer. New spaces and platforms open typography up to other disciplines and different audiences.

Like the movie star who wins their first Oscar, typography—in reaching such public attention today—needs to be careful in how it chooses its next role. The typographer is caught between a rock and a hard place. The autonomy of the unknown craftsman is now exposed: the success of such films as Gary Hustwit's documentary *Helvetica* (2007; page 178) has, in a sense, 'outed' the skills, processes and people involved in the manufacture and creation of type. These have been fine-tuned since 1455, when the Gutenberg printing press opened up a new specialism in the creative arts. If moveable type and mass-production democratized knowledge—through books and magazines—it has taken until now truly to do the same for the typographic process itself.

This democratization has added the knowledgeable connoisseur to the mix of typographer and designer/typographer: a mixture of Helvetica T-shirt-wearing groupies and the type hipsters who claim that type alone will change the world. An example of the latter is the Homeless Signs project, which gives out laminated signs—*correctly* typeset in Helvetica—to the homeless. The project's website claims the signs are 'impossible to ignore'.[3]

The minutiae of type design are discussed on blogs by a burgeoning number of enthusiasts every day, delivering blow-by-blow accounts of 'beautiful'/'outrageous'/'historically inaccurate!' uses of Gill Sans here or hand-painted Gotham there. This is compounded by the appeal of, say, the FontBook app with its scroll-through categories and constantly updated profiles. Is this a typographer's dream, or a new kind of connoisseurship: type as butterfly collection?

It's liberating that anyone with digital access can deploy or design a font and print a newspaper or book on demand. And yet it takes time, training and passion to learn not to let type drop into the gutter, to understand the balance of a bowl or the shy curve of an ellipse. What is often missing, in the new democracy, is an understanding that design is a composite of skilled practices. In the differences between typographer, designer/typographer and type connoisseur we see typography (and its authorship) falling between two defined areas of cultural advocacy: type as geek badge of honour and type as something that can deliver (or at least approximate) aesthetic experience and cultural resonance.

Typography as aesthetic experience

'Style' has for many become a dirty word. And yet, in order to think about practice repositioned, and its cultural and technological possibilities, it's useful to re-engage with it as a reflection of the process of its making. Rather than style over content or substance, we are trying to define style over fashion.[4]

2
A classic text from the early digital era is Erik Spiekermann and E.M. Ginger, *Stop Stealing Sheep & Find Out How Type Works* (Mountain View, CA: Adobe Press, 1993).

3
homelesssigns.wordpress.com

4
We are reminded of Susan Sontag's rehabilitation of style, not as decoration but as a reflection of the process of its making whereby 'what is inevitable in a work of art is the style' ('On Style', *Against Interpretation* [New York: Farrer, Straus & Giroux, 1966]).

Of course, there is the fashionability of the handmade, but the root of this attraction and popularity is the inherent sense of skilled craft. Non-Arabic readers might be attracted to a modern Arabic typeface, because it still has a trace of its origins in calligraphy, beautifully rendered. In this case, fashionability dissolves into the root of its style at the point of technical and aesthetic consideration.

In another example, the Marian family by Paul Barnes (page 126) is a series of classic typefaces stripped back to a hairline to reveal the structure of the letterforms. In doing so, it recalls the way they were crafted types of their time. The style is in this root. An essay by Barnes explains the development of Marian, partly through style. He addresses the monoline form through references such as eighteenth-century marble inscriptions where 'one can imagine that the production of it informed the style'. And, on the stylistic qualities of thinness: 'Letters that are based on single-stroke weights work most successfully when thinner. As the stroke becomes heavier, the letter begins to deform.' Defining style in terms of technical and aesthetic qualities is to define it *against* fashion. Finally, Barnes explains how serif book-faces were chosen because they could be reduced to a line without losing their intrinsic qualities—'the life and spirit of the letters'—for digital redeployment today.[5]

We would argue that it is this understanding of root—as epistemology—that one sees in the bespoke, skilled work of many typographers and designer/typographers, even as they are deployed in manifold contexts and platforms. To push the metaphor a bit further, it is about transplanting the root rather than simply grafting one stock on to another (which, in design terms, would simply be fashionable pastiche). It corresponds to our earlier metaphor of modernism as meme, where type styles—like a cultural baton—move from hand to hand, from typographer to typographer, reflecting each new cultural context.

This process of generating innovation can be seen in many of the projects initiated by the Khatt Foundation, which is dedicated to advancing Arabic typography and design research. In the project 'Typographic Matchmaking in the City', this involves collaborating with Western typographers.[6] Khatt Foundation director Huda Smitshuijzen AbiFarès observes: 'Lots of scripts come from a similar origin. This becomes a starting point or a going-back-to point to reconsider cultural connections for the future.'

Smitshuijzen AbiFarès is forthright in arguing that typography has a role in challenging the status quo. In contrast to the kind of 'social design' that simply provides a new typeface for, say, a homeless charity—or the homeless themselves—the point of connection, for her, 'is in talking about our cultures through what we make and through making them together'. The crux is 'learning from the applied art traditions and taking the essence of this but applying it in an open way'.[7]

The once clear division between typographer and designer/typographer who creates fonts for the task at hand is increasingly becoming blurred, and is bridged by projects like 'Typographic Matchmaking in the City'. They also provide a structural link between typography's aesthetic and cultural possibilities. What is instructive, for us, is the way typography is imagined as an object *and* as an art form in context.

Elsewhere, it is new technology that brings the two experiences —typography as object *and* as art form in context—together. Consuming on the screen, one experiences the beauties of the page layout—the panache, the joke or the stillness of space. Yet with the gesture interface, the simple manipulation of finger and thumb

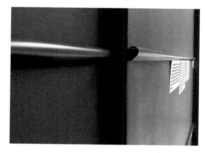

New Simplicity exhibition
Julia
2010–ongoing

5
Paul Barnes, specimen/essay to accompany the exhibition *Thieves Like Us*, dedicated to Marian, New York, October 2011.

6
Huda Smitshuijzen AbiFarès (ed.), *Typographic Matchmaking in the City: Propositions for a Pluralist Public Space* (Amsterdam: Khatt Books, 2010).

7
Huda Smitshuijzen AbiFarès, interviewed at *Design Indaba*, Cape Town, February 2011.

Installation view, Marian Typeface
Commercial Type
2012

Defining style in terms of technical and aesthetic qualities is to define it *against* fashion.

P776 PETER AND THE COCK 1931
The Four Gospels

Peter and the Cock
Eric Gill
1931

zooms us on to the typographer's plane. The page layout recedes and we see instead the sculptural forms that were first articulated in sketchbooks and imaginations. To see typography as, once, only the typographer saw it on the page can be a magical experience for the user and consumer.

The experience of typography is intrinsically about *reading*. The two main ways of reading typography on screen in tablet form are the dedicated readers, such as the Kindle, and the more expressive iPad-type tablets. In the former, the dedicated readers, the hardware provides basic navigation tools while the screen acts as a facsimile of a traditional book page, but one the reader can personalize to make it more legible: dimming or brightening the screen, changing the typeface or colour. This provides the essential requirements for reading where, as with early modernist typography, the aim is to facilitate the experience of reading alone, uninterrupted by clutter. Dedicated readers like the Kindle arguably *remove design*—certainly from the control of typographers. One response to this is AXIS Mincho, a typeface commissioned by the Japanese design magazine *AXIS*.[8] Thinking about the way in which people personalize displays for reading in a range of environments prompted the design of a typeface on an axis of high to low contrast in precise increments, from thick vertical lines with thin horizontals to thin vertical lines with thick horizontals. This allows readers to select the most comfortable intensity for reading. Here, a challenge to typographic authorship provides the rationale for design innovation; the implications of this adjustable function remain to be seen.

iPad-type tablets, on the other hand, encapsulate a more experiential environment than dedicated readers, offering not only the technological hardware of an interactive screen but also a rudimentary set of *gesture metaphors* (swiping, pulling, pinching, tapping). Manipulating the layout with the tips of your fingers—visually 're-editing' it in real time—not only adds a more personal dimension to navigation, but also gives a new cognitive experience.

There is a shift from earlier desktop metaphors—files, folders and tools—to the new, *physical* metaphors. Now a pinch between finger and thumb, unlike selecting the magnifying-glass icon or changing the page size in a drop-down menu, is a purely

8
For a demonstration of the adjuster function, see typeproject.com/demo/axis_mincho.html (accessed January 2014).

phenomenological event—momentarily at least. Touch, here, is still partly metaphorical, but the *feel* of writing on the screen, with either finger or stylus, maps against the actual memory of pen, ink and paper in the analogue world. This brings the multi-dimensionality of the experience of writing to the new informational design 'landscape'.

This mixture of new metaphors and cognitive experiences represents a huge leap forward. The implications for typography and design remain to be seen, but understanding typography—not only as object but also as art form in context—will remain as crucial as ever. And the research is still unfolding ...

In the main, typography's new digital formats still follow the book metaphor—and that is not a bad thing. Many experiments in this area are simply that, experimental journeys rather than holistic re-imagining. In this future for the book, what is lost in the turning of the page is gained by the ability to be visually inquisitive through moving and scaling—but, crucially, without the loss of narrative coherence. Mostly, you return to a page unaltered by your excursion. For, just as in a physical book, bookmarks, page numbers and so on anchor your experience to a place in the document. For all the discussions over multi-narratives that accompanied the birth of the web, it is often more a subject of rhetoric than a paradigm shift. The need for a beginning, middle and end to our reading experience is proving difficult to shift.

The to-ing and fro-ing between analogue and digital experiences goes in both directions, as book metaphors and narratives have returned in tablet formats, and print is re-imagined in the light of digital's 'fragmented and intimate, tactile engagement'. In a commercial context, this leads to predictions that 'magazines will ape their apps'.[9] But as so many of the projects selected here and beyond remind us, it's about understanding the relationship between typography and the experience of reading, taking its essence, and applying it in an open way.

One paradigm shift happening in many of the print-on-demand platforms is that authors can change text 'in-vitro', as it were, simply editing the digital original without republishing (or even letting the reader know). The ramifications for writing are yet to be seen, but those for typography are largely positive. Publications can be updated beyond the simple redesign of jackets, etc. It will be interesting to see how the typographer/designer updates the typographic layout of a digital publication over time.

The sticking point here is copyright. This paradigm of the 'seamlessly updated' could lead to the commercial value of these works being contested and exploited in relation to the design and use of typography. And in due course, the more type-literate the general public becomes, the greater the commercial pressure to use typography to provide validation and cultural capital, as with stars on the red carpet, where the choice of fashion designer reinforces a person's taste over fashion alone. This is a double-edged sword, but exploitation of the commercial value and intellectual property of type design is nothing new to typographers (or designers). Platforms like Typeright.org become the bridge between previously defined areas of cultural advocacy by bringing together diverse sectors, to advocate for typefaces as *creative works*.

It must not be forgotten that the democratization of typographic processes is being accompanied by the first additions of digital typefaces to institutional collections, such as that of the Museum of Modern Art in New York. Or that concept stores like Copenhagen's Playtype—an initiative by e-Types' type foundry of the same

Beyond Postmodern excess, beyond techno-fetish, beyond fashion, something new is going on: a renewed emphasis on the process of type and design as a site of cultural engagement.

9
Robert Andrews, 'Two Become One: How Magazines Will Ape Their Apps', 17 February 2012; paidcontent.org/2012/02/17/419-two-become-one-how-magazines-will-ape-their-apps (accessed January 2014).

10
See playtype.com/store (accessed January 2014).

name (page 140)—provide, quite literally, 'street-level entry to typography'.[10] The more typography becomes publically recognized as an art form, the greater the legal leverage to introduce, say, a royalty scheme for typographers and their descendants. In the atomized, hybridized, distributed design landscape, the repositioning of typographic practice is accompanied by new possibilities for advocacy.

So far, we have plotted the aesthetic developments technology brings to the uses and audiences of typography. The other thread to our analysis is a cultural mapping. Typography reflects the context of its making, and the thin line between fashion and style. Certainly, Eric Gill (page 50)—active in the early twentieth century—was aware of the conventions of his time, but his work is still relevant because he did not simply appropriate the signs of his times. He used the skill and rules of type-making to reflect contemporary culture rather than make fashionable statements. Compare this to work from the Punk era in the 1970s. To contemporary eyes it might still be beautiful and effective, but within the context of the time. Or take the layouts of the magazine *Ray Gun* from the early 1990s; much so-called Postmodern typography/design is unreadable without the context (the baggage) of the time to enlighten the viewer.

In the second decade of the new millennium, typography is again Modern, integral to the physical and intellectual world of the high street, of protest, of corporate headquarters and the world of publishing. In the system for the Adidas Design Center in Herzogenaurach, Germany, the 'Laces' signage and typeface by Büro Uebele are intended to reflect a networked, dynamic world, 'fast and light, [which] leaps and bounds across walls and balustrades, its form vibrating and altering in the process'.[11] There is nothing new there, of course. Le Corbusier, the Bauhaus tutors, even the Futurists would recognize a typography that is vivid, active and fully integrated into its environment.

11
See uebele.com/en/projekte/orientierungssystem/ adidas-laces.html (accessed January 2014).

Typography has always been in the vanguard—think of Stéphane Mallarmé's typeset poems, Surrealist advertising or the typographic screams of Futurist letterpress. And today, beyond Postmodern excess, beyond techno-fetish, beyond fashion—and far from needing to defend itself—typography can relax. Type design can transcend fashion because the integrity of type—its beauty?—remains at the root of the design, rather than its context or fashionable epoch.

Today the cultural trajectory of the avant-garde is introduced into the economic sphere of 'innovation', as we have seen in examples ranging from the Khatt Foundation to *AXIS* magazine. Here, old top-down, structured formulas of development are being replaced with a bottom-up approach open to different audiences, other cultures, new technology and many disciplines.[12] If it remains both rooted *and* open—a practice of possibility—typography will maintain its position in the new modern world of technology and human scale and all the things as yet uninvented.

12
One might think of the open-source movement or the improvisation advocated in Navi Radjou, Jaideep Prabhu and Simone Ahuja, *Jugaad Innovation: Think Frugal, Be Flexible, Generate Breakthrough Growth* (San Francisco, CA: Jossey-Bass, 2012).

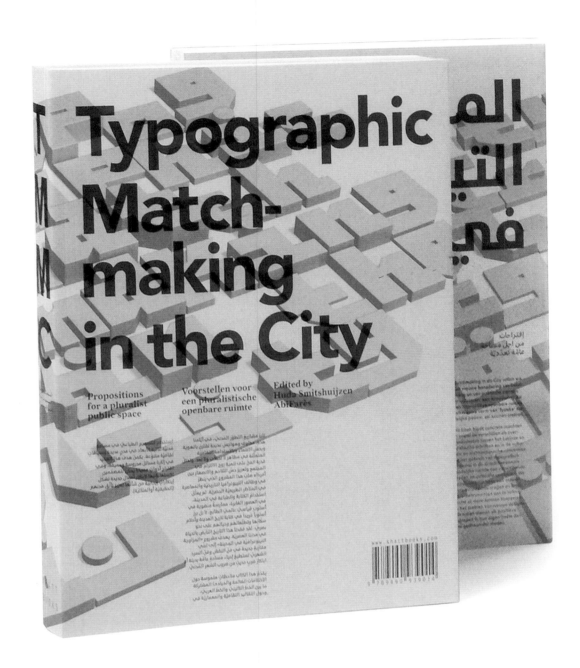

Typographic Matchmaking in the City
Khatt Books; illustration by Naji El Mir,
design by Studio Carvalho Bernau
2010

Emily King

Artists and Type

Text is part of the commonplace palette of contemporary art. Where in 1970 the inclusion of words alongside or instead of images was a decidedly radical gesture, since the mid-1990s it has become absorbed into the normal range of art practice. That span has of course grown to encompass flotation tanks and soup kitchens, so perhaps it's not surprising that the use of text no longer causes a stir. Of the collection of text-based art in this book, the only work that might prompt a frisson is Gelitin's exhibition *Das Kackabet* (Nicola van Senger gallery, Zürich; see opposite), an alphabet made out of faeces, likely human. This reaction would have less to do with a specific art-world sensibility than with the fundamentally repulsive quality of shit.

While the meeting of art and shit is a singular disgust-driven topic, the meeting of art and text has spawned multiple ongoing themes. Where once it was allied to certain movements or schools, these days artists who use text do so in diverse and even contradictory ways. There is no other context in which the art grouped on these pages would be presented as one. In an essay published in 2009, Charles Harrison, the late art historian and one-time member of the group Art & Language, described the contemporaneous practice of using text as 'a kind of filigree added to an avant-garde product'. For certain artists, wrote Harrison, text had become no more than a 'customary component' of their 'brand'.[1] Arguing from the perspective of a 40-year association with the pioneers of Conceptual art, and in light of his early ambitions to create 'an art altogether without objects, a kind of *tabula rasa*', Harrison is understandably disillusioned, yet his dismissal is unfair. The model and language of branding has become so powerful that it sweeps both its proponents and its enemies into its worldview. Among the latter, the term is often used as a licence to avoid interrogating a work's particular qualities.

Tracing the longer history of the inclusion of text in art, before the rise of Conceptual art in the late 1960s, requires the pursuit of several threads. Conceptualism came about as a direct response to the dominance of modernist abstract painting and the voices of critics such as Clement Greenberg in the 1950s. According to Harrison, the by-product of the movement's desire to start from scratch was a tendency to overlook its possible antecedents in text-and-image movements such as Dada. Harrison argued that he and his cohorts in Art & Language desired to be 'mainstream' and 'serious' in the vein of Abstract Expressionism, rather than 'alternative' in the style of Dada, Marcel Duchamp, neo-Dada and Fluxus. This was a state of affairs he later regretted.[2]

1
Charles Harrison, 'Think Again', in *Art and Text* (London: Black Dog, 2009), p. 25.

2
Ibid., p. 20.

Das Kackabet
Gelitin
2007

Running alongside, and related to the evolution of both Conceptual art and the Dada/Fluxus strand, was the notion of Pop. Art's appropriation of the text and imagery of popular culture has origins in the early twentieth century. In the 1910s, such artists as Georges Braque and Juan Gris incorporated fragments of printed texts into complex painted surfaces, a method later called Synthetic Cubism. Pop art was proclaimed as a movement only in the late 1950s and lost currency as a term a decade later, yet the explicit reference to the products and publications of popular culture in fine art both predated that period and continues to this day.

Contemporary artists who use text, but wish to avoid being placed in relation to the twentieth century's march of movements, might claim another, much longer history for their work. An artist like David Shrigley (page 57) can be linked to the Dada/Fluxus-associated urge to disrupt the status quo with humour, but equally could be placed in a 250-year tradition of satirical illustration. Surveying the collection of late twentieth-/early twenty-first-century art gathered in this book, the influence of twentieth-century antecedents is very obvious, but similarly apparent is the blurring and confusion of historical influences and formerly distinct motives to use text in artworks. To pick one of many examples, a work such as Christopher Wool's painting *Fuckem* (1992) seems to be equal parts Pop art appropriation and Conceptualist *tabula rasa*.

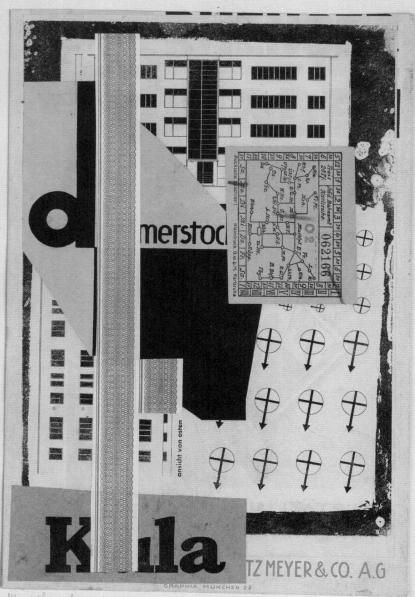

Kurt Schwitters 1928   Karlsruhe

So, there are various allegiances between strands of contemporary art and historical precedents, but it no longer makes sense to organize contemporary artworks into clear-cut categories of the Conceptual/Pop/Dada kind. It might appear that everything is up for grabs, but that is not quite the case. There is one area of art activity that remains taboo for the most part: its very close relationship with design, and in the case of art that uses text, graphic design. The artworks shown on these pages cover a wide range of materials and processes, but in every case, the artist making them made a series of formal decisions about their appearance that are akin to, if not indistinguishable from, the processes of design.

Long-term advocates of Conceptual art find the notion of art being designed troublesome because of the myth that form can be entirely dictated by ideas. To return to Harrison and his argument that contemporary artists use text as part of their 'brand', for him the process of making formal decisions appeared to imply an uncomfortably close relationship with the processes of commerce. Artists who admit to thinking about the appearance of their work risk the accusation that they have been reduced to making mindless consumer objects. In his seminal article 'Art after Philosophy' of 1969, the key Conceptual artist Joseph Kosuth wrote: 'Aesthetic considerations are ... always extraneous to an object's function or "reason to be".'[3] In fact, many graphic designers share the same reservations about form. Influenced by the powerful rhetoric of Conceptual art, graphic designers of the generation that emerged in the late 1980s and early 1990s tend to argue that form springs directly from concept. Even those most associated with formal elaboration, such as Jonathan Barnbrook, insist that each of their graphic twirls had its basis in intellectual rigour.

VOLUME 1 NUMBER 1   MAY 1969

Art-Language
The Journal of conceptual art

Edited by Terry Atkinson, David Bainbridge,
Michael Baldwin, Harold Hurrell

Contents

Art-Language is published three times a year by
*Art & Language Press 84 Jubilee Crescent, Coventry CV6 3ET
England, to which address all mss and letters should be sent.
Price 7s.6d UK, $1.50 USA   All rights reserved*
Printed in Great Britain

Cover of Art-Language
Art & Language
1969

3
Joseph Kosuth, 'Art after Philosophy', *Studio International*, October 1969; ubu.com/papers/kosuth_philosophy.html
(accessed January 2014).

Karlsruhe
Kurt Schwitters
1929

Imagine the Green is Red
David Shrigley
1998

Work No. 1092: MOTHERS
Martin Creed
2011

4
Susan Hapgood, 'Fonts of Wisdom', *Frieze*,
no. 29, June–August 1996; frieze.com/issue/
article/fonts_of_wisdom (accessed January 2014).

Reviewing exhibitions by Kosuth and Lawrence Weiner, perhaps the two most significant Conceptual artists, the art critic Susan Hapgood took issue with the denial of form. Analysing the shows in detail, she concluded that 'an artist's aesthetic eventually turns up, despite efforts to neutralize or thwart it'.[4] Not only individual artists, but also collectives, might find that they have generated a distinctive and even imitable aesthetic. The group Art & Language published the journal *Art-Language* sporadically between 1968 and 1985 (page 57). For the most part adopting the apparently neutral typographic template of the academic journal, the publication, however inadvertently, set a graphic format for Conceptual art that remains in use more than 40 years later. An unremarkable serif or sans serif face set in black on an open sea of white space still tends to denote to the art audience that they are in the territory of the Idea. Mark Wallinger's self-portrait 'I' is a perfect example (opposite).

Progressing from setting type in ink on paper, Kosuth and his contemporary Bruce Nauman also began to make words in neon. The effect of these signs, such as Nauman's *100 Live and Die* (1984; page 60), is to render language theatrical, and in so doing call its mechanisms into question. A great many artists have used similar strategies in the decades since, among them Martin Creed and Cerith Wyn Evans. Both acutely tuned to the nuances of form, Creed's and Wyn Evans's references are anything but naïve. Rather, they are a deliberate means of recalling the wrestling with and relish of language that was so vivid for the generation of the late 1960s.

Discussing his work, Creed often refers to very straightforward processes and basic emotions. Interviewed by Paul Morley about the exhibition *Mothers* of 2011 (Hauser & Wirth Gallery, London; above), he claimed: 'I hope [my work] leads to better feelings ... for me, and ... for others, because if other people get something from it like a feeling that's nice for them, then that is nice for me,

Self-Portrait (Freehand 2)
Mark Wallinger
2007

100 Live and Die
Bruce Nauman
1984

5
'Paul Morley's Showing Off: Martin Creed',
The Guardian, 30 January 2011; theguardian.com/
music/2011/jan/30/martin-creed-david-byrne.

6
Jennifer Higgie, 'Cerith Wyn Evans', *Frieze*, no. 47,
June–August 1999; frieze.com/issue/review/
cerith_wyn_evans1 (accessed January 2014).

because [they might] like me.' Pressed by Morley on this point, Creed insisted: 'It is sincere ... as far as I'm able to tell ... I can't think of a reason that rings more true that I do things other than that I want to be loved.'[5]

At something of an opposite extreme, Wyn Evans's work is founded on an intricate and even self-consciously poetic frame of reference. Quoting from philosophy, literature and poetry in neon and fireworks, he tempers the elaborate nature of his language and materials with very simple typographic form. Reviewing the artist's film *Firework Text (Pasolini)* of 1998 (opposite), the art critic Jennifer Higgie called the piece 'grandiloquent yet a little forlorn. The achingly romantic words are, at first, hard to read, before the poem, letter by letter, bursts into flames, explodes and fades. It's a wonderful image—words as fireworks, erupting joyfully before their own annihilation.'[6] Creed and Wyn Evans are pursuing different muses, yet in using a typographic style that prompts memories of the early Conceptual art, both reassert the movement's argument that language is an appropriate material for art.

This use of typographic form to refer to a certain philosophical position has echoes in the terrain of graphic design proper. More engaged graphic designers had long been aware of the possibility that letterforms carried meaning, but in the early 1990s this became the subject of lively debate, much of it conducted on the pages of the Californian magazine *Emigre*. The upshot was that the use of Helvetica became near forbidden among liberal North American

Still from *Firework Text (Pasolini)*
Cerith Wyn Evans
1998

designers on the grounds of its association with corporate America. In flagrant opposition to this lore, the Dutch designers Experimental Jetset have used the typeface consistently since they formed their group in the late 1990s. Acknowledging that the 'neutrality' of the face, the idea that it carries no meaning, is 'a myth', nevertheless they argue that it is a 'myth that created its own reality ... The neutrality of Helvetica, real or imagined, enables us and the user to fully focus on the design as a whole, neutralizing the typographic layer as a way to keep the concept as clear and pure as possible.'[7]

Experimental Jetset shares the quest for an approximation of typographic neutrality with a number of artists, among them the aforementioned Weiner, who began using text in his art in 1967. Usually painted directly on to the wall, Weiner's pieces typically describe physical relationships in language so basic that it becomes poetic, such as *Water with Salt + Water without Salt* (page 64). He refers to these text works as sculptures, yet on occasion he uses such lowly materials as cardboard and canvas to make physical structures that would more conventionally merit the description. As such, it seems safe to assume that the letterforms he uses, usually something close to Franklin Gothic, are intended to be the typographic equivalent. Recently he has started using his own typeface, a set of sturdy capitals he calls Margaret Seaworthy Gothic. In an exhibition catalogue published in 1969, Weiner claimed that 'presentation ... has very little to do with the art',[8] yet the minute attention he pays to the nuance of typographic restraint would suggest otherwise.

7
Interview with Rudy VanderLans, *Emigre*, no. 65, May 2003; experimentaljetset.nl/archive/helveticanism.html (accessed January 2014).

8
January 5–31 1969 (New York: Seth Siegelaub Gallery, 1969).

IT'S
NOT
ART
(THAT COUNTS NOW)

ARE
YOU
CRYING?

WHAT
SHOUL
I
DO?

NOTHING

★

NOBODY

EVERYTHING IS OVER
everything is over
Everything Is Over
everything is over
EVERYTHING IS OVER
Everything is over
everything is over
Everything Is Over
EVERYTHING IS OVER
everything is over
EVERYTHING IS OVER
everything is over
Everything Is Over
everything is over
EVERYTHING IS OVER

A
D
U
L
T

O·N·L·Y
PLEASE

WATER WITH SALT ✚ WATER WITHOUT SALT

Water with Salt + Water without Salt
Lawrence Weiner
1987

In formal terms, as Experimental Jetset would testify, engineering the typographic unremarkable is as much of a challenge as creating the flamboyant. Contrary to Experimental Jetset's views, however, Weiner is said to avoid Helvetica on the grounds that he finds it authoritarian.

The artist Ed Ruscha is also very strongly associated with the use of text, and similarly, he was moved to design his own set of capital letters, a font that he calls Boy Scout Utility Modern. 'I wanted to come up with a typeface that didn't have any curves in it,' he has said of the face.[9] Floating over beautiful but blank scenes of mountains and sunsets and spelling out gnomic yet banal messages such as 'So it is the Amazing Earth' (opposite), the sharp-cornered letters are intended to emphasize the dissonance between word and image. Over the last two decades, however, Ruscha's style, the way he meshes image, letterform and language, has become so well known that the mismatch has been all but obscured. What might once have looked uncanny now looks like a Ruscha; Boy Scout Utility Modern deployed in the making of Ruscha Typographic Deadpan. Ruscha's typeface design is artless, yet his graphic style is powerful enough to become part of the common visual culture.

Ruscha's possibly inadvertent design triumph could be a by-product of his having studied typography in the 1950s. The artist Barbara Kruger likewise trained as a designer and similarly formulated a style of text and image that is immediately recognizable as her own. With the aim of exploring the relationship between the structures

9
Dana Goodyear, 'Moving Day', *New Yorker*, 11 April 2011; newyorker.com/talk/2011/04/11/ 110411ta_talk_goodyear (accessed January 2014).

So it is the Amazing Earth
Ed Ruscha
1984

of language and power, Kruger sets texts such as 'I shop therefore I am' (below) in her signature face, Futura Bold Italic, on red bands over found black-and-white imagery (on occasion she also uses Helvetica Ultra Condensed). Writing on the online forum Design Observer, the designer Michael Bierut instigated furious debate when he related an incident involving a student reproducing Kruger's style apparently in complete ignorance of her work.[10] At issue was the point when a certain graphic style becomes unmoored from its origins or its author and is open for use as a free-standing entity.

While Ruscha and Kruger have design skills of their own, other artists who use text have chosen to collaborate with graphic designers to ensure that their work is typographically correct. In the late 1990s the artist Damien Hirst teamed up with the designer Jonathan Barnbrook to create a set of prints entitled *The Last Supper*. Adopting the graphic language of Swiss medicine packaging, Hirst spelled out a menu of greasy-spoon delicacies including 'Steak and Kidney Pie' and 'Beans & Chips'. The success of the prints hinges on the precision of their graphic execution, and Barnbrook got every detail just right, including the appearance of a Hirst logo in a different format on every package. In this instance the alliance of the use of text with the idea of branding is completely apt.

The artist Pierre Huyghe similarly employs the skills of graphic designers, but to different ends. Sustaining a long-standing relationship with the partnership M/M (Paris), he argues that not only do they have an expertise he needs in his work, but also it is important that they make their contribution visible. 'An expert is someone who knows perfectly the language of his or her field and so is able to translate it,' he has said. 'If I try and translate it, I make a mistake. And translation always involves interpretation— I like the fact that Michael and Mathias [Amzalag and Augustyniak, of M/M (Paris)] make that clear.'[11] For their part, M/M talk about revisiting and developing the 'language of Pierre' each time they

10
Michael Bierut, 'Designing Under the Influence', Design Observer, 26 February 2005; observatory. designobserver.com/feature/designing-under-the-influence/2727/ (accessed January 2014).

11
Pierre Huyghe, interview with the author, 5 May 2010.

Untitled (I shop therefore I am)
Barbara Kruger
1987

work with the artist. [12] There are many parts to this idiom, but perhaps the most distinctive single element is the neon typeface that he uses for his ongoing disclaimer series, for example *I do not own Tate Modern or the Death Star*.

Venturing further than collaboration, some contemporary artists have made typography the subject of their work. In the late 1990s Fiona Banner began to explore punctuation marks, and this led to her rendering the full stops of various widely used typefaces, including Gill Sans and Palatino, in three dimensions and producing them at different scales in a range of materials, including polystyrene and bronze (above). These works prompt us to notice and marvel at the minute differences in typeface designs. By omitting any mention of the designers of the faces or the context in which they were designed, Banner appears to scrutinize type in the way an amateur lepidopterist might look at rare butterflies.

Among the subjects most commonly explored in art since 1990 has been that of historical modernism or, as it is sometimes put, modernisms. Unsurprisingly, much of this work has touched on design, and alongside pieces dwelling on architecture and product design, there is also a body of recent art that delves into modernist ideas about typography. In 2001 the then 25-year-old Polish artist Paulina Olowska devised a series of physical exercises entitled *Bauhaus Yoga*, which were photographically recorded four years later. The pictures show the artist wearing a loose red dress that harks back to the Victorian 'dress reform' movement, enacting physical poses that are reminiscent of early modern ballet and at the same time hint at letterforms. The work is a collage of ideas, a mesh of Olowska's impressions of various early twentieth-century sensibilities. A few years later, in 2008, the British artist Ryan Gander made a piece entitled *The New New Alphabet* in collaboration with the graphic designer Rasmus Spanggaard Troelsen. A reworking

12
M/M (Paris), interview with the author, 21 October 2011.

Slipstream, Palatino, Nuptial, Times, Gill Sans Condensed, New Century Schl BK Polystyrene Full Stops
Fiona Banner
1998

Handle with Care!
Sister Corita
1967

of Wim Crouwel's New Alphabet, a radical technology-driven typeface designed in 1967, it was made by adding features of the late 1950s Swiss typeface Helvetica to Crouwel's spare forms, rendering them infinitely less elegant, but much more readable. Like Olowska before him, Gander combined two related but quite different twentieth-century modernist design philosophies to create an odd early twenty-first-century hybrid.

This essay has touched on but failed to do justice to the range of the contemporary text-based artworks shown on these pages. There are also the so-sharp-they-cut-themselves compositions of Scott King (pages 190–91), to name one more. The subject of all these works is language, but in taking physical form they place themselves in a web of typographic influence, with strands taken from both art and design. As long as artists deal with words, as long as they create text, their concerns and processes will overlap with those of graphic designers and typographers. Rather than denying the importance of appearance and muttering about branding, it would be more productive to acknowledge the common territory, and for artists and designers to mine each other's disciplines for all they're worth.

Alphabet
Paulina Olowska
2005–12

Rick Poynor

The Typographic Voice

The most intriguing question typography poses is, oddly, one that is rarely addressed, or addressed only in the vaguest of terms. In a given piece of design, what does the typography itself say to us? It's a commonplace of student projects and professional design advice that type endows a communication with its distinctive voice. The usual way of demonstrating this point is to take a few meaning-laden words—'I love you' is an example I saw on a typography blog—and set them in a range of contrasting typefaces to demonstrate how the type can reflect the words' sentiment with the proper finesse and sincerity, or bungle the tone and take the communication in entirely the wrong direction. This is fine as far as it goes, but it reduces the subject of typographic meaning to the simplest and least nuanced of terms, and suggests that the allocation of typefaces is the prime consideration when a designer constructs graphic messages that involve words and typography.

Most graphic communication is much more complicated, as confirmed by the selection of contemporary pieces that follows. These representative examples of type and typography since the year 2000 indicate some of but not necessarily all the typographic concerns of this period. Looking through them, I am struck at once by the problem of typographic voice and how to talk about it with precision. Design specialists tend to explain developments in the discipline, such as the impact of technology on type design, from the inside, while ordinary viewers and readers will inevitably focus not on unseen processes and factors, but on the visual outcome encountered on the page or in the street. Being vaguely 'type aware', with an enhanced sensitivity to the look of letterforms that comes from routinely making type choices on a computer, is not the same as the contextual understanding possessed by professional designers or historians of the subject. For the non-specialist viewer, the success or failure of a communication must depend in large part on the effectiveness of its voice, but how should the semiotic timbre of this voice be determined and described?

Remarkably little work has been done on the question. As Theo van Leeuwen noted in 2006 in an essay entitled 'Towards a Semiotics of Typography', 'despite the fact that a number of linguists have begun to explore this new field … we do not yet have a systematic framework for the analysis of the communicative work done by typography today.'[1] Moreover, as anyone involved in graphic design knows implicitly and as Van Leeuwen spells out, typography is 'multi-modal' rather than a unitary matter of type alone, because it is 'integrated with other semiotic means of expression such as colour,

1
Theo van Leeuwen, 'Towards a Semiotics of Typography', *Information Design Journal + Document Design*, vol. 14, no. 2, 2006, pp. 139–55.

texture, three-dimensionality, and movement'. Space and imagery are also important factors within complex visual designs. Van Leeuwen goes on to itemize different typographic resources, such as weight, expansion, slope, curvature, connectivity and orientation, and to assign them particular meanings. For instance, roundness can signify 'smooth', 'soft', 'natural', 'organic' or 'maternal', while angularity signifies 'abrasive', 'harsh', 'technical' or 'masculine'. Van Leeuwen's analysis takes us only so far, and he admits that we are still in the early stages, but it does indicate the complexity of the semiotic frameworks required to account for every interlocking component in a piece of typographic design. His illustrative examples are rudimentary in form compared to the graphically challenging examples in the following pages.

In 2011 a research project undertaken by the Simplification Centre and Jeanne-Louise Moys, a researcher at the University of Reading, made some unexpected discoveries about how typographic voice is perceived.[2] Fifteen people with no connection to graphic design were questioned about their reaction to several magazines chosen because of their typographic complexity. Moys found that the participants were sensitive to the tone of documents and that they formed judgments on this basis. This tone came from content, images, colour and paper, as well as typographic presentation. However, the participants did not share designers' strong concern with typefaces and type categories, and they sorted the publications into related groups using more general criteria. 'When it came to typeface,' writes Moys, 'they were more likely to discuss its treatment than its choice: whether something was in bold, capitals, italics, colour, had a drop shadow or other effects, seemed to influence its distinctiveness far more than the choice of typeface.' This leads Moys to propose that the way type is treated and the 'impression of busyness' is possibly 'far more influential on the typographic voice than what typeface is used'. Here, again, considerably more research is needed into a wider range of typographic materials before firm conclusions can be drawn and perhaps some day applied by designers (although designers have tended to resist such prescriptions). What comes across strongly, though, is the sense that, in the absence of formulated guidelines, designers can rely only on a tacit professional understanding of how designs will be received, which might not coincide with the way viewers perceive them.

It would be illuminating to see the examples here subjected to this kind of investigation, particularly the less orthodox pieces. Without such a framework, a typographic insider—and that probably includes you, the reader—can examine these designs only from a position that might take too much for granted. Consider, for instance, a device that seems very contemporary: the way in which designers float type across similarly unanchored elements as though the visual field consists of separate layers, one above the other. Variations on this manner of construction can be seen in work by Hort, Rasmus Koch Studio, Karel Martens, Richard Turley, Cornel Windlin and Zak Group. Ludovic Balland's three posters, meant to represent three perspectives on architecture—A, B and C— in an exhibition, evolve towards ever greater architectonic density. How would Van Leeuwen's semiotic reading of letterforms deal with customized characters that awkwardly fuse rounded and angular strokes, loosely framed by grids of dots and mesh-like modules, in a layout in which classical centring and modernist asymmetry collide? Is it necessary to be an architect to gain full semiotic value from this manipulation, or would a controlled test with non-specialist viewers reveal it to embody meanings other than those notionally intended?

2
Jeanne-Louise Moys, 'Typographic Voice: Researching Readers' Interpretations', Technical paper 6, Simplification Centre, April 2011, pp. 1–15; simplificationcentre.org.uk/resources/ technical-papers (accessed March 2014).

Despite the fact that a number of linguists have begun to explore this new field … we do not yet have a systematic framework for the analysis of the communicative work done by typography today.
Theo van Leeuwen

Balland's posters display another contemporary tendency that can be found, expressed in differing ways, in many of the designs shown here: the tension between structure and informality, function and playfulness. In the mid-1990s, when new kinds of typographic voice were a pressing issue for radical typographers of the early digital era, there were many assaults on convention (a reminder of these transgressions can be seen in the jumbled sizes and crossing-out in Jonathan Barnbrook's *Heathen* graphics for David Bowie, one of the older pieces here). Today typographers can take the relaxation of rules as a given, rather than something to be fought for, and blend moments of waywardness with a careful concern for structural soundness and even a reassuring sobriety. The letterform can be distorted—see Ed Fella and Metahaven—or physically connected by extensions to other elements, as found in designs by Philippe Apeloig and karlssonwilker. Alphabets can be improvised from three-dimensional objects, such as flower petals and pasta shapes (Marian Bantjes), fluorescent tubes (Change is Good), twigs and water drops (Doyle Partners), the landscape photographed from above (Pablo Martin) or huge inflatable cushions (Cornel Windlin). Such designers as Laurent Benner, Stuart Bailey, FUEL, Julia and Studio Frith produce typography with traces of whimsy, quirkiness and off-handedness that is always cultivated and knowing rather than naïve or oblivious of its effect. But even as I write this, I am conscious that I am seeing these pieces from the designers' point of view, with an eye trained to spot small departures from well-understood conventions of typography. If these designs work for their audiences, this might suggest a similarly educated taste, but at this point, without rigorous viewer surveys, we cannot say for sure.

This quirkiness is, in any case, not the norm in contemporary typography, where functional solutions in the spirit and style of modernist typography before Postmodernism now flourish—see Cartlidge Levene's WalkRide wayfinding system, e-Types' Medilabel Safety System for Danish hospitals, or Mark Porter's work for *The Guardian*. Such designers as Bibliothèque, Farrow and Made Thought continue to practise a fashionably stylized modernism for the tasteful consumer, while work by Experimental Jetset and Gavillet & Rust shows that a conceptual, implicitly critical version of modernism remains just about possible, even now. Other designers —Anthony Burrill, Atelier Carvalho Bernau, De Designpolitie—prefer a plainness and directness that can verge on childlike simplicity. There is a sense in such designs that in order to be clear about 'What Design Can Do!'—as a Dutch conference puts it—typography must purify itself of unnecessary elaboration or adornment, return to basics and start again. New systematic frameworks for investigating viewers' responses to its manner of multi-modal address would undoubtedly assist in that task.

Designers

Philippe Apeloig
ARC (RCA) journal
Phil Baines
André Baldinger
Ludovic Balland
Marian Bantjes
Jonathan Barnbrook
Nick Bell Design
Jop Van Bennekom
    & Veronica Ditting
Laurent Benner
Pierre Bernard
Bibliothèque
Michael Bierut
Peter Bil'ak
Nicholas Blechman
Sara De Bondt Studio
Irma Boom Office
Erich Brechbühl
Anthony Burrill
Cartlidge Levene
Atelier Carvalho Bernau
Change is Good
Commercial Type
De Designpolitie
Dot Dot Dot magazine
Doyle Partners
Markus Dreßen/Spector
    Bureau
Atelier Dyakova
Esterson Associates
e-Types
Experimental Jetset
Farrow
Ed Fella
Frost✲ Design
FUEL
Till Gathmann
Gavillet & Rust
James Goggin
Graphic Thought Facility
Julia Hasting
Jonathan Hoefler &
    Tobias Frere-Jones

Hort
Thomas Huot-Marchand
Gary Hustwit
David James
    & Gareth Hague
Julia
karlssonwilker inc
Zak Kyes/Zak Group
Scott King
Alan Kitching
Joerg Koch
Rasmus Koch Studio
Kontrapunkt
L2M3
Jürg Lehni
Made Thought
Karel Martens
Pablo Martin
Peter Mendelsund
Metahaven
Niels Shoe Meulman
J. Abbott Miller
Monocle
Julian Morey
John Morgan Studio
Norm
North
Optimo
OurType
David Pearson
David Pidgeon
Playtype/e-Types
Mark Porter
Project Projects
Sagmeister Inc.
Office of Paul Sahre
Peter Saville
Paula Scher
Ralph Schraivogel
Erik Spiekermann
Spin
Astrid Stavro
Stockholm Design Lab
Studio Dumbar
Studio Frith
Suburbia
Jeremy Tankard
Thonik
Triboro
Troika
Niklaus Troxler
Richard Turley
Andreas Uebele
Value and Service
Vier5
Micha Weidmann Studio
Why Not Associates
Cornel Windlin
Martin Woodtli

le premier
opéra africain

création

Musique   **Zé Manel Fortes**
Livret   **Koulsy Lamko**

Direction artistique   **Wasis Diop**
Mise en scène   **Jean-Pierre Leurs**
Lumière   **Jacques Rouveyrollis**
Décors et costumes   **Oumou Sy**

châ
-te-
let

THÉÂTRE
MUSICAL
DE PARIS

Bintou Wéré

un opéra

25, 26 et 27 octobre 2007 à 20 h

du Sahel

Théâtre du Châtelet poster
Philippe Apeloig
2007

Type
Customized version of Akkurat

Concert
exceptionnel

**Vendredi
30 Mai 2008
à 21 h**

Roy Hargrove
et RH Factor
invitent
MC Solaar
et Ron Carter

châ
-te-
let

THÉÂTRE
MUSICAL
DE PARIS

T. 01 40 28 28 40 / chatelet-theatre.com

Théâtre du Châtelet poster
Philippe Apeloig
2008

Type
Customized version of Akkurat

Festival de danse

CCN – Ballet de Lorraine
Bronislava Nijinska /
Tero Saarinen
Hunt, Noces, Mariage
4 et 5 avril

Ballet d'Europe
Jean-Charles Gil
Folavi, Mireille
8 et 9 avril

Ballet de Hambourg
John Neumeier
Mort à Venise
16, 17, 18, 19 et 20 avril

Aterballetto
Mauro Bigonzetti
Wam, Cantata
23, 24 et 25 avril

Compañía Nacional de Danza
Nacho Duato /
Tomaz Pandur
Alas
12, 13, 14, 15 et 16 mai

Design Philippe Apeloig 2008

T. 01 40 28 28 40 / chatelet-theatre.com

Théâtre du Châtelet poster
Philippe Apeloig
2008

Type
Customized version of Akkurat

Philippe Apeloig 77

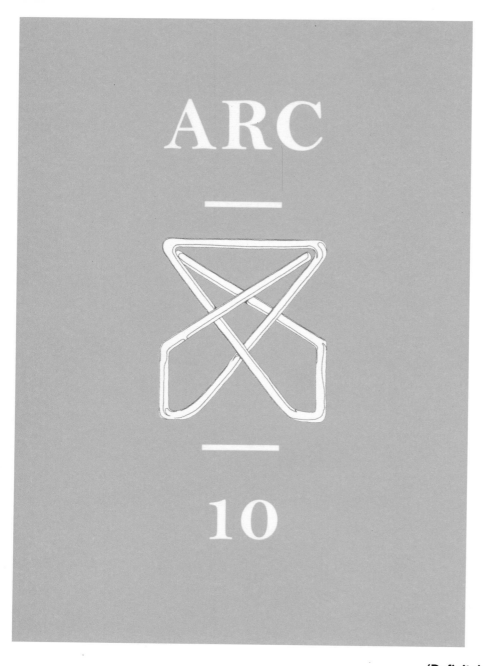

ARC
—
10

ARC (RCA) journal
Various designers
2004–2012

Type
Various

'Definitely not a brochure for the college,' according to its final editor, Charmian Griffin, _ARC_ was created by RCA students for RCA students, as a platform to experiment with publishing, writing, editing, design, typography and art direction. Its original incarnation, _Ark_, was produced from 1950 to 1978 and provided early outings in print for a host of creative luminaries, such as Alan Fletcher and David Hockney.

ARC (RCA) journal
Various designers
2004–2012

Type
Various

7 July 2005 Memorial
Phil Baines (typography) and
Carmody Groarke (memorial design)
2009

Type
Custom made type

Exactly four years after the London bus and Tube bombings of 7 July 2005, a memorial was unveiled in Hyde Park of 52 stainless steel pillars in four clusters, each one cast with the date, time and place of death of a different victim. Asked for typography that suggested London, Phil Baines drew a bespoke font based on the Victorian sans serif sign-maker's lettering seen on older buildings around the city, and arranged the text to read vertically, like a book spine. The names of the victims are listed on a separate plaque, also designed by Baines.

7 July 2005 Memorial
Phil Baines (typography) and
Carmody Groarke (memorial design)
2009

Type
Custom made type

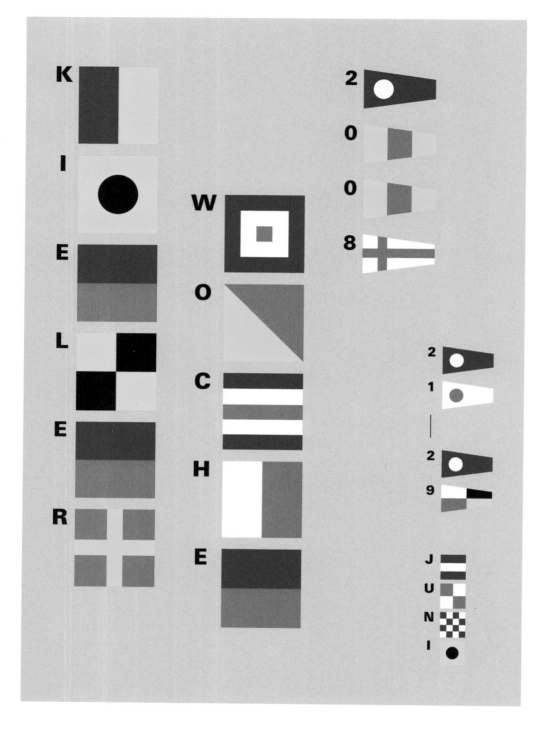

Kieler Woche regatta poster
André Baldinger
2008

Type
Univers 75

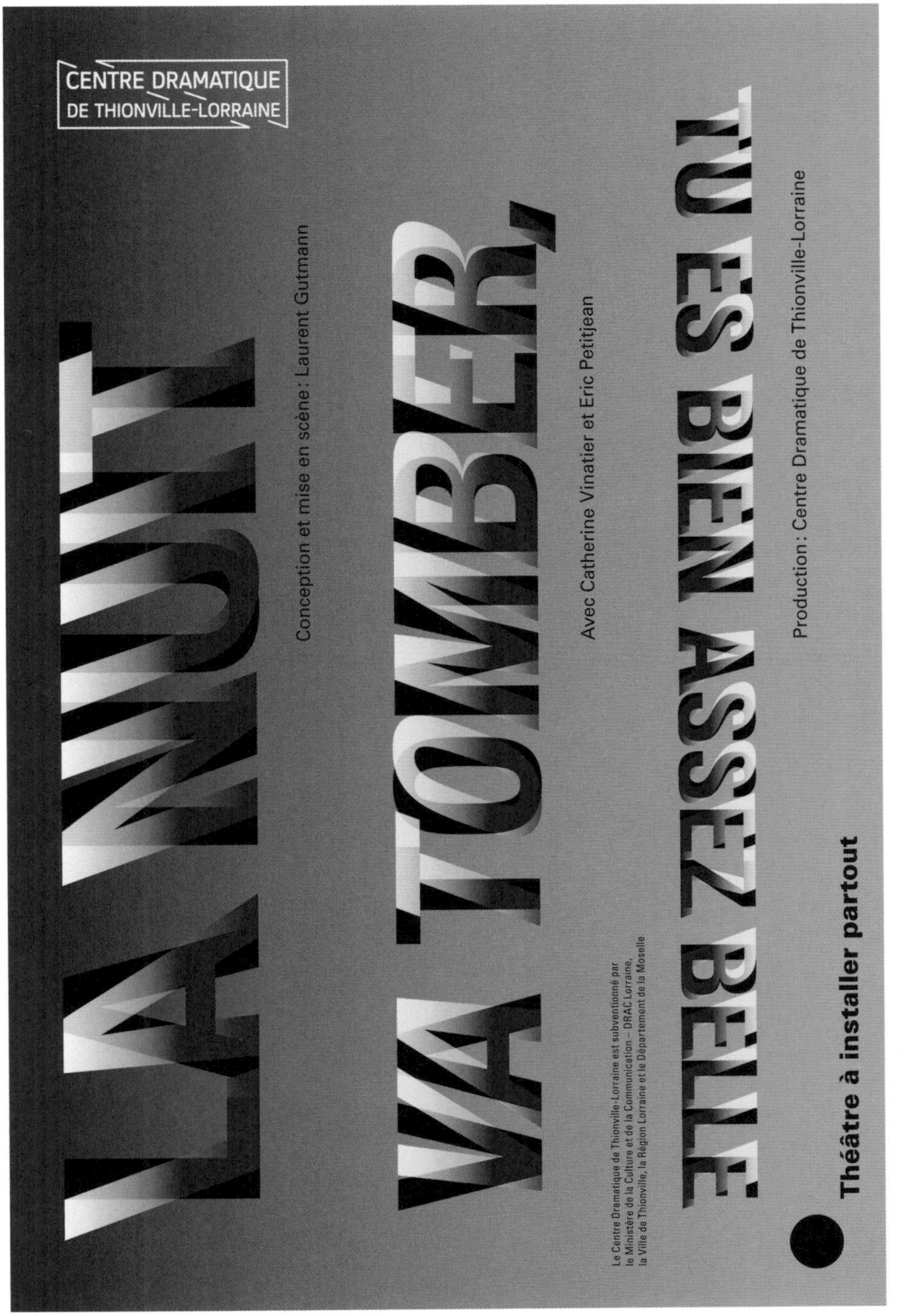

CENTRE DRAMATIQUE
DE THIONVILLE-LORRAINE

Conception et mise en scène : Laurent Gutmann

LA NUIT

VA TOMBER,

Avec Catherine Vinatier et Eric Petitjean

TU ES BIEN ASSEZ BELLE

Production : Centre Dramatique de Thionville-Lorraine

Le Centre Dramatique de Thionville-Lorraine est subventionné par
le Ministère de la Culture et de la Communication – DRAC Lorraine,
la Ville de Thionville, la Région Lorraine et le Département de la Moselle

Théâtre à installer partout

La Nuit va Tomber ('Night Will Fall') theatre poster
André Baldinger
2005

Type
Univers

Istituto Svizzero di Roma
Sede di Venezia   presents

Campo Sant'Agnese, Dorsoduro 810
(tra Accademia e Zattere)

Teaching Architecture.

3 positions (A) B C

B : Durata mostra :
7 ottobre–
30 ottobre
2010

C : Durata mostra :
9 novembre–
27 novembre
2010

Made in Switzerland
Emanuel Christ e Christoph Gantenbein

Durata mostra

Hong Kong in Zurich. A Typological Transfer

26 agosto–
25 settembre
2010

ETH
Eidgenössische Technische Hochschule Zürich
Swiss Federal Institute of Technology Zurich

Orari
martedì–venerdì
ore
11.00–13.00 /
15.00–18.00
sabato ore
14.00–18.00
Chiuso lunedì,
domenica e festivi

Istituto
Svizzero

Roma
Milano
Venezia

Hong Kong in Zurich?

This exhibition in Venice as part of the Architecture Biennale in 2010 featured three individual perspectives on urban architecture from architects at three Swiss architecture schools. Ludovic Balland designed a catalogue and poster for each, denoting them A, B and C and deploying the same eye-catchingly anarchic typography across the set to give the three-part exhibition a distinctive, coherent single identity.

Teaching Architecture:
3 Positions Made in Switzerland **identity**
Ludovic Balland
2010

Type
Agenda

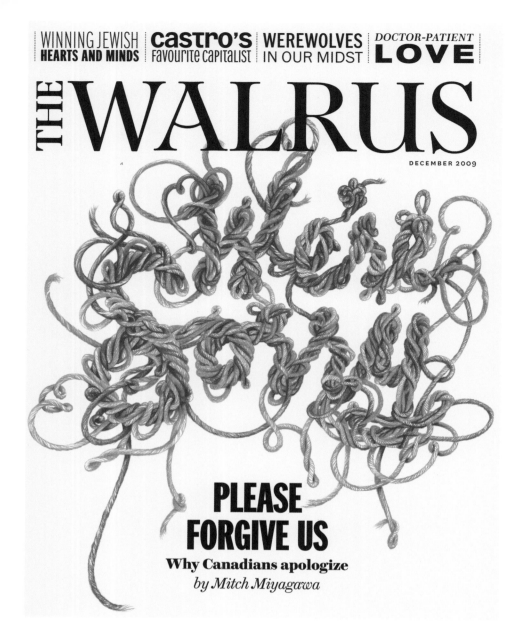

THE WALRUS

DECEMBER 2009

PLEASE FORGIVE US

Why Canadians apologize

by Mitch Miyagawa

We're Sorry for The Walrus
Marian Bantjes
2009

Type
Custom made lettering

Commissioned by *The Walrus* to illustrate its cover story on the Canadian propensity to apologize, and the difficulties that ensue from public apologies for past national crimes, Bantjes created a visual metaphor of knotted and twisted yarn. 'I quite like the way, from a distance this looks like some gruesome viscera ... but on closer inspection it reveals itself to be only harmless, friendly yarn.'

Bantjes' chapter opener for her book, *I Wonder,* is created entirely in pasta pieces of different shapes. Her aim was to reflect the sense of honour in which the ordinary is elevated and made the object of attention, praise and, in extreme cases, worship.

Honour
Marian Bantjes
2010

Type
Custom made lettering

'My peonies were wilting and sighing, and I decided to immortalize them, one afternoon.'

I Want It All
Marian Bantjes
2006

Type
Custom made lettering

heathen

The title and theme of David Bowie's 2002 album found their perfect typographic accompaniment in Jonathan Barnbrook's Priori font, derived from the carved lettering of religious buildings and memorials. 'We took the theme of heathen defined as "one who is regarded as irreligious, uncivilized, or unenlightened." To express this visually, I thought about how religious icons have been destroyed in the past. We then treated the graphics in the same way. The majority of the text is crossed or scribbled out.

Heathen **by David Bowie**
Jonathan Barnbrook
2002

Type
Priori

'Finally, in a simple visual way,
we tried to say "anti" by putting
the word heathen upside down
on the cover.'

Heathen **by David Bowie**
Jonathan Barnbrook
2002

Type
Priori

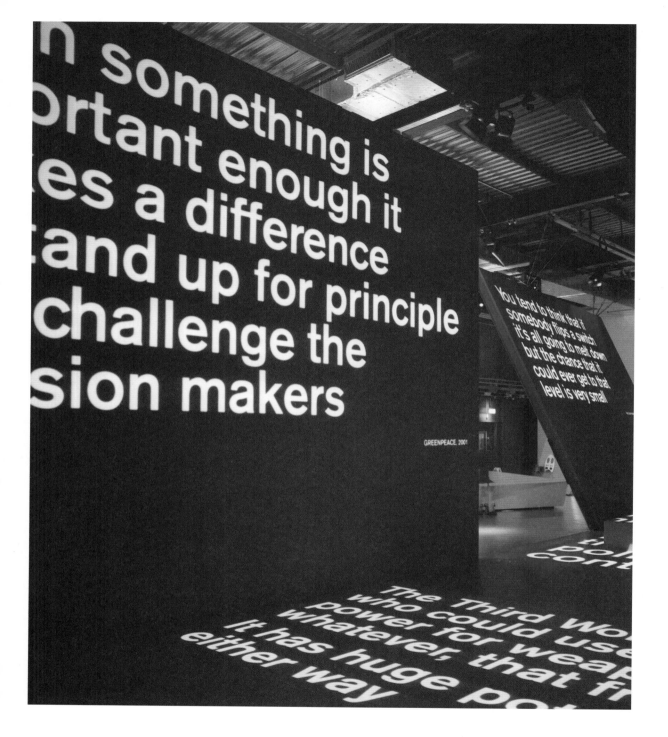

Sparking Reaction at BNFL Visitors' Centre, Sellafield, for the Science Museum
Nick Bell Design
2002

Type
Akzidenz-Grotesk BQ, Beta Sans

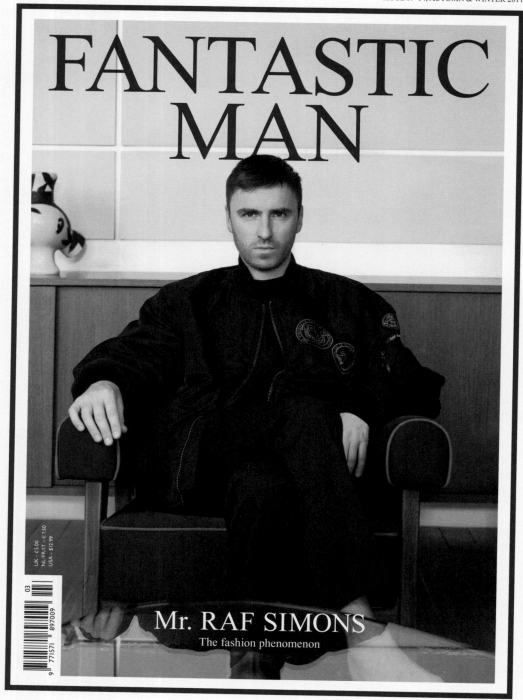

FANTASTIC MAN

UK – £5.00
NL/FR/IT – €7.50
USA – $12.99

Mr. RAF SIMONS
The fashion phenomenon

Fantastic Man (issue 14)
Jop Van Bennekom
2011

Type
Times New Roman, Engravers Gothic, Gill Sans

The Brothers

FABIO and FAUSTO COVIZZI are the glamorous security specialists for Milan's giants of fashion. Neither naturally bald nor twins, the brothers watch over the fashion shows of JIL SANDER, DOLCE & GABBANA, PRADA, CALVIN KLEIN and BOTTEGA VENETA, among many more. FABIO and FAUSTO are friends of the designers, as well as their protectors, and they make fabulous emblems of the industry they serve.

MILAN

Photography by Daniel Riera, styling by Simon Foxton

FABIO (left) is three years older than FAUSTO. They are both wearing suits, shirts and ties by D&G.

– 210 –

– 211 –

Presse Papier

GLASS RECTANGLE
Albeit see-through, this glass rectangle holds great substance. The paperweight, which belongs to stylist Mr. SAM LOGAN, is resting on an A4 ruled pad and a red-bordered card and envelope from SMYTHSON, with a sheet of graph paper from COWLING & WILCOX. The grey 'Reform' table is from VAN DER MEERSCH & WESTON.

The paperweight is the most useless of all desk accessories, but it's utterly fabulous nonetheless. It's a fetching friend to the inkpot, the pen and the paper it perches upon.

Photography by Zoë Ghertner
Styling by Sam Logan

– 124 –

– 125 –

Fantastic Man (issue 14)
Jop Van Bennekom
2011

Type
Times New Roman, Engravers Gothic, Gill Sans

Text by Susie Rushton
Portraits by Daniel Riera

Sara Pérez
the revolutionary force behind modern Spanish wine

With brave new ideas about wine at a time of great gastronomic experimentation in her country, Sara Pérez is the chief winemaker at the ambitious Mas Martinet and Venus vineyards in northeast Spain. Thirty years ago, when her family moved there, harsh and mountainous Priorat had all but fallen off the map as a wine-producing region. Now, Sara is breathing new life into their pioneering work, bringing very radical changes

74

Sara Pérez

Sara was interviewed and photographed at her vineyard in Falset,
Spain, in a selection of multipurpose looks suited to the shifting demands of her days.
Styling by Bernat Sobrebals

75

Knots

Knots

Five exquisite updos for summer. Peter Gray, a prominent celebrity hair stylist if ever there was one, here shares his expert advice on how to roll, twist, spin, scrape, fold and tie all unruly strands into hair heaven. The knots were photographed in New York City by Zoë Ghertner, styling was provided by Haidee Findlay-Levin, and Peter's explanations were noted by Felix Burrichter.

112

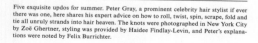

A – THE VERTICAL ATHENIAN
For this 21st-century take on the Horizontal Athenian knot, section the hair from the top of one ear to the other. Then gather both halves into separate ponytails. This requires four hands rather than two to ensure all strands are simultaneously twisted into S-shapes. Wind the bottom tail around the base of the top tail and vice versa, interlock-ing and meshing the different hair sections. The repeated twisting provides the hair with such rigidity that no hairpin is required. To finish, simply tuck the loose ends in underneath with a tail comb. It's a wonderful daytime look, albeit a complex and time-consuming one. The black-and-white striped silk dress with epaulettes and attached neck scarf is by CÉLINE.

113

The Gentlewoman (no. 1)
Jop Van Bennekom & Veronica Ditting
2010

96 Jop Van Bennekom & Veronica Ditting

Type
Futura and Times Ten

The Gentlewoman
Issue n° 1
Spring Summer 2010

the gentlewoman

New! From the makers of FANTASTIC MAN

UK £ 5.00
Europe € 7.50
USA $ 10.95

Phoebe Philo photographed by David Sims

9 771879 869005

Modernist

Designer PHOEBE PHILO and the return of modern fashion,
see page 48...

The Gentlewoman (no. 1)
Jop Van Bennekom & Veronica Ditting
2010

Type
Futura and Times Ten

DRK–018. All tracks written, arranged and produced by Stefan Schwander, Düsseldorf. Published by Italic, Berlin.

Antonelli; A-Side — Disconnected, B-Side — Operatore

Dreck Records, 23 — 25 Redchurch Street, London E2 7DJ © 2009 Dreck Records ℗ 2009 Dreck Records www.dreck-records.com. Made in the EU. Distributed by Rubadub, Glasgow. Designed by Kammer-orchester Kloten, 1970.

drkrec

'Disconnected' (12 inch) by Antonelli
Laurent Benner
2010

Type
Various

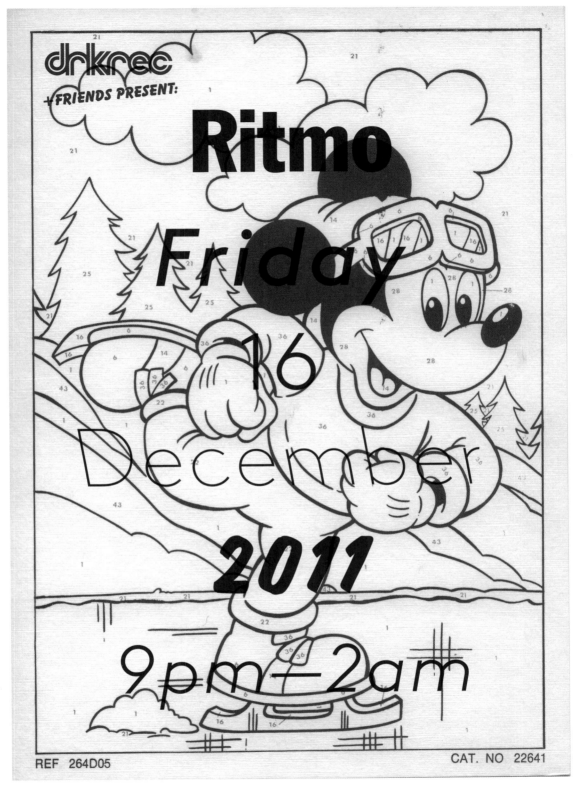

Ritmo club night poster
Laurent Benner
2011

Type
Various

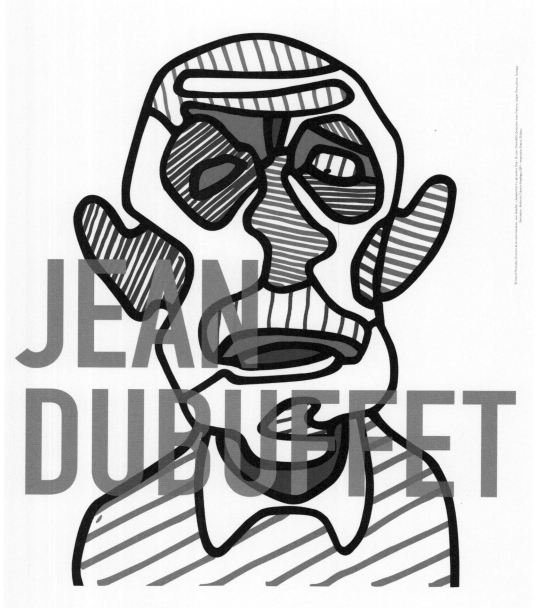

JEAN
DUBUFFET

Centre
Pompidou

exposition du centenaire
13 septembre — 31 décembre 2001

réservation Fnac 0892 684 694 www.fnac.com

LVMH
AVEC LE SOUTIEN DE MOËT HENNESSY . LOUIS VUITTON

Centre Pompidou poster
Pierre Bernard
2001

Type
DIN Engschrift

Centre Pompidou poster
Pierre Bernard
2009

Type
DIN Engschrift

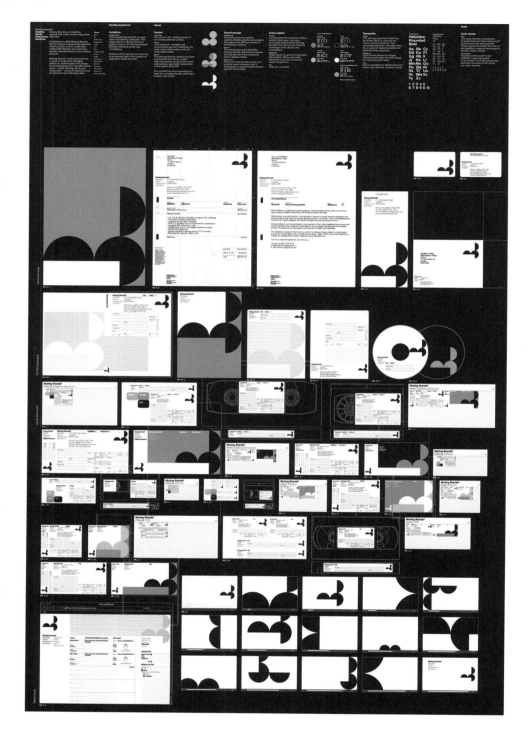

Moving Brands identity
Bibliothèque
2005

Type
Helvetica Rounded

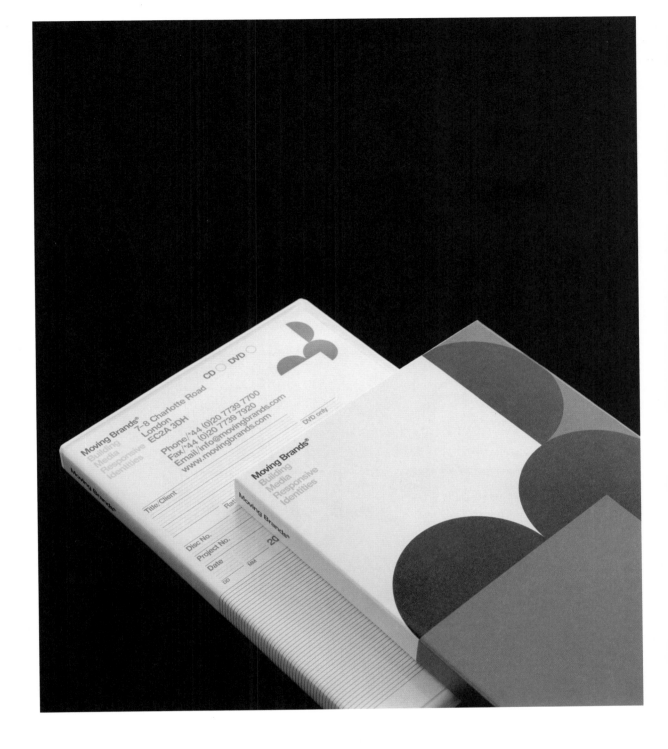

Moving Brands identity
Bibliothèque
2005

Type
Helvetica Rounded

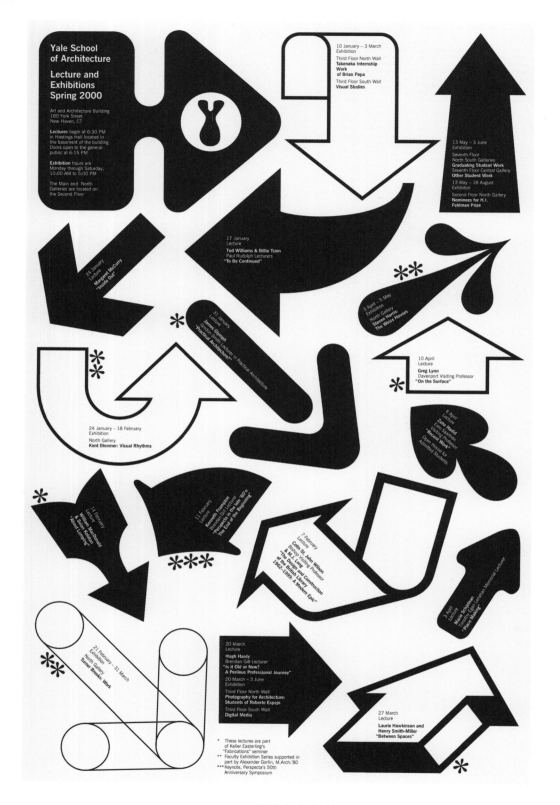

Yale School
of Architecture

Lecture and
Exhibitions
Spring 2000

Art and Architecture Building
180 York Street
New Haven, CT

Lectures begin at 6:30 PM
in Hastings Hall located in
the basement of the building
Doors open to the general
public at 6:15 PM

Exhibition hours are
Monday through Saturday,
10:00 AM to 5:00 PM

The Main and North
Galleries are located on
the Second Floor

10 January – 3 March
Exhibition
Third Floor North Wall
**Takenaka Internship
Work
of Brian Papa**
Third Floor South Wall
Visual Studies

13 May – 3 June
Exhibition
Seventh Floor
North South Galleries
Graduating Student Work
Seventh Floor Central Gallery
Other Student Work
13 May – 18 August
Exhibiton
Second Floor North Gallery
**Nominees for H.I.
Feldman Prize**

17 January
Lecture
Tod Williams & Billie Tsien
Paul Rudolph Lecturers
"To Be Continued"

24 January
Lecture
Margaret McCurry
"Inside Out"

31 January
Lecture
James Glymph
Gordon Smith Lecturer in Practical Architecture
"Practical Architecture"

24 January – 18 February
Exhibition
North Gallery
Kent Bloomer: Visual Rhythms

3 April – 5 May
Exhibition
North Gallery
**Steven Harris:
The Weiss Houses**

10 April
Lecture
Greg Lynn
Davenport Visiting Professor
"On the Surface"

6 April
Lecture
Zaha Hadid
Eero Saarinen
Visiting Professor
"Recent Work"
Open House for
Admitted Students

11 February
Lecture
Kenneth Frampton
Brendan Gill Lecturer
**"Perspecta in the late '90's:
The End of the Beginning"**

14 February
Lecture
**William MacDonald
& Sulan Kolatan**
"About Living"

7 February
Lecture
Colin St. John Wilson
Bishop Visiting Professor
& M. J. Long
**"The Design and Construction
of The British Library
1962–1999: A Modern Epic"**

3 April
Lecture
Mario Schjetnan
Timothy Egan Lenahan Memorial Lecturer
"Place Making"

21 February – 31 March
Exhibition
North Gallery
Turner Brooks: Work

20 March
Lecture
Hugh Hardy
Brendan Gill Lecturer
**"Is it Old or New?
A Perilous Professional Journey"**
20 March – 3 June
Exhibition
Third Floor North Wall
**Photography for Architecture:
Students of Roberto Espejo**
Third Floor South Wall
Digital Media

27 March
Lecture
**Laurie Hawkinson and
Henry Smith-Miller**
"Between Spaces"

*   These lectures are part
of Keller Easterling's
"Fabrications" seminar
** Faculty Exhibition Series supported in
part by Alexander Gorlin, M.Arch.'80
***Keynote, Perspecta's 50th
Anniversary Symposium

Yale School of Architecture poster
Michael Bierut, Pentagram
2000

Type
News Gothic

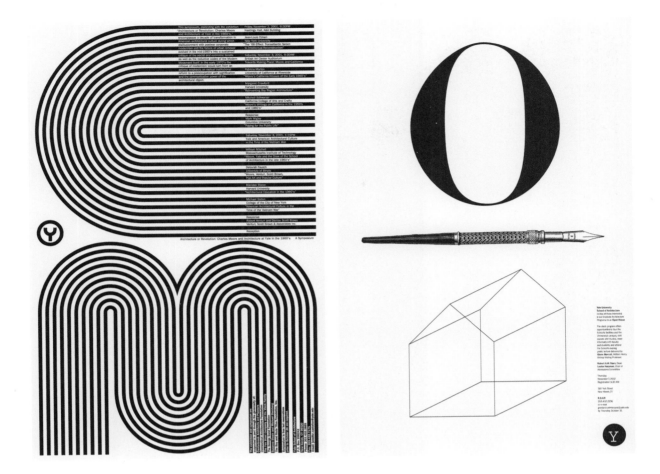

Michael Bierut's inspiration in designing more than 40 posters for events and programmes at the Yale School of Architecture has been Willi Kunz's long-running poster series for Columbia University's School of Architecture. Kunz consistently used Univers in very few weights as the basis for his designs. Bierut, in contrast, has opted for typographic diversity, employing different fonts for every poster while sticking to the same design parameters: one colour (black), one size and no images, just typographic characters and glyphs. It's a different kind of consistency, and one that's recognizable as YSA's from as far as the eye can see.

Yale School of Architecture posters
Michael Bierut, Pentagram
2000

Type
News Gothic

Naïve, uneven and playful, Julien was inspired by the radically simplified, cutom-made geometric letterforms that announced the meetings and manifestos of early twentieth-century avant-garde movements such as Dada, Futurism and the Bauhaus. Bil'ak developed two weights, each with three different styles based on circles, squares and a mixture of the two. There are also numerous letter variants and a pseudo-randomization script for OpenType substitutions, with specific rules for repeated letters. Alternatively, users can overwrite the rules and insert their choice of shapes from the glyph palette.

Julien font
Peter Bil'ak, typotheque
2011

Type
Julien

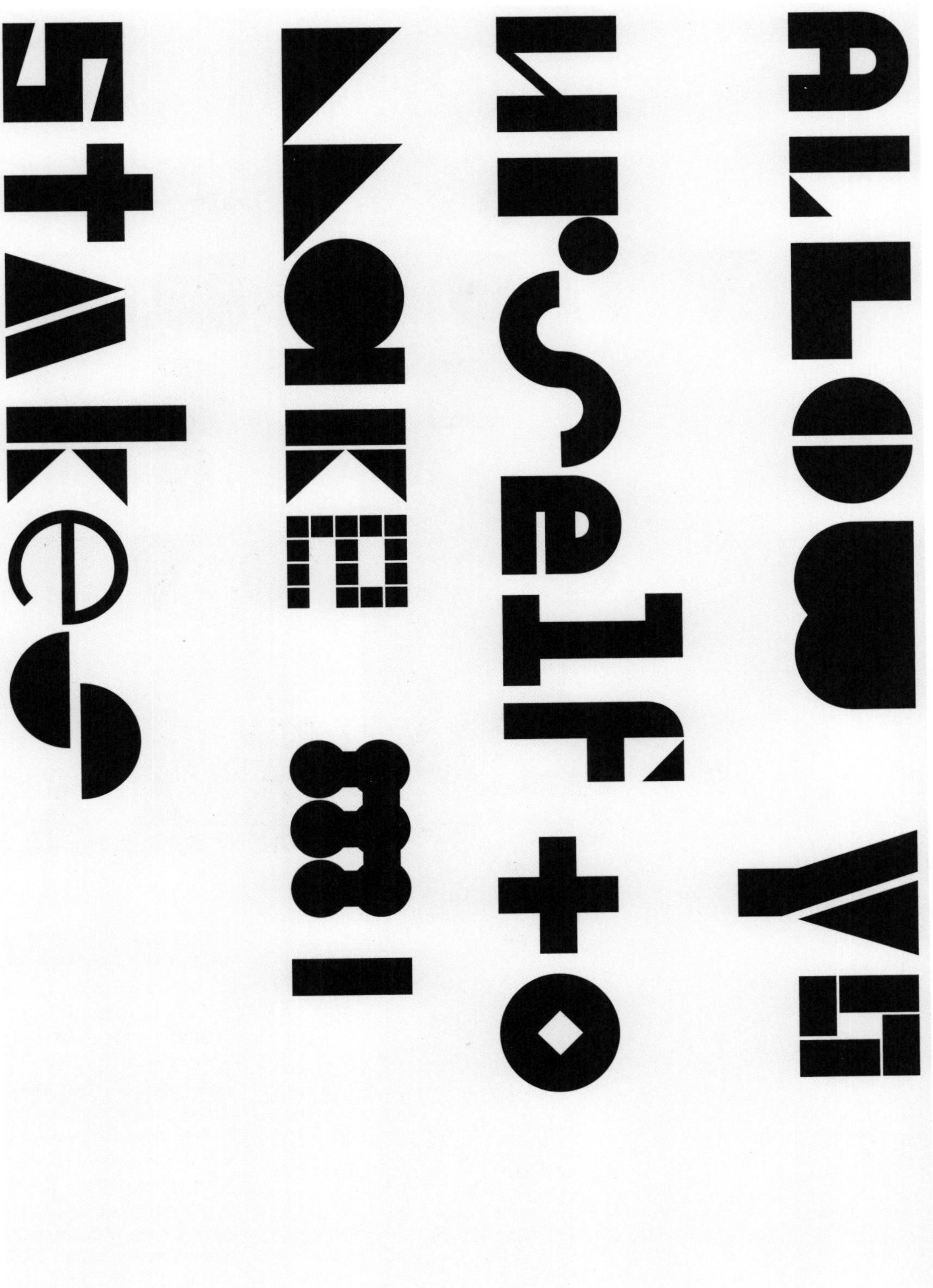

STAKE NAKED YRSELF & ALLOW YS

Julien font
Peter Bil'ak, typotheque
2011

Type
Julien

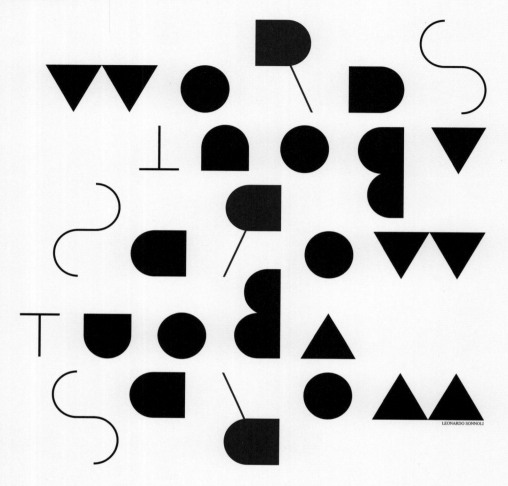

LEONARDO SONNOLI

Why Criticism Matters

SAM ANDERSON / ELIF BATUMAN / STEPHEN BURN / ADAM KIRSCH / PANKAJ MISHRA / KATIE ROIPHE

The New York Times Book Review
Nicholas Blechman (art direction) and Leonardo Sonnoli (design)
2011

Type
Hand lettering, Cheltenham, Franklin Gothic, Imperial

The New York Times
Book Review

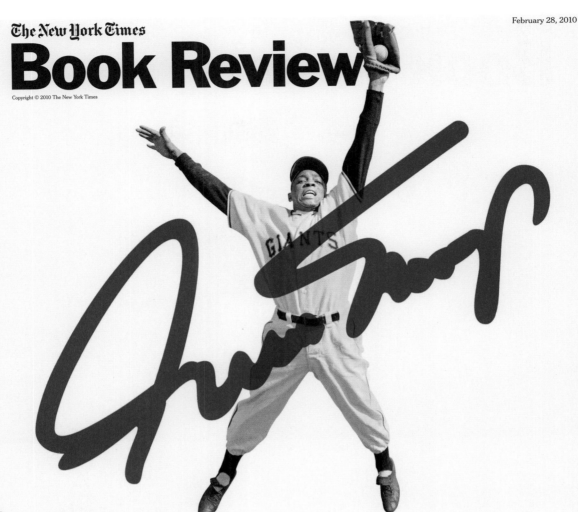

Say Hey

By Pete Hamill

WILLIE MAYS The Life, the Legend. *By James S. Hirsch. Illustrated. 628 pp. Scribner. $30.*

A long time ago in America, there was a beautiful game called baseball. This was before 30 major-league teams were scattered in a blurry variety of divisions; before 162-game seasons and extended playoffs and fans who watched World Series games in thick down jackets; before the D.H. came to the American League; before AstroTurf on baseball fields and aluminum bats on sandlots; before complete games by pitchers were a rarity; before ballparks were named for corporations instead of individuals; and long, long before the innocence of the game was permanently stained by the filthy deception of steroids.

In that vanished time, there was a ballplayer named Willie Mays.

Continued on Page 8

ROGER BOYLAN: **GILBERT SORRENTINO'S** LAST NOVEL PAGE 7 | **CATHLEEN SCHINE:** MY ILLITERACY EPIPHANY PAGE 23

The New York Times Book Review
Nicholas Blechman (art direction) and Rodrigo Corral (design)
2010

Type
Hand lettering, Cheltenham, Franklin Gothic, Imperial

Bob Gill once said, 'A good piece of graphic design is something you can explain over the telephone,' and it's an axiom that Sara De Bondt holds close. Her logotype for WIELS, a contemporary art centre in Brussels, is as far from complex as you could get, yet as specific and distinctive as any client would want. The centre's home, a 1930s former brewery, contains four strong horizontal concrete bands in its façade—a defining feature that De Bondt was able to incorporate into the 'E' of the client's name.

WIELS identity
Sara De Bondt Studio
2006–ongoing

Type
Custom made lettering by Sara De Bondt and Jo De Baerdemaeker

Irma Boom: Biography in Books
Irma Boom Office
2010

Type
Plantin and Neuzeit S

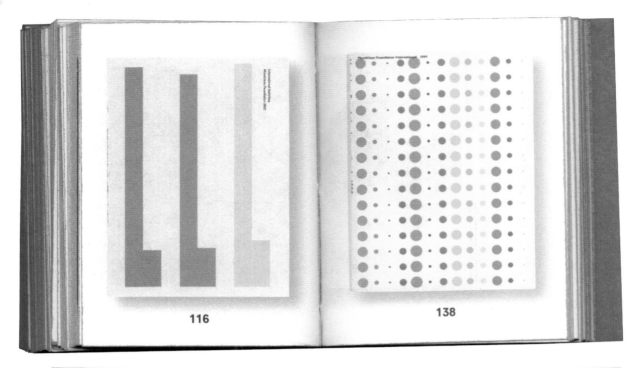

116

138

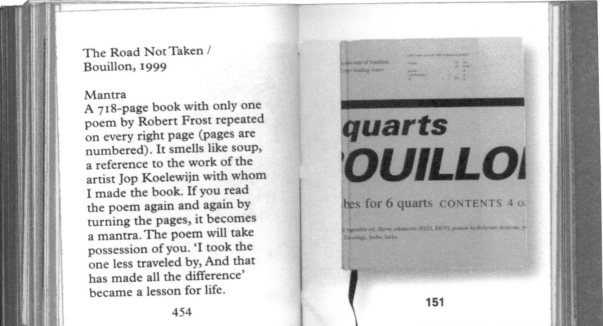

The Road Not Taken /
Bouillon, 1999

Mantra
A 718-page book with only one
poem by Robert Frost repeated
on every right page (pages are
numbered). It smells like soup,
a reference to the work of the
artist Jop Koelewijn with whom
I made the book. If you read
the poem again and again by
turning the pages, it becomes
a mantra. The poem will take
possession of you. 'I took the
one less traveled by, And that
has made all the difference'
became a lesson for life.

454

151

Irma Boom: Biography in Books
Irma Boom Office
2010

Type
Plantin and Neuzeit S

Die Arabische Nacht ('The Arabian Night'), *Frühlings Erwachen* ('Spring Awakening') and *The Old School* theatre posters
Erich Brechbühl
2004–2007

Type
Custom made type

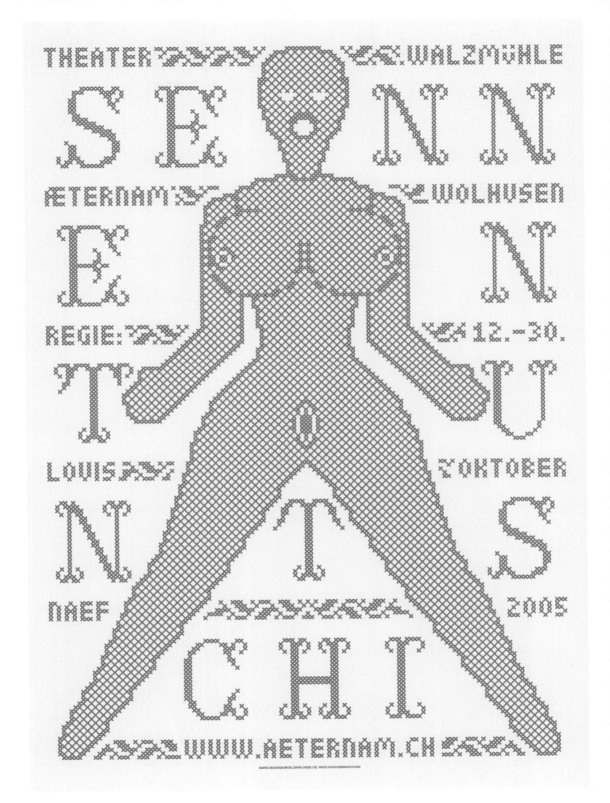

Sennentuntschi theatre poster
Erich Brechbühl
2005

Type
Custom made lettering

Yes series
Anthony Burrill
2004

Type
Champion, Accidental Presidency, Akzidenz-Grotesk

Woodblock poster series
Anthony Burrill
2004–11

Type
Antique woodblock

WalkRide urban wayfinding system
Cartlidge Levene and City ID
2005

Type
Basic Commercial

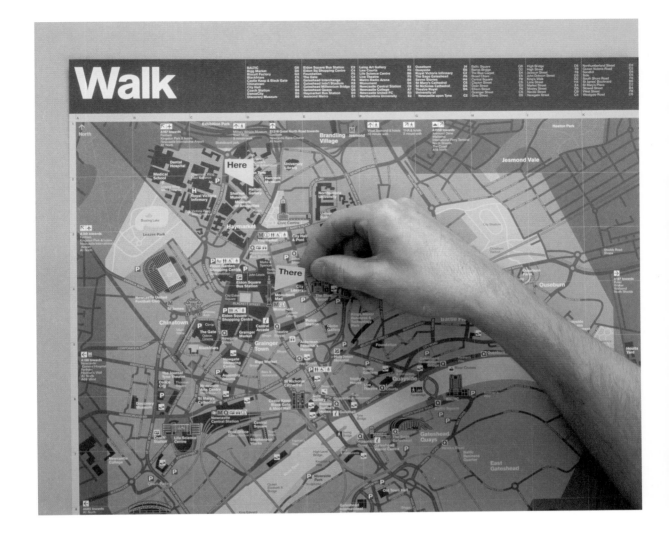

WalkRide is a wayfinding system for both pedestrians and public transport users in Newcastle and Gateshead. Its identity is expressed through the clarity and flexibility of its typography, which is applied with absolute consistency, from the logotype for the system and the QuayLink electric bus service to the complex practical information contained in maps and bus timetables.

WalkRide urban wayfinding system
Cartlidge Levene and City ID
2005

Type
Basic Commercial

Millennium Point (Birmingham) wayfinding and signage
Cartlidge Levene
2002

Type
DIN

Millennium Point (Birmingham) wayfinding and signage
Cartlidge Levene
2002

Type
DIN

The art of today is the heritage of tomorrow

De Zaak Nu identity
Atelier Carvalho Bernau
2010

Type
Platform

De Zaak Nu arrives in the wake of deep austerity measures by the Dutch government that have roused the cultural sector in the Netherlands to protest and action. Its aim is to network small art spaces and galleries, following in the footsteps of De Zaak in Groningen, one of the first independent artist-run spaces.

The logotype and display typography employ Platform, a geometric sans serif by Berton Hasebe whose purposefully unsophisticated letterforms, in conjunction with simple shapes and strong colours, evoke the spirit of protest and agitation that *De Zaak Nu* represents. The crossed box of the logo also echoes De Zaak, reversing its 'Z' in a rectangle to create a clear 'No' in visual shorthand.

De Zaak Nu **identity**
Atelier Carvalho Bernau
2010

Type
Platform

Gare Saint Sauveur, Lille
Change is Good
2009

Type
Saint Sauveur

In a former railway station quite central to Lille, a new cultural centre has been created that makes a virtue out of economy and announces itself on a gable wall with an array of fluorescent tubes. The letters, composed of three different lengths of tube and spaced at consistent intervals, project a warm neon-like glow at night but keep the feel of something temporary, like an art installation that shouldn't be missed.

Gare Saint Sauveur, Lille
Change is Good
2009

Type
Saint Sauveur

Typefaces
Type Test!

Search...
About
News

User License
Licensing FAQ
Technical FAQ

Austin Collection
Austin
Austin Hairline
Austin Cyrillic

Austin

Dala Floda

Dala Floda

Giorgio Collection
Giorgio
Giorgio Sans

Giorgio

Graphik

Graphik

Guardian Collection
Guardian Egyptian Headline
Guardian Egyptian Text
Guardian Sans Headline
Guardian Sans Headline Narrow
Guardian Sans Headline Condensed
Guardian Sans Headline X Condensed
Guardian Agate Sans

Guardian Egyptian Headline

Lyon Collection
Lyon Display
Lyon Text

Lyon Display

Marian

Marian

Platform

Platform

Publico Collection
Publico Headline
Publico Text

Publico Headline

Stag Collection
Stag
Stag Sans
Stag Dot
Stag Stencil
Stag Sans Round

Stag Stencil

Commercial Type fonts
Commercial Type: Paul Barnes and Christian Schwartz
2007–ongoing

Type
Various

Paul Barnes and Christian Schwartz established Commercial Type after creating the Guardian Egyptian headline and text typefaces, which were the bedrock of the newspaper's award-winning redesign led by Mark Porter. The company publishes retail fonts developed by the two designers, individually and in partnership, and by external collaborators.

Its fonts are both influential and, as the name suggests, commercial, and combine those developed for clients with others that started as self-initiated projects. Graphik, a Schwartz font, has been adopted by *Wallpaper**, CondeNast's *Portfolio* magazine and *T, The New York Times Style Magazine*. Marian, by Barnes, was released in 2012, and was an experiment in imagining classic historical serif fonts reduced to their basic skeletal forms, while trying to retain their original character.

PLATFORM, PROPORTION, SKELETON, CRAFT, GEOMETRY & COMMERCIAL TYPE

It all started when our uber geek, Platform, woke up in a lemur-infested moor. It was the ninth time it had happened. Feeling alarmingly frustrated, Platform attacked a dull pencil, thinking it would make him feel better (but as usual, it did not). Suddenly inspired by the wise teachings of Confuscious, he realized that his beloved Skeleton was missing! Immediately he called his enemy in training, Proportion. Platform had known Proportion for [plus or minus] 153 years, the majority of which were eccentric ones. Proportion was unique. She was intelligent though sometimes clueless. Platform called her anyway, for the situation was urgent.

Proportion picked up to a very distressed Platform. Proportion calmly assured him that most albino cats sigh before mating, yet South American hissing sloths usually sassily turn red after mating. She had no idea what that meant; she was only concerned with distracting Platform. Why was Proportion trying to distract Platform? Because she had snuck out from Platform's with the Skeleton only seven days prior. It was a curious little Skeleton...how could she resist?

SS01

It didn't take long before Platform got back to the subject at hand: his Skeleton. Proportion turned red. Reluctantly, Proportion invited him over, assuring him they'd find the Skeleton. Platform grabbed his canoe and disembarked immediately. After hanging up the phone, Proportion realized that she was in trouble. She had to find a place to hide the Skeleton and she had to do it aptly. She figured that if Platform took the curb-jumping ghetto sled [Donk], she had take at least six minutes before Platform would get there. But if he took the Craft? Then Proportion would be really screwed.

Before she could come up with any reasonable ideas, Proportion was interrupted by nine dimwitted Geometrys that were lured by her Skeleton. Proportion cringed; *'This can't be happening again'*, she thought. Feeling frustrated, she deftly reached for her potato and skillfully backhanded every last one of them. Apparently this was an adequate deterrent—the discouraged critters began to scurry back toward the lemur-infested moor, squealing with discontent. She exhaled with relief. That's when she heard the Craft rolling up. It was Platform.

SS02

As he pulled up, he felt a sense of urgency. He had had to make an unscheduled stop at Texaco to pick up a 12-pack of wolverines, so he knew he was running late. With a hasty leap, Platform was out of the Craft and went scandalously jaunting toward Proportion's front door. Meanwhile inside, Proportion was panicking. Not thinking, she tossed the Skeleton into a box of bananas and then slid the box behind her rhinocerus. Proportion was frustrated but at least the Skeleton was concealed. The doorbell rang.

'Come in', Proportion explosively purred. With a skillful push, Platform opened the door. *'Sorry for being late, but I was being chased by some oafish social outcast in a time machine'*, he lied.

Platform spcimen
Commercial Type: Berton Hasebe and Hyo Kwon
2010

WE'VE WE
DONE DO
IT BE IT
FORE FO
WE'LL WE
DO IT DO
AGAINAG

What Design Can Do! poster
De Designpolitie
2011

Type
Century Old Style, Franklin Gothic

What Design Can Do! is an annual two-day conference in Amsterdam that examines the impact of design as a catalyst for social change and renewal. The event was initiated, organized and designed by De Designpolitie, and its marketing material carries an undesigned, unselfconscious but strident tone, with centred, all-caps Century Old Style and Franklin Gothic dominating, and red type on bright yellow adding to the air of urgency.

1

• • •

Why another graphic design magazine?

This pilot issue of ...
        (a graphic design / visual culture magazine)
hopes to answer itself
        being an encyclopaedia of previous attempts
        with extended articles on a select few

During this field trip we hope to plot the next issue
        i.e.   how?
                    where?
                    when?
                    who?
        based on the experiences of those who
        tried already

Those 3 dots were chosen as the title for being
something close to an internationally-recognised
typographic mark
but now they seem even more appropriate as
a representation of what we intend the project to become:
        A magazine in flux
        ready to adjust itself to content

and here is the first list of our aims to date:
(to be)   critical
           flexible
           international
           portfolio-free
           rigorous
           useful

Dot Dot Dot magazine
Stuart Bailey, Peter Bil'ak and David Reinfurt
2000–10

Type
Various

DOT DOT DOT 9: elementary mathematics

In the candid spirit of a few publications and products which have exposed their process and production costs,† DDD9 begins—or ends—by taking into account its current financial state. In all innocence it has taken us nine issues to understand why independent publishing is an oxymoron, or at least impossible without third-party sponsorship: basically, we're too small to afford a solicitor. If our distributors and bookshops paid all outstanding debts (dating from up to three years ago) the magazine could sustain itself, but however FINAL, the growing list of debtors repeatedly ignore demands—we assume because they arrive without any (convincing) threat of legal action. So the independent can be ignored as long as 'solicitors' costs' is not in the vocabulary of arts funding applications.

† Rem Koolhaas, S,M,L,XL (1995), spread itemising OMA's expenditure

† Reverse of sleeve for TV Personalities' 7" EP Where's Bill Grundy Now? with production-costs (1978)

SBN 90 77620 03 6

51495

9 789077 620038

This open presentation of our accounts is, then, a surrogate solicitor, some kind of commercial hari-kiri attempt to embarass our debtors into settling outstanding bills. We're reasoning that if we piss them off in the process it doesn't really make much difference either way. Until then we remain in a circle of funding for which we're eternally grateful but would rather be able to do without.

Based on DDD8, a single issue (print run 3,000) costs this much to produce:

(all figures in ℮)

Printing
Authors
Editorial/Office
Postage
Miscellaneous
—

of which this much is typically generated from advertising: and this much made from combined shop and subscription sales: (that's ℮2.75 (USA) or ℮5 (Europe) per each ℮12.50 copy sold) so we are typically subsidised this much by Dutch arts funding:

The list below details all outstanding debts as DDD9 goes to print, which can be made payable to *Dot dot dot VOF*, account no. 50 26 69 659. This information is correct as of 01/01/2005:

03/08/2002	Hennessey & Ingalls, USA
20/10/2002	Actar, Spain
05/12/2002	CCA bookstore, Canada
18/01/2003	Actar, Spain
14/04/2003	Actar, Spain
20/08/2003	Actar, Spain
16/10/2003	Actar, Spain
30/11/2003	goodwill, NL
23/12/2003	Athaeneum books, NL
23/03/2004	Actar, Spain
15/04/2004	Actar, Spain
23/04/2004	Nijhof & Lee books, NL
11/07/2004	Actar, Spain
16/07/2004	Nijhof & Lee books, NL
04/08/2004	Nijhof & Lee books, NL
26/04/2004	Nijhof & Lee books, NL
30/08/2004	Secretonix, Portugal
12/10/2004	Magma books, UK
15/10/2004	Nijhof & Lee books, NL
21/10/2004	Praktaly SRO, Czech Rep.
25/10/2004	Actar, Spain

TOTAL AMOUNT OWED:

Whole Earth Catalog Cash Flow 69-70   599

438

† The Last Whole Earth Catalogue (1971), detail of Money spread from the section 'How to make a Whole Earth Catalogue' in the closing pages of the 1960s/70s counterculture bible. See DDD8 pp.104-5 for a legible reproduction.

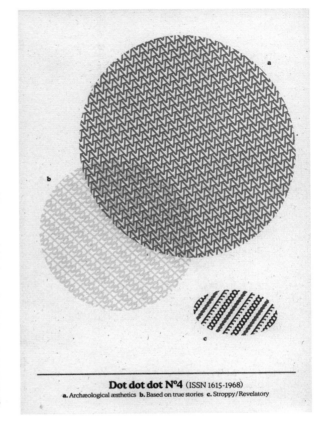

Dot dot dot Nº4 (ISSN 1615-1968)
a. Archæological æsthetics **b.** Based on true stories **c.** Stroppy/Revelatory

Dot Dot Dot originated from a desire on the part of Stuart Bailey and Peter Bil'ak, two designers and occasional writers, to create a publication about design that they could regularly reinvent. There was no editorial policy and no design philosophy, according to Bil'ak.

Up until issue 10, a different typeface was used to match the tone of each self-consciously loosely designed edition. *DDD* then aimed for a more standardized design, and commissioned the Mitim font by Radim Peško, which would be characterized by its triangular serifs. *DDD*11 featured the basic roman version of Mitim, and then each new edition of the magazine used a new member of the Mitim family, added to respond to the changing conditions and demands of the magazine's production.

DOT
DOT
DOT

Nº19 is assembled from PDFs of THE FIRST/LAST NEWSPAPER (TF/LN) which was issued from Port Authority in New York City every Wednesday & Saturday during the first 3 weeks of November 2009

TF/LN AT THE TIME OF WRITING

***The Druid King* by Norman Spinrad**
Doyle Partners
2003

Type
Custom made lettering

AIGA *Fresh Dialogue* poster
Doyle Partners
2006

Type
Custom made lettering

Irreguläre Tage ('Irregular Days') by Michael Schade
Markus Dreßen/Spector Bureau
2013

Type
Vergil BQ, Book: Akzidenz-Grotesk BQ, Medium Condensed

Ingenieure waren ihr sowieso suspekt: Mein
Großvater war tagelang in schlammigen Tagebauen
verschwunden, um Gefrierverfahren gegen
hereinbrechendes Grundwasser zu testen. Sein
Rechenschieber in der linken Brusttasche leuchtete
in der Sonne wie ein Sheriffstern, erzählte sie.

Und abends hatte er im Bett neben ihr gelegen.
Die Zeitung weit aufgeschlagen, mit Watte in
den Ohren, um nicht auf ihre Fragen antworten
zu müssen.

Irgendwann nahm sie ihre Tochter an der
Hand und ging für immer. Wilde Verfolgungsjagden
begannen und für meine Mutter eine Odyssee.
Mein Großvater heiratete die Schwester meiner Großmutter. Aus Rache. Meine Mutter wurde in einem
Verfahren dem Großvater und der Tante zuge-
sprochen. »Eine politische Entscheidung!«, sagte
meine Großmutter. »Damit er nicht in die Westzone
abhaut.« Die Russen taten fast alles, um ihn bei
Laune zu halten. Sie fürchteten sogar um sein Leben:
Er war ein katastrophaler Autofahrer. Deshalb
stellten sie ihm einen Chauffeur und verboten ihm,
selbst zu fahren. Er war eine ›Very Important Person‹.
Später leitete er den riesigen Tagebau Welzow-Süd.
Er starb 1971. Von ihm erbte ich meine erste Kamera.
Eine Contax D.

Meine Großmutter zog Anfang der 6oer in ihren
Geburtsort zurück und arbeitete dort als Kranken-
schwester. Sie starb 1995 an einem Herzanfall.
Im Bad, als sie sich wusch. Das Letzte, was sie sah,
muss ihr Gesicht im Spiegel gewesen sein.

12

FÜNF KURZE GESCHICHTEN ÜBER DIE ENTTÄUSCHUNG

BÖSCHUNG

Ich rannte durch eine Landschaft. Als ich sie wahr-
nahm, wusste ich, dass ich mich noch nie so weit
von unserem Dorf entfernt hatte. Erschrocken blieb
ich stehen. Es herrschte absolute Stille. Dann,
nachdem eine Hupe ertönte: ein langgezogenes,
dauerhaftes, eindringliches Geräusch, als ob gleichzeitig Stahl auf Stein und Stahl auf Stahl träfe.
Ich schaute mich um, sah vom Sand verwehte
Straßen, wild wuchernde Gärten, verlassene Häuser.
Ich lief in Richtung des Geräusches. Die Häuser
links und rechts verwandelten sich mehr und mehr
in Ruinen. Fast mit jedem Schritt. Die Landschaft
wurde karger, bis ich auf einer spärlich mit Gras
bewachsenen Ebene stand, über die der Wind strich.
Ich ging weiter. Das Geräusch war verstummt.
Dann stand ich an einer Böschung. Das ist das Ende
der Welt, dachte ich.

»Das ist der Rand des Tagebaus«, erklärte mir
mein Vater zwei Wochen später, als wir fast an
derselben Stelle standen. Klein zwischen Himmel
und Erde. Indem ich mich an die erste Begegnung
mit dem vermeintlichen Ende meiner Welt erinnerte,
zum Vater aufblickte und eine Frage formulierte,
spürte ich zum ersten Mal, dass zu antworten nicht
immer möglich ist. Auch nicht für einen Vater.

13

Irreguläre Tage ('Irregular Days') by Michael Schade
Markus Dreßen/Spector Bureau
2013

Type
Vergil BQ, Book: Akzidenz-Grotesk BQ, Medium Condensed

Creamier: Contemporary Art in Culture
Atelier Dyakova
2012

Type
Tribute, Neuzeit

Sculpture Today
Atelier Dyakova
2007

Type
Paper Alphabet

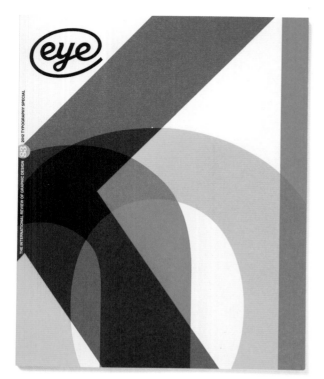

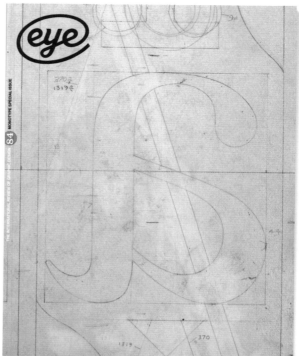

Eye magazine (issues 83, 84 and 86)
Esterson Associates
2012–13

Type
Times New Roman, Cargo

Eye magazine (issue 79)
Esterson Associates
2011

Type
Calypso

Unclear labelling accounted
for many of the 5,000 incidences
of wrongful medication reported
to the Danish National Board
of Health in 2006. In response,
e-Types developed the Medilabel
Safety System for Danish
hospitals, which presented
a clear, logical, consistent
hierarchy of information, and
a typeface (Medic) specifically
designed for the purpose.

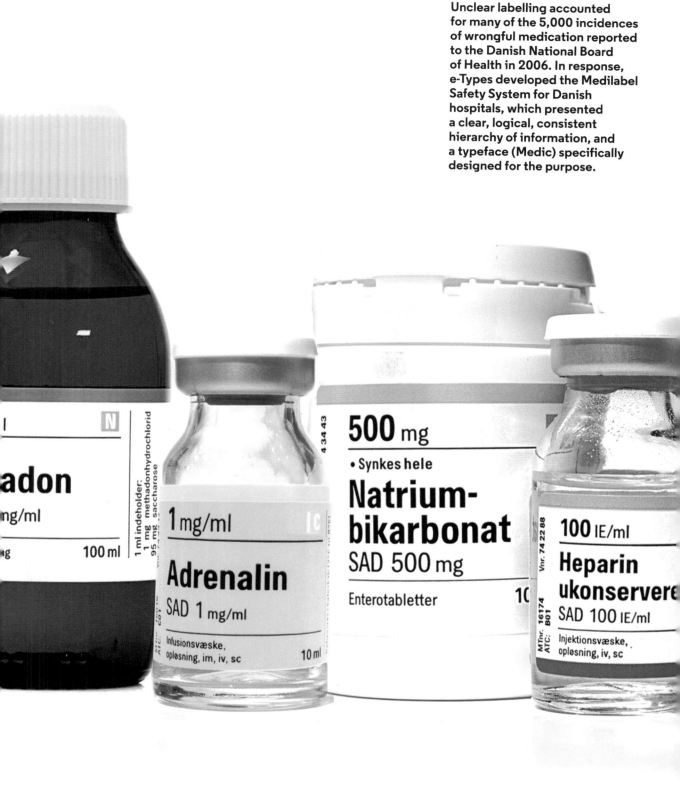

The clarity of text on even tiny ampoule labels owes much to the narrowing of certain strokes in key areas of letters to increase definition, and the adoption of Tallman lettering (eg NORadrenaline) in place of all-upper-case text.

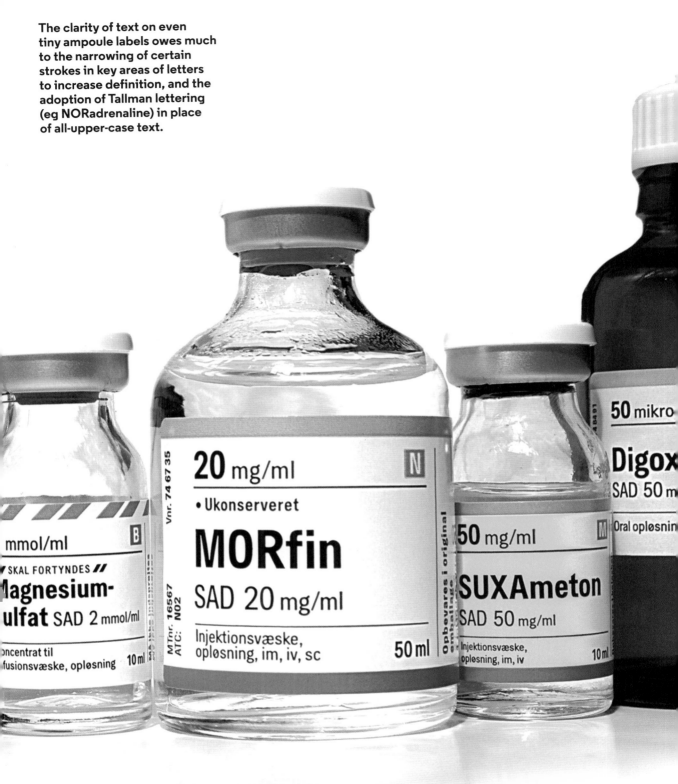

Medilabel Safety System
e-Types
2007

Type
Medic

Whitney Museum of American Art graphic identity
Experimental Jetset
2012

Type
Customized version of Neue Haas Grotesk

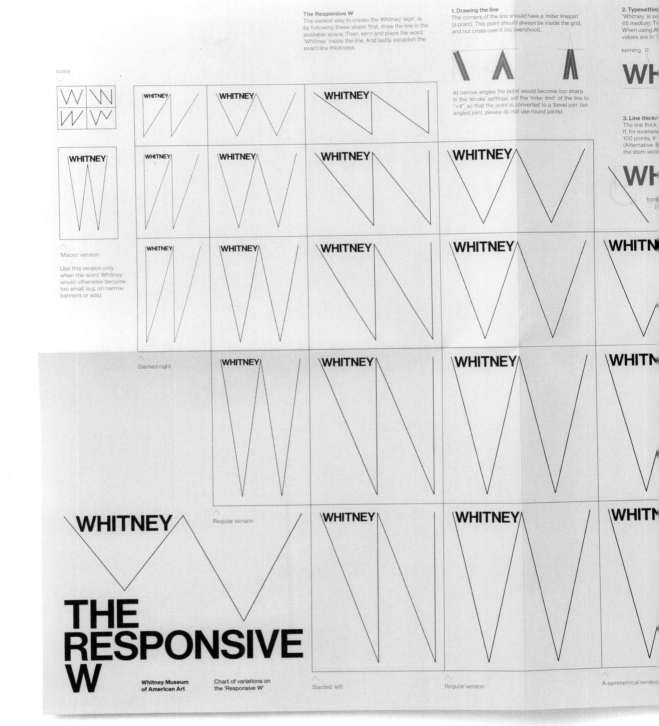

The Responsive W

The easiest way to create the Whitney 'sign', is by following these steps: first, draw the line in the available space. Then, kern and place the word 'Whitney' inside the line. And lastly, establish the exact line thickness.

1. Drawing the line

The corners of the line should have a 'miter linejoin' (a point). This point should always be inside the grid, and not cross over it (no overshoot).

At narrow angles the point would become too sharp. In the 'stroke' settings, set the 'miter limit' of the line to "×4", so that the point is converted to a 'bevel join' (an angled joint, please do not use round joints).

2. Typesetting

'Whitney' is se... 65 medium. T... When using A... values are in 1...

kerning 0

3. Line thickn...

The line thick... If, for example... 100 points, th... (Alternative: If... the stem widt...

font...

Icons

'Macro' version

Use this version only when the word 'Whitney' would otherwise become too small (e.g. on narrow banners or ads).

Slanted right

Regular version

Slanted left

Regular version

A-symmetrical versio...

WHITNEY

THE RESPONSIVE W

Whitney Museum of American Art

Chart of variations on the 'Responsive W'

Whitney Museum of American Art graphic identity
Experimental Jetset
2012

Type
Customized version of Neue Haas Grotesk

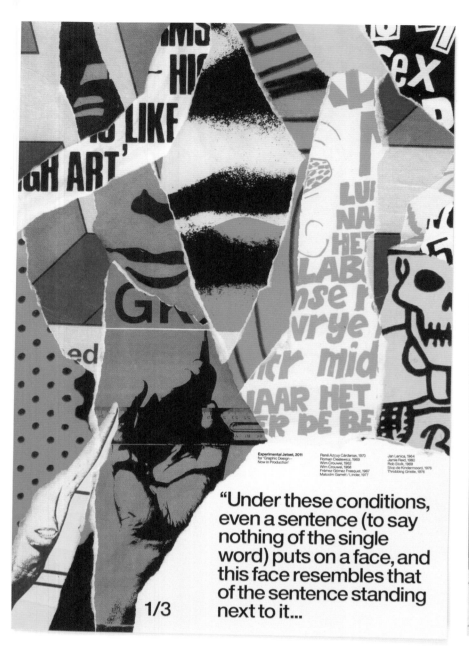

...in this way, every truth points manifes to its opposite.

Experimental Jetset, 2011
for 'Graphic Design –
Now in Production'

René Azcuy Cárdenas, 1970
Roman Cieslewicz, 1969
Wim Crouwel, 1962
Wim Crouwel, 1968
Frémez Gómez Fresquet, 1967
Malcolm Garrett / Linder, 1977

Jan Lenica, 1964
Jamie Reid, 1980
Rob Stolk, 1969
Stop de Kindermoord, 1976
Throbbing Gristle, 1976

"Under these conditions, even a sentence (to say nothing of the single word) puts on a face, and this face resembles that of the sentence standing next to it...

1/3

These posters were for a major touring exhibition from the Walker Art Museum, and they recall the collages of torn posters made by the French *affichistes* of the early 1950s, creating a kind of billboard archaeology—as well as a mini-exhibition—of influential graphic and typographic languages. The clash of these fragments spanning early modernism to post-punk design represents a portrait of the graphic sensibilities of the Experimental Jetset partners, and strongly evokes the 'culture of making', of print on paper, which was one of the key themes of the exhibition.

According to Experimental Jetset, the quote from Walter Benjamin offers a model for the interpretation of graphic design: 'as a landscape of conflicting voices, in which truth becomes something living.'

3/3

"Truth becomes something living; it lives solely in the rhythm by which statement and counter-statement displace each other, in order to think each other."
—W. Benjamin

Graphic Design—Now in Production exhibition posters
Experimental Jetset
2011

Type
Various

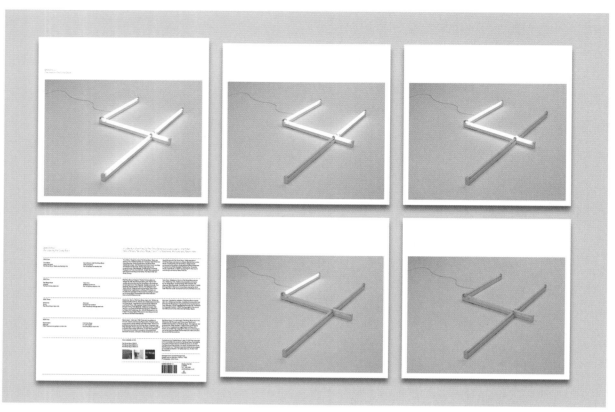

Disco 4 by the Pet Shop Boys packaging
Farrow
2007

Type
Neue Helvetica

Carroll Dunham Hydra Workshop catalogue
Farrow
2008

Type
Handwritten cover, Neue Helvetica

Mark Farrow and his eponymous studio are known for a minimalist approach to typography and imagery, powerful use of colour and an unswerving attention to detail that, together, over time, have forged indelible, understated identities for a range of clients. These include the Pet Shop Boys, for whom Farrow have designed all album packaging since 1986, Sadie Coles (the London gallery that helped stage Carroll Dunham's 2008 exhibition at the Hydra Workshop in Greece) and the bakery and café brand, Peyton and Byrne.

Peyton and Byrne tea packaging
Farrow
2010

Type
Gill Sans

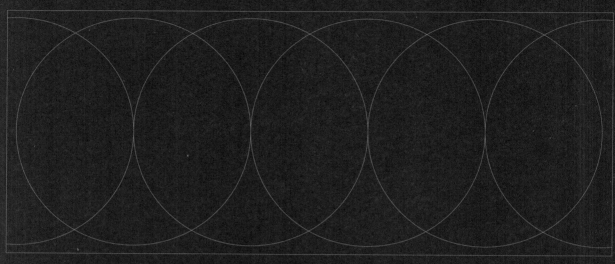

Spiritualized®

Ladies and gentlemen we are floating in space B P

14 tablets 180 min

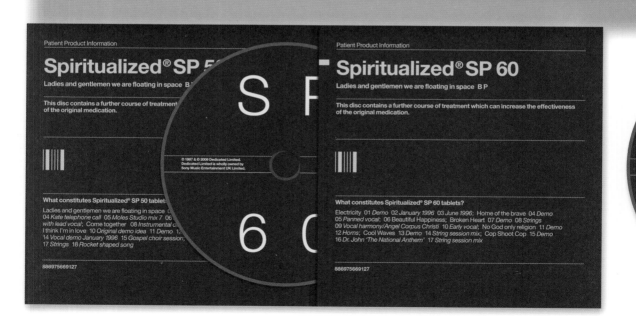

Patient Product Information

Spiritualized® SP 5

Ladies and gentlemen we are floating in space B

This disc contains a further course of treatment
of the original medication.

℗ 1997 & © 2009 Dedicated Limited.
Dedicated Limited is wholly owned by
Sony Music Entertainment UK Limited.

What constitutes Spiritualized® SP 50 tablet

Ladies and gentlemen we are floating in space
04 *Kate telephone call* 05 *Moles Studio mix 7* 06
with lead vocal; Come together 08 *Instrumental*
I think I'm in love 10 *Original demo idea* 11 *Demo*
14 *Vocal demo January 1996* 15 *Gospel choir session*;
17 *Strings* 18 *Rocket shaped song*

886975669127

Patient Product Information

Spiritualized® SP 60

Ladies and gentlemen we are floating in space B P

This disc contains a further course of treatment which can increase the effectiveness
of the original medication.

What constitutes Spiritualized® SP 60 tablets?

Electricity 01 *Demo* 02 *January 1996* 03 *June 1996*; Home of the brave 04 *Demo*
05 *Panned vocal*; 06 Beautiful Happiness; Broken Heart 07 *Demo* 08 *Strings*
09 *Vocal harmony/Angel Corpus Christi* 10 *Early vocal*; No God only religion 11 *Demo*
12 *Horns*; Cool Waves 13 *Demo* 14 *String session mix*; Cop Shoot Cop 15 *Demo*
16 *Dr. John 'The National Anthem'* 17 *String session mix*

886975669127

℗ 1997 & © 20
Dedicated Li
Sony Music E

Ladies and Gentlemen We Are Floating in Space (remastered edition) by Spiritualized
Farrow
2009

Type
Neue Helvetica

Vasi Comunicanti
Paesaggi della grafica contemporanea
Ottobre 02 / Maggio 03

5 manifesti di Ed Fella
Palazzo Fortuny
13.10 / 8.12.02

Palazzo Fortuny
Campo San Beneto 3780
Venezia

Orario 10 / 18
Biglietteria 10 / 17
Chiuso lunedì

Per informazioni
mkt.musei@comune.venezia.it
www.vasicomunicanti.org

Venice poster
Ed Fella
2002

Type
Custom made lettering

This Is What Will Never Do
Ed Fella
1995

Type
Custom made lettering

Sydney Dance Company identity
Frost* Design
2004–09

Type
Futura

COMPANY

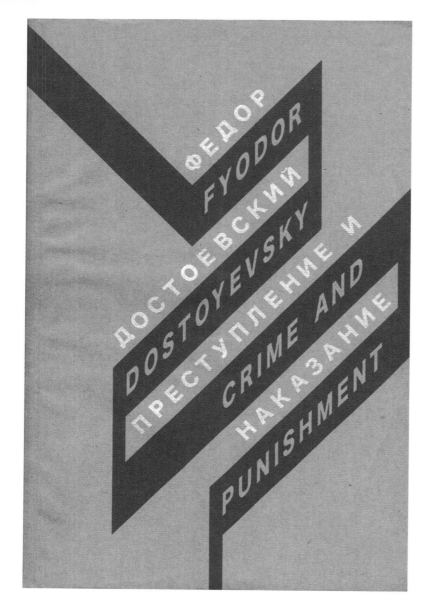

ФЕДОР
FYODOR
ДОСТОЕВСКИЙ
DOSTOYEVSKY
ПРЕСТУПЛЕНИЕ И
CRIME AND
НАКАЗАНИЕ
PUNISHMENT

FUEL—Stephen Sorrell and Damon Murray—have been interested in Russian culture since a visit to Moscow in 1992. Their cover for the Penguin Classics edition of *Crime and Punishment* uses brown craft paper to reflect the poverty that pervades the book. The typography—in both English and Cyrillic script—aims to convey the tension and intensity of the writing in the style of Russian Constructivist art.

Crime and Punishment **by Fyodor Dostoyevsky**
FUEL
2006

Type
Custom made lettering

Between 1948 and 1986, Russian prison guard Danzig Baldaev made more than 3,000 detailed ink drawings of skulls, swastikas, naked women, medieval knights, Christs, tanks and other outlandish icons with which convicts had chosen to identify themselves. FUEL purchased the archive of 739 drawings from Baldaev's widow and have presented his drawings and photographs in three volumes, each fronted by a kind of unsophisticated, retro typography that highlights the strangeness of the chosen image.

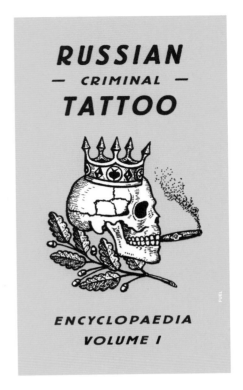

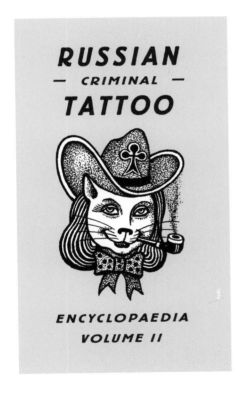

Russian Criminal Tattoo Encyclopaedia 2004 vols. I–III
FUEL
2004–2008

Type
Custom made lettering

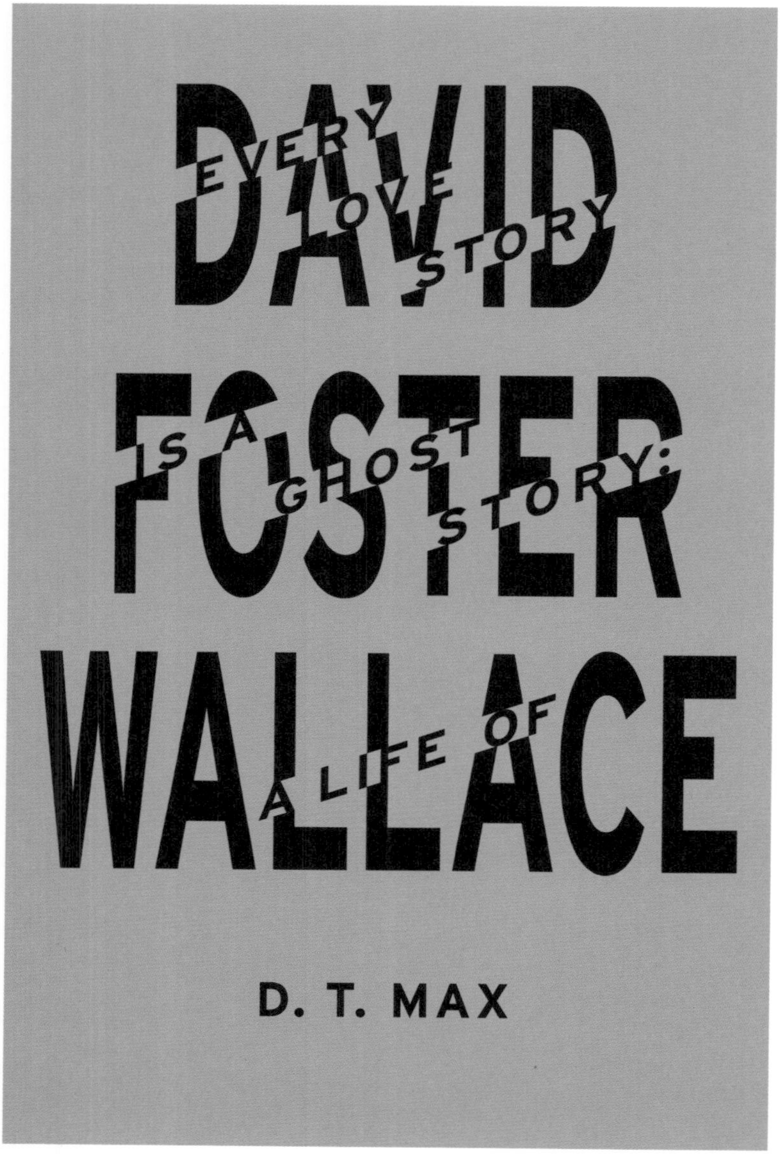

DAVID
FOSTER
WALLACE

EVERY
LOVE
STORY

IS A
GHOST
STORY:

A LIFE OF

D. T. MAX

Every Love Story is a Ghost Story: A Life of David Foster Wallace
FUEL
2012

Type
Custom made lettering

Cream 3
FUEL
2003

Type
Avant Garde

Robert Morris

Hearing

Edited and commented
by Gregor Stemmrich

Spector Books

Hearing **by Robert Morris**
Till Gathmann
2012

Type
Times LT Std, AG Book

Gregor Stemmrich

Listening to *Hearing*

Avoid the idea of a puzzle which could be solved. (Jasper Johns)[1]

Morris created his installation *Hearing* in 1972 and first exhibited it at the Leo Castelli Gallery that same year. It consists of an ensemble of furniture with surfaces of various metals that stands on a cruciform platform and a three-and-a-half-hour tape recording of a fictive hearing, to be played back through stereo speakers. The platform is square and measures twelve feet across, is six inches high, and is surrounded by a bronze molding. On its four corners, square sections of twenty-four inches a side are cut out, giving it an emblematic quality. Standing parallel to each other on it are a bed covered with lead and a table covered with zinc; between these two pieces of furniture in grayish metal, shifted slightly to the rear, stands a copper chair. Opposite the chair, between the bed and the table, is a bronze trough holding six wet-cell batteries, each of which is attached to one leg of the bed and one leg of the table. The trough is recessed into the 15cm tall platform, which is covered with reddish sand ("casting sand"), a color similar to that of the copper chair.[2] The grayish shades of the table and bed thus contrast with the reddish shades of the chair, the bronze, the sand, and the metal molding. The uniform surfaces and the harmonized proportions, materials, and shades lend the entire ensemble a suggestive aesthetic effect. The minimalism of the design seems to have entered into an unholy alliance with the martial. Warning signs indicate to the viewers that they should not, for their own well-being, touch the furniture. The chair is filled with water, which is kept at a constant boil by an immersion heater. They can indeed verify empirically the heat radiating from the chair, and the concrete demonstration that the table and chair are electrically charged by the wet-cell batteries in the trough makes the warning signs almost superfluous.

Description of the work (a) Installation of objects

1   Jasper Johns, "Sketchbook Notes [S-39. Book B, c. 1968.]," in Jasper Johns, *Writings, Sketchbook Notes, Interviews*, ed. Kirk Varnedoe, comp. Christel Hollevoet (New York: Museum of Modern Art, 1996), 64.
2   This indication of the color of the material covering the platform refers to the installation of *Hearing* in the Guggenheim retrospective in 1994. During the preparations for Morris's exhibition at the Museum Abteiberg in Mönchengladbach in 2010, however, it became clear that Morris had not clearly specified the material or its color; rather, he accepts that an appropriate material and an appropriate color will be selected from the materials and colors available in each case. A gray granular material was used for the exhibition in Mönchengladbach. Thus the gray was increased in the color combination while the colors of the metal furniture remained the same.

99

***Hearing* by Robert Morris**
Till Gathmann
2012

Type
Times LT Std, AG Book

Fabrice Gygi monograph
Gavillet & Rust
2005–06

Type
Autobahn

11th Swiss Sculpture Exhibition: Utopics poster
Gavillet & Rust
2009

Type
Theinhardt

Sat, Jul 20, 6pm

Somewhere to Haunt

Patrick Keiller's British Psychogeographic Cinema

(270)
(450)
(600)
750
(900)
(1200)

Regulatory Sign 616 The Traffic Signs Regulations and General Directions 2002, Her Majesty's Stationery Office

616
No entry for vehicular traffic

The North (M 1)
Derby A 38

Toyota

Presented by James Goggin,
Graphic Designer, Practise

Excerpts from *London* (1994) and *Robinson in Space* (1997), screening of *Robinson in Ruins* (2010).

This presentation will show excerpts, a trailer, and one feature-length film from the Robinson trilogy by British filmmaker and architect Patrick Keiller. Using his signature technique of subjective camera and voiceover, Keiller creates a reflective narrative, driven by the exploits of an unseen and unheard character, Robinson. The running commentary is relayed to us by Robinson's unnamed friend (and apparent onetime lover), the Narrator, voiced by noted English actor Paul Scofield in *London* and *Robinson in Space*, and by equally noted English actress Vanessa Redgrave in *Robinson in Ruins*.

Layering moving and static images, music, and quotation, Keiller's films describe his character's search for utopia in the cities, suburbs and industrial landscapes, while simultaenously grappling with wider "problem of England". Drawing upon the Situationist theory of psychogeography— an update of Charles Baudelaire's *flâneur*, the inquisitive urban explorer further articulated by Walter Benjamin— Keiller's films enable us to experience the unique pleasures and quandaries presented by wandering through the environment with open eyes.

Robinson in Ruins (still)
Patrick Keiller, 2010

Robinson in Space (still)
Patrick Keiller, 1997

Black Cinema House
6901 S. Dorchester Ave.
Chicago, Il 60637
blackcinemahouse.org

BLACK
CINEMA
HOUSE **SAIC**

balloon

Image, Building, Object. Exploring Architecture & Design on Film

A monthly film series at Black Cinema House, 6901 S Dorchester

Somewhere to Haunt poster
James Goggin
2013

Type
Plak, Library Seven

After ten years of running his own graphic design studio, Practise, with wife and partner Shan James, Goggin moved to Chicago to become Director of Design, Publishing and New Media at the Museum of Contemporary Art. Together with a small team of designers, editors and producers, Goggin used the museum's exhibitions, events, publications and videos to establish an ongoing, in-flux beta identity informed by curators, artists and the museum's visitors.

These approaches allowed for a shifting palette of type and colour relating to specific exhibitions, including the strategic appropriation of ultimate 1980s art and commerce typeface Futura Extra Black Condensed for *This Will Have Been: Art, Love & Politics in the 1980s.*

In spring 2013, Goggin left the MCA and returned to running Practise with James.

This Will Have Been **exhibition and catalogue**
James Goggin, Scott Reinhard, Alfredo Ruiz
2012

Type
Futura Extra Black Condensed

This permanent exhibition at the Science Museum explored new digital technologies. In a semi-dark space, many of the texts provided their own illumination, including this, the title panel. GTF adapted 11 thin, low-energy electro-luminescent lamps, commonly used in electronic products, to create the panel at the gallery entrance. The eight characters—D, I, G, T, O, P, L, S —were created by breaking circuits with a hole punch and illuminating selected areas of each lamp.

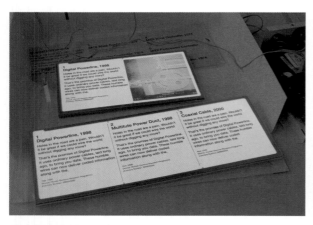

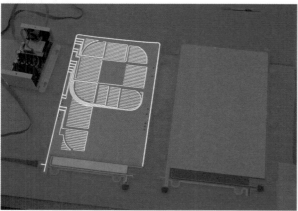

Digitopolis **exhibition**
Graphic Thought Facility
2000

Type
Neue Helvetica

9/10
Opens 20 July
Edward II
By Christopher
Marlowe

The Men's Company An all male
production exploring clothing,
music, dance and settings possible
in the original Globe of 1603

Edward II Liam Brennan

Master of Play Timothy Walker

ROBIN JEFFREY, DRESSING ROOM, 2002

11/12
Opens 10 August
*The Taming
of the Shrew*
By William
Shakespeare

The Women's Company An all
female production exploring
clothing, music, dance and
settings possible in the original
Globe of 1603

Master of Play Barry Kyle

COLIN HURLEY, GREEN ROOM, 2002

The Taming of the Shrew is one
of Shakespeare's most famous,
funny and controversial plays.
It tells the story of Petruccio,
a young man from Verona
in search of great wealth in Padua.
He meets Katherine, a strong-
willed soul, notorious for her wit
and independence. Tempted by
the promise of a favourable dowry,
and eager to help his friend woo
Katherine's younger sister Bianca,
Petruccio sets about courting the
reluctant 'shrew'.

With its infamous final scene,
when the bond between Petruccio
and Katherine is finally put to the
test, *The Taming of the Shrew*
is a tale of the change of regime
between an independent man and
woman when they unite in love
and marriage.

ALBIE WOODINGTON, SMOKERS' BALCONY, 2002

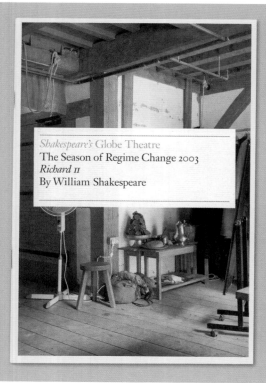

Shakespeare's Globe Theatre
The Season of Regime Change 2003
Richard II
By William Shakespeare

Shakespeare's Globe Theatre
Graphic Thought Facility
2003

Type
Janson Text, Linotype Univers

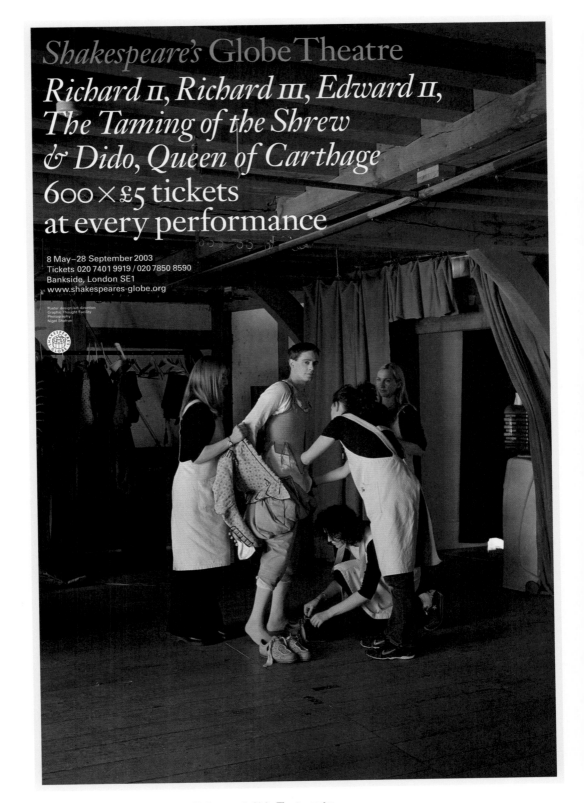

Shakespeare's Globe Theatre

Richard II, *Richard* III, *Edward* II,
The Taming of the Shrew
& Dido, Queen of Carthage
600 × £5 tickets
at every performance

8 May–28 September 2003
Tickets 020 7401 9919 / 020 7850 8590
Bankside, London SE1
www.shakespeares-globe.org

Poster design/art direction
Graphic Thought Facility
Photography
Nigel Shafran

Shakespeare's Globe Theatre poster
Graphic Thought Facility
2003

Type
Janson Text, Linotype Univers

Andy Warhol catalogue raisonné
Julia Hasting
2002–10

Type
Trade Gothic, handmade script

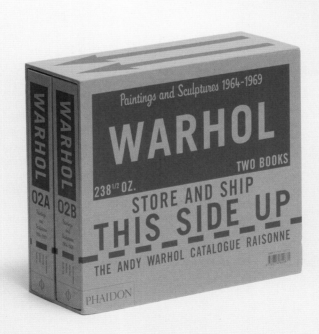

Andy Warhol catalogue raisonné
Julia Hasting
2002–10

Type
Trade Gothic, handmade script

Hoefler & Frere-Jones was established in Manhattan by Jonathan Hoefler and Tobias Frere-Jones in 1989, and is today one of the world's most influential type foundries. Since the early 1990s, its focus has been on creating fonts for editorial use by publications such as *Rolling Stone*, *The New York Times*, *Harper's Bazaar*, *Wired* and *The Wall Street Journal*.

Gotham, designed by Frere-Jones in 2000, was inspired by the basic, matter-of-fact, unassuming lettering found engraved in stone, cast in bronze or glowing in neon on buildings all over New York—hence the familiar, trustworthy but assertive tone that brought it to prominence in the Obama campaign of 2008.

In the vein of the Humanist fonts of the early twentieth century, such as those by Eric Gill and Edward Johnston, Ideal is a sans serif with classical rather than industrial proportions—a handmade rather than machine aesthetic, with an absence of straight lines and symmetries.

Gotham font
Jonathan Hoefler & Tobias Frere-Jones
2000

1001 FIFTH AVENUE 101

1166 SIXTH AVENUE 120

ROAD STREET 127 JOHN STRE

REET 140 WEST 57TH STREET

ROADWAY 17 STATE STREET

21 WEST STREET BUILDING 23

ECINCT STATION HOUSE 275 M

Water (%)	negligible (2.830 km²)¹

POPULATION

2008 estimate	9,689,800¹ (86th)
1999 census	10,045,200
Density	49/km² (142nd)
	127/sq mi

GDP (PPP) 2007 estimate
Total	$105.292 billion² (58th)
Per capita	$10,948² (IMF) (65th)

GDP (nominal) 2007 estimate
Total	$44.773 billion²
Per capita	$4,655² (IMF)

		GDP (nom
		Total
		Per capita

BUL

CAPITAL	
LARGEST M	
LANGUAGE	
DEMONYM	
GOVERNME	

King
Prime Min

INDEPEND
Declared
– Recogni

EU ACCESS

BELARUS

CAPITAL (and largest city)	Minsk 53°55'N 27°33'E
LANGUAGES	Belarusian, Russian
DEMONYM	Belarusian
GOVERNMENT	Presidential republic
President	Alexander Lukashenko

Store Hours

Monday	10:00am–9:00pm
Tuesday	10:00am–9:00pm
Wednesday	10:00am–9:00pm
Thursday	10:00am–9:00pm
Friday	10:00am–9:00pm
Saturday	10:00am–9:00pm

26

Flight Number
NA920

Destination
Amsterdam

Scheduled Departure
6:00pm

Carrier
National Airways

joins with both gover
industry leaders to s
boycott of the endar
bluefin tuna. Often c
foodstuff, the bluefir
extraordinary specim
ten feet long (2.5m),
more than 1,200 pou
warm-blooded, and a
temperature — a ne
migratory pattern ac
cold Atlantic waters.
predators who exhib
at speeds of up to 8c
migrating schools are
cross the *ocean* in as
a few weeks. Their st
fins, bluefins are kno
have been seen by m
for centuries, but no

ne space embraces a

pirit and physical well

lance finding relaxatio

secluded desert settin

rsonalized experience

Grow.

Jean-Paul Béringer

with a new foreword by ANUSHKA RAO SAHAB
editor of THE ORESTEIAN REVIEW

Ideal Sans font
Jonathan Hoefler & Tobias Frere-Jones
2011

Die neue Linie

19.5. bis 24.8. 2011

DIE NEUE LINIE
DIE MÖBELWERKSTÄTTEN AM BAUHAUS

Ausstellung vom 19.5. bis 24.8.2011
Im Werkstattflügel des Bauhausgebäudes
Geöffnet täglich von 10 bis 18 Uhr
Eintritt: € 6,- / 4,-

Stiftung Bauhaus Dessau
Gropiusallee 38
D-06846 Dessau-Roßlau
www.bauhaus-dessau.de

Bauhaus Dessau identity
Hort
2011

Type
Dessauer Courier, Arial Black

Stiftung Bauhaus Dessau

Stiftung Bauhaus Dessau
Gropiusallee 38
06846 Dessau-Roßlau
Telefon: +49-340-6508-250
www.bauhaus-dessau.de

Freikarte
Preis: 0,00 €

1

30.07.2010 11:02 Frau Gäbler
036943

Bauhaus Dessau identity
Hort
2011

Type
Dessauer Courier, Arial Black

Stiftung Bauhaus Dessau
Postfach 1405
06846 Dessau-Roßlau
Germany

An: HORT
       Eike König
       Hagelberger Straße 52
       10965 Berlin

B
A
U
H
A
U
S

D
E
S
S
A
U

Prof. Philipp Oswalt   Direktor

Stiftung Bauhaus Dessau
Gropiusallee 38
06846 Dessau-Roßlau
Germany
Telefon +49-(0)340-1234-567
Fax   +49-(0)340-1234-567
E-Mail abcdefg@bauhaus-dessau.de
www.bauhaus-dessau.de

Diana Schmidt   Servicebereich

Stiftung Bauhaus Dessau
Gropiusallee 38
06846 Dessau-Roßlau
Germany
Telefon +49-(0)340-1234-567
Fax   +49-(0)340-1234-567
E-Mail abcdefg@bauhaus-dessau.de
www.bauhaus-dessau.de

The Bauhaus Dessau Foundation is housed in the original Bauhaus building and is dedicated to conserving and researching the Bauhaus legacy.

Hort's typographic system for the foundation's new identity consists exclusively of common system fonts and an approach that connects to the original Bauhaus ideology of functionality, based on the potential of mass-production: strict typography, a minimalist layout, standardized formats and no colour.

As the most 'generic and incidental' typeface, Courier was selected as the new, corporate font. For uniqueness, the capital 'A' of Courier was redesigned to better match that of Herbert Bayer's vertical Bauhaus logo, which still runs down the front of the Bauhaus building. In another echo, the new logotype is also set vertically at all times.

Bauhaus Dessau identity
Hort
2011

Type
Dessauer Courier, Arial Black

Prof. Philipp Oswalt
Direktor

Stiftung Bauhaus Dessau
Gropiusallee 38
06846 Dessau-Roßlau
Germany

Telefon +49-(0)340-1234-567
Fax   +49-(0)340-1234-567
E-Mail abcdefg@bauhaus-dessau.de

Telefon +49-(0)340-6508-250
Fax   +49-(0)340-6508-226
www.bauhaus-dessau.de

An: HORT
        Eike König
        Hagelberger Straße 52
        10965 Berlin

Betreff: Neukonzeption des visuellen
Erscheinungsbildes

Dessau-Roßlau,
den 5. Juli 2010

Lieber Eike König,

Die aktuelle Brisanz des Bauhauses liegt nicht in konkreten Objekten oder
Formen, sondern in seiner Programmatik, in den Bauhausideen und -methoden.
Genau genommen müssen wir hierbei vom Plural sprechen, von den Bauhäusern,
und nicht dem Bauhaus. Soweit sich das Bauhaus aus der Bewegung der
klassischen Moderne heraushebt und vielleicht tatsächlich einzigartig
ist, so deshalb, weil es dem historischen Bauhaus gelungen ist, eine
Vielfältigkeit und Widersprüchlichkeit von modernen Gestaltungspraktiken
im Rahmen eines Projektes zu bündeln, wie es sonst nie erreicht wurde. Das
ungemein fruchtbare lag nicht zuletzt darin begründet, dass an einem Ort
Maler, Grafiker, Architekten, Typografen, Theatermacher, Medienkünstler,
Städtebauer, Produktdesigner und auch Wissenschaftler, Techniker und
Ingenieure zusammenwirkten, sich austauschten, stritten und immer wieder
gemeinsam Projekte realisierten.

Wir haben geordnete Vorstellungen von der Moderne, der Architektur der
modernen Sachlichkeit, der abstrakten Kunst, des funktionalen Designs
usw. Doch das Eigenwillige des Bauhauses war, dass es eben genau diese
Kategorien überwand und die heterogene Gleichzeitigkeit der modernen
Avantgarden nicht nur akzeptierte, sondern auch operativ nutzte. Um es
mit den letztendlich untauglichen Stilrichtungen und Moden zu umreißen:
Es gab am Bauhaus Expressionismus, Konstruktivismus, Funktionalismus,
DeStijl, Neue Sachlichkeit, ja auch Dadaismus und vieles mehr. Obgleich es
in den einzelnen Phasen der Bauhausgeschichte dominante Haltungen gab, so
ist der eigentliche Befund, dass diese Widersprüchlichkeiten an einem Ort
gleichzeitig präsent waren.

mit freundlichen Grüßen

Prof. Philipp Oswalt

Seite
1/1

Bauhaus Dessau identity
Hort
2011

Type
Dessauer Courier, Arial Black

Hort 175

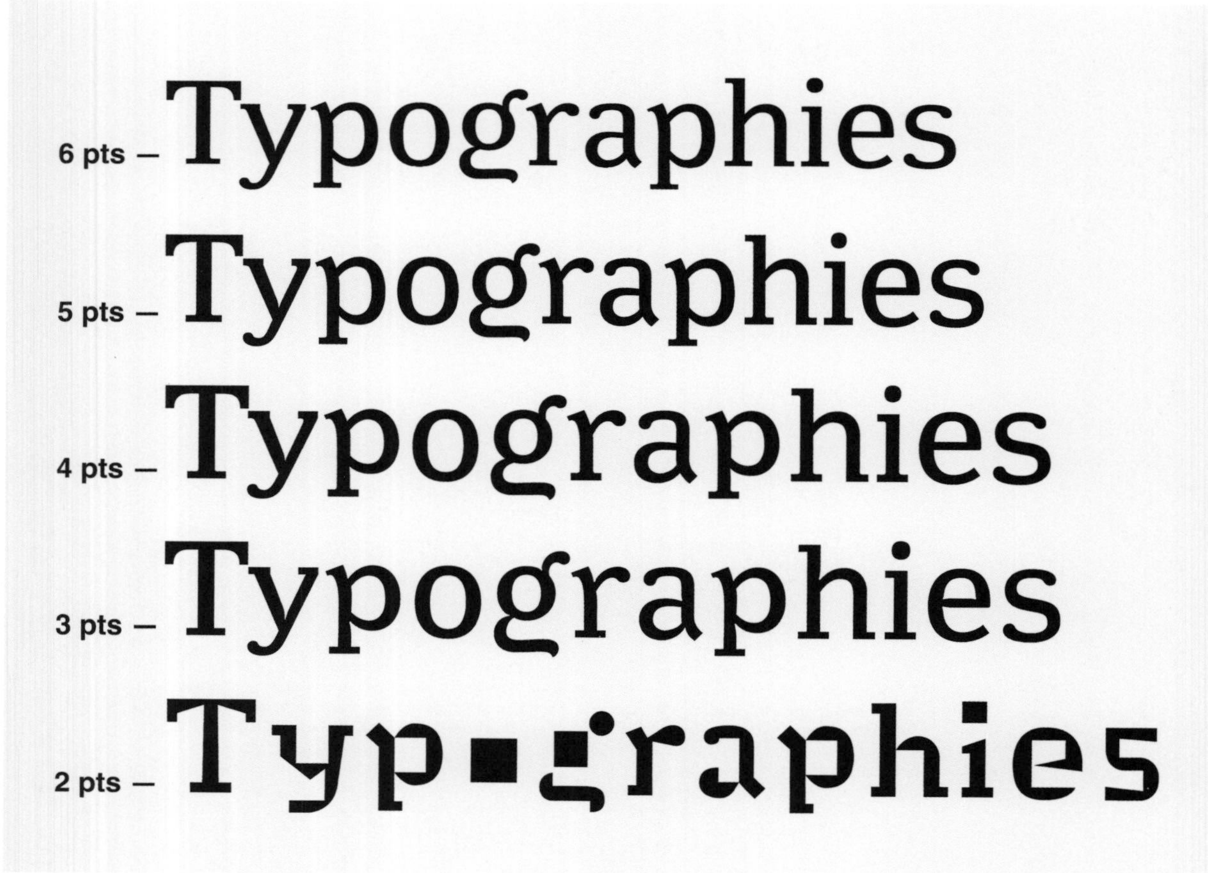

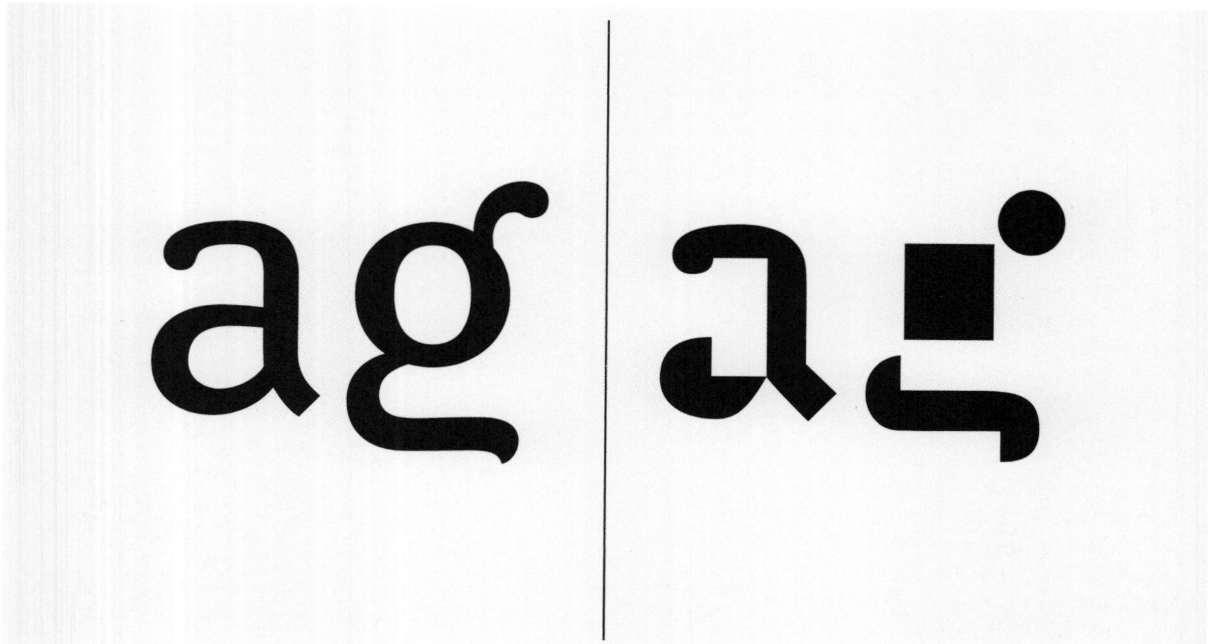

6 pts – Typographies

5 pts – Typographies

4 pts – Typographies

3 pts – Typographies

2 pts – Typ■graphies

ag a■

Minuscule
Thomas Huot-Marchand
2002–07

Type
Minuscule 6, 5, 4, 3 & 2

Like e-Types' Medilabel font, Minuscule is designed for reading at very small sizes, with a master for use at each point size from 6pt down to 2pt. Its characteristics include a large x-height, robust slab serifs, a vertical stress, an open structure and large counters.

It was inspired by the research into the physiology of reading carried out by Louis Émile Javal, a nineteenth-century ophthalmologist who was the first to analyse eye movements during reading. He reported that, rather than moving continuously along a line of text, eyes make short jumps and stops, taking in sections of sentences at each interval.

Minuscule
Thomas Huot-Marchand
2002–07

Type
Minuscule 6, 5, 4, 3 & 2

Meet the cast:

ABCD EFGHIJK LMNOP QRSTUV WXYZ

Now see the movie:

Helvetica

A documentary film by Gary Hustwit

A Swiss Dots
production,
in association
with Veer

swiss dots Veer

Helvetica
A documentary film
by Gary Hustwit

Featuring:
Michael Bierut
Neville Brody
Matthew Carter
David Carson
Wim Crouwel
Experimental Jetset
Tobias Frere-Jones
Ottmar Hoefer
Jonathan Hoefler
Alfred Hoffmann

Lars Müller
Norm
Mike Parker
Michael C. Place
Rick Poynor
Stefan Sagmeister
Leslie Savan
Paula Scher
Manfred Schulz
Erik Spiekermann
Bruno Steinert

Massimo Vignelli
Hermann Zapf

**Produced and
Directed by**
Gary Hustwit

Editor:
Shelby Siegel

helveticafilm.com

**Director of
Photography:**
Luke Geissbühler

**Additional
Photography:**
Colin Brown
Gary Hustwit
Pete Sillen
Chris Wetton
Ben Wolf

Additional Editing:
Laura Weinberg

Sound Editor:
Brian Langman

Sound Mixer:
Andy Kris

Motion Graphics:
Trollbäck & Co.

**Sound
Recording:**
Nara Garber
Victor Horstink
Dan Johnson
Jörg Kidowski
Sam Pullen
Reto Stamm

Poster by
Experimental Jetset

Music:
The Album Leaf
Battles
Caribou
Chicago Underground
Quartet
El Ten Eleven
Four Tet
Kim Hiorthøy
Motohiro Nakashima
Sam Prekop

**Associate
Producers:**
Andrew Dreskin
John Goldsmith
Sharon Hustwit
Michelle Hustwit
Jakob Trollbäck
Antoine Wilson
Chris Levinson Wilson

(c) 2007 Swiss Dots

'A rock documentary, but about a typeface,' is how film-maker Gary Hustwit described *Helvetica* to uncomprehending listeners before he started making the film.

'Since millions of people see and use Helvetica every day, I guess I just wondered, "Why?". How did a typeface drawn by a little-known Swiss designer in 1957 become one of the most popular ways for us to communicate our words fifty years later?

'And what are the repercussions of that popularity? Has it resulted in the globalization of our visual culture? And what about the effects of technology on type and graphic design, and the ways we consume it? Most of us use computers and digital fonts every day, so are we all graphic designers now, in a sense?

'So let's just say I had a few questions, and I thought making a film would be a good way to answer them.'

Helvetica: A Documentary Film
Gary Hustwit
2007

Type
Helvetica

Gary Hustwit 179

THE NIHIL
HATH WILL
CIVIL I

AnOther Magazine (issue 3)
David James & Gareth Hague
2002

Type
Ano Serif

IS IMM OF T HE

DESTOY ESROY

SAITON

N S U I
E A T
A X L Y

Collections
Autumn/Winter 2008

Text
Susannah Frankel
Photography
Sølve Sundsbø
Styling
Marie Chaix

AnOther Magazine is a fashion and culture magazine published twice a year by Dazed Group. All of its text and headlines are set in versions of Anoserif, a font developed by David James and Gareth Hague, working as their joint venture type foundry, Alias.

Anoserif is a mix of ideas and reference points—from Berthold Wolpe's Faber and Faber book cover designs to blackletter typography and lettering for toilet roll and cereal packaging—produced as a typeface in angular, brush and script versions.

AnOther Magazine (issue 15)
David James & Gareth Hague
2008

Type
Ano Serif

Text
Alex
Marashian
Photography
Jim
Goldberg

Pla st iki Kon -Ti ki

For *AnOther Man,* the male
fashion spin-off from *AnOther
Magazine,* Alias created Ano,
a sans serif font drawn in nine
styles and six weights.

Its mathematical circular
construction and monolinear
framework, reminiscent
of Futura, is emphasized
through its various versions.
The difference between weights
is calculated to give consistency
of line thickness when used at
set sizes, allowing for a variety
of layout options.

AnOther Man explored different
typography and layout ideas
for each issue. Issue 9 used
Ano Black for headlines, with
words broken to fit super-short
line lengths.

AnOther Man (issue 9)
David James & Gareth Hague
2009

Type
Ano

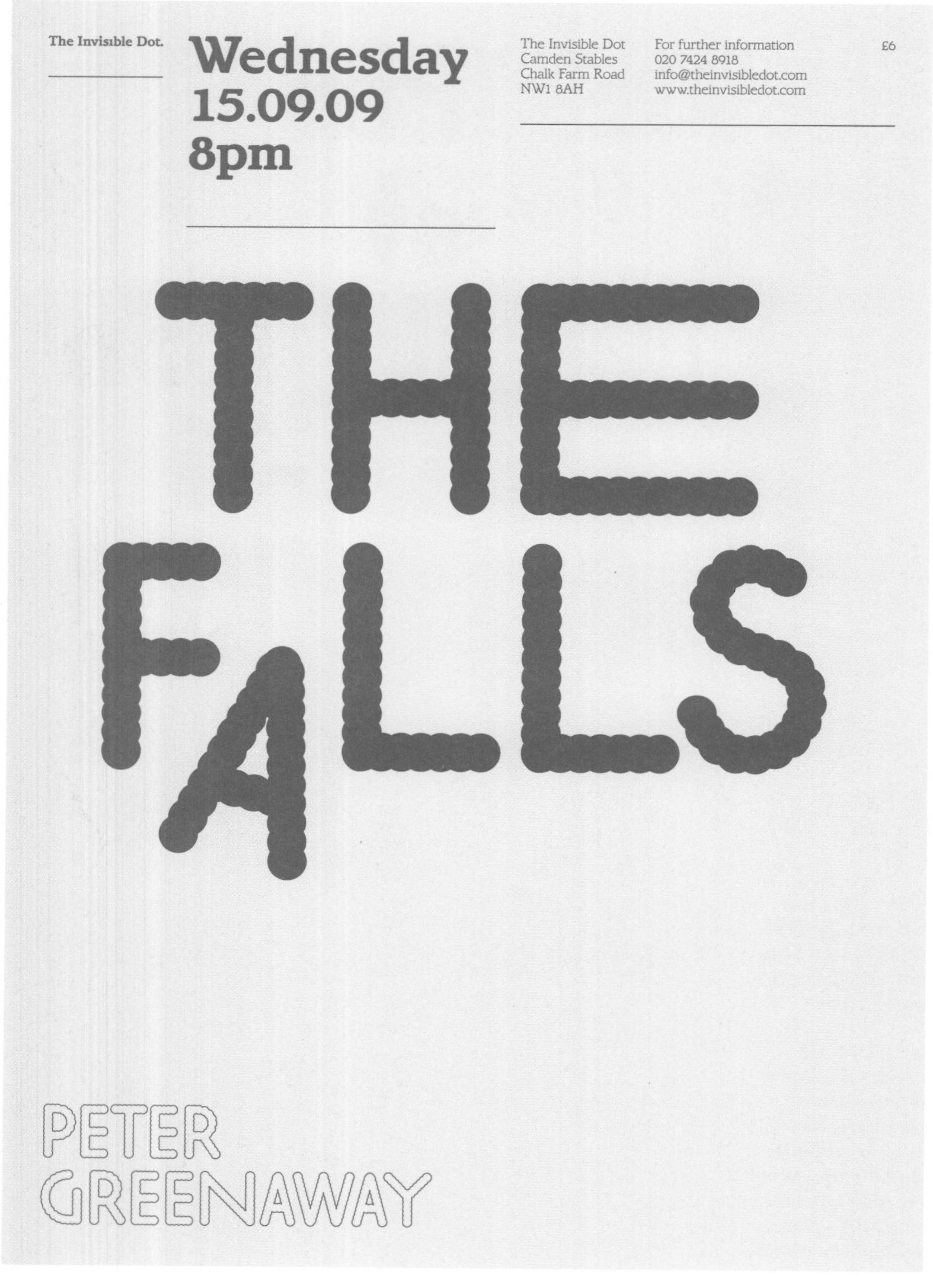

Wednesday
15.09.09
8pm

The Invisible Dot
Camden Stables
Chalk Farm Road
NW1 8AH

For further information
020 7424 8918
info@theinvisibledot.com
www.theinvisibledot.com

£6

THE FALLS

PETER
GREENAWAY

The Falls **poster**
Julia
2010

Type
Riso

JOHN-LUKE ROBERTS

DISTRACTS

YOU

FROM

A

MURDER

4th – 30th 8.10pm
pleasance.co.uk
0131 556 6550

An Invisible Dot
production

DOME
PLEASANCE
0131 556 6550

John-Luke Roberts Distracts You from a Murder theatre poster
Julia
2010

Type
Tail Gothic (Julia)

Allora &
Calzadilla
Bock
Dean

THE HUGO BOSS PRIZE 2006

Ortega
Ruilova
Sehgal

Guggenheim Museum Hugo Boss Prize catalogue
karlssonwilker inc
2006

Type
Akzidenz-Grotesk

Guggenheim Museum Hugo Boss Prize catalogue
karlssonwilker inc
2006

Type
Akzidenz-Grotesk

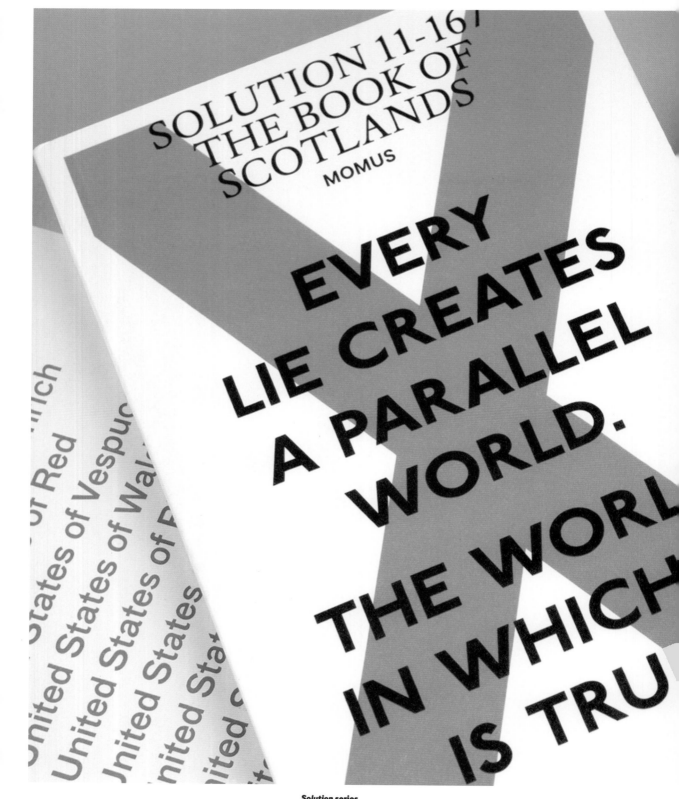

SOLUTION 11-167
THE BOOK OF
SCOTLANDS
MOMUS

EVERY
LIE CREATES
A PARALLEL
WORLD.

THE WORL
IN WHICH
IS TRU

Solution series
Zak Kyes/Zak Group
2008–11

Type
DTL Elzevir, Stempel Schneidler, Neuzeit

SOLUTION 214-238
THE BOOK OF JAPAN
MOMUS

THINGS ARE CONSPICUOUS

SOLUTION 214-238 THE BOOK OF J

אנחנו us نحن

SOLUTION 196-213 PALESTINE-ISRAEL

SLEAZENATION

AN IDEAL FOR LIVING THROUGH HONEST FASHION, ART, MUSIC AND DESIGN

I'M WITH STUPID

JARVIS COCKER & BARRY 7 • ARAKI FASHION EXCLUSIVE • BIBA • THE HIVES

DJ BIRD • KILLED BY DEATH • CHARLIE LUXTON • RAPING STEVEN SPIELBERG

NOV 2001 £3.20 MADE IN THE UK

9 771460 473055

11 >

Sleazenation (vol. 4 issue 10)
Scott King and Earl Brutus
2001

Type
Sleazenation stencil font, Helvetica, Eurostile Bold Condensed, Eurostile Condensed

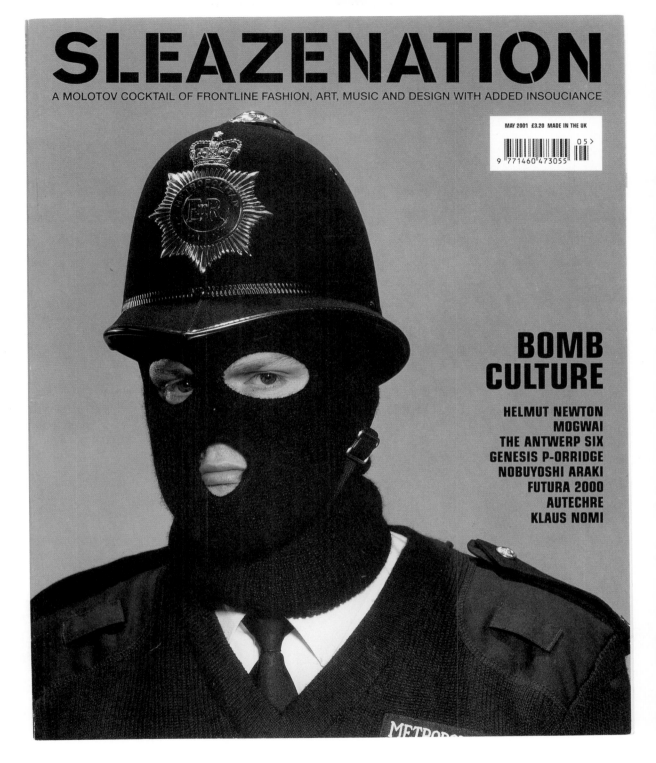

SLEAZENATION

A MOLOTOV COCKTAIL OF FRONTLINE FASHION, ART, MUSIC AND DESIGN WITH ADDED INSOUCIANCE

MAY 2001 £3.20 MADE IN THE UK

9 771460 473055

BOMB CULTURE

HELMUT NEWTON
MOGWAI
THE ANTWERP SIX
GENESIS P-ORRIDGE
NOBUYOSHI ARAKI
FUTURA 2000
AUTECHRE
KLAUS NOMI

Sleazenation (vol. 4 issue 4)
Scott King
2001

Type
Sleazenation stencil font, Helvetica, Eurostile Bold Condensed

DR JOHNSON'S
London

Broadside* 10

* Broadside is
a series of experiments
in typography & printing
published by
The Typography Workshop
since 1989.

Broadside 10 is printed & published to celebrate the tercentenary of the birth of Dr. Samuel Johnson LL.D. in 1709 at Lichfield in the county of Staffordshire, England & the twentieth anniversary of the establishment of The Typography Workshop by Alan Kitching in November 1989 at the Clerkenwell Workshops in Clerkenwell, London EC1.

Edited, produced & published 2009/10 ©
by Alan Kitching & Celia Stothard
at The Typography Workshop, 19 Cleaver Street,
Kennington, in the London Borough of Lambeth SE11 4DP
& printed letterpress at their Workshop in Pullens Yards,
in the London Borough of Southwark SE17

BIBLIOGRAPHY

James Boswell, *Life of Johnson*, Oxford University Press, 1980
(First published 1791)
Alvin Kernan, *Printing Technology, Letters & Samuel Johnson*,
Princeton University Press, 1987
Peter Martin, *Samuel Johnson – A Biography*, Weidenfeld & Nicholson, 2008
David Nokes, *Samuel Johnson – A Life*, Faber & Faber, 2009
Charles Norman, *Mr. Oddity – Samuel Johnson LL.D.*, John Murray, 1951

Text set in Stephenson Blake's (Founders 1901) Caslon Old Face

This edition of twenty copies is printed on 300gsm Somerset Satin

LONDON
Based on R & J Dodsley's
map of 1761

1717
HE HAD A LITTLE MONEY WHEN he came to town, he knew how he could live in the cheapest manner. His first lodgings were at the house of Mr. Norris, a staymaker, in Exeter-street, adjoining Catherine-street, in the Strand.

'I dined very well for eight-pence, with very good company, at the Pine Apple in New-street, just by. Several of them had travelled. They expected to meet every day; but did not know one another's names. It cost the rest a shilling, for they drank wine; but I had a cut of meat for six-pence, and bread for a penny, and gave the waiter a penny; so that I was quite well served, nay, better than the rest, for they gave the waiter nothing.'

Spring 1738
... he was now enlisted by Mr. Cave as a regular coadjutor in *The Gentleman's Magazine*. Thus was Johnson employed, during some of the best years of his life, as a mere literary labourer

'for gain not glory'

Tuesday, 20 July 1762
'...Last winter I went down to my native town, ... I wandered about for five days, and took the first convenient opportunity of returning to a place, where, if there is not much happiness, there is, at least, such a diversity of good and evil, that slight vexations do not fix upon the heart.'[1]

[1] This is a very just account of the relief which London affords to melancholy minds.

Tuesday, 5 July 1763
'Sir, if you wish to have a just notion of the magnitude of this city, you must not be satisfied with seeing its great streets & squares, but must survey the innumerable little lanes and courts. It is not in the showy evolutions of buildings, but in the multiplicity of human habitations which are crouded together, that the wonderful immensity of London consists.'

Saturday, 30 September 1769
'The happiness of London is not to be conceived but by those who have been in it. I will venture to say, there is more learning & science within the circumference of ten miles from where we now sit, than in all the rest of the kingdom.'

1770
'No place, cured a man's vanity or arrogance so well as London; for as no man was either great or good per se, but as compared with others not so good or great, he was sure to find in the metropolis many his equals, and some his superiours.'

1770
We dined *tête à tête* at the Mitre, as I was preparing much leaving London, where I had formed many agreeable connexions: 'Sir, (said he,) I don't wonder at it; no man, fond

of letters, leaves London without regret.'

Tuesday, 13 April 1773
'Nay, Sir, I say that is not luxury a walk from Charing-cross to [...] through, I suppose, the greatest s[...] in the world; what is there in any [...] (if you except gin-shops,) that can [...] man being any harm?'

Thursday, 15 April 1773
'Sir, any man who [...] name, or who he [...] power of pleasing [...] be very generally [...] ed in London.'

Tuesday, 26 March 1776
'Why, Sir, you have Edinburgh, where the gentlemen of counties meet, and which is not so large but that the[...] There is no such common place of collection in London, where from its great size and diffusion, m[...] reside in contiguous counties of England, may [...] meet [...] in each other.'

Friday, 5 April 1776
'It is wonderful, Sir, [...] best London [...] literary conversation [...] enjoyed, was at the tab[...] Ellis, a money-scrivener [...] the Royal Exchange, w[...] I at one period used to d[...] ally once a week.'[1]

[1] This Mr. Ellis was, I believe [...] that profession called Scrivener [...] one of the London companies [...] the business is no longer carried [...] ely, but is transacted by attorn[...]

HIGH HOLBORN

COVENT GARDEN MARKET

RUSSELL ST

DRURY LN

CHANCERY LN

GRAY'S INN LN

HO

GETTER IN

Gray's Inn
Johnson's
home
1759-60

Staple Inn
Holborn
Johnson's
home
1759

Thomas Davies's bookshop
↓
Where Johnson met Boswell
1763

Drury Lane Theatre
Johnson's play *Irene* performed here in 1749

THE STRAND

FLEET

St Clement's Dane
Johnson's regular London church

Mitre Tavern
Fleet Street

Turk's Head
Johnson's club first met here

Essex Head
Johnson's last London club 1783

ESSEX ST

INNER TEMPLE LN

Inner Temple Lane
Johnson's home
1760-65

RIVER TH

Dr Johnson's London
Alan Kitching
2009–10

Type
Letterpress

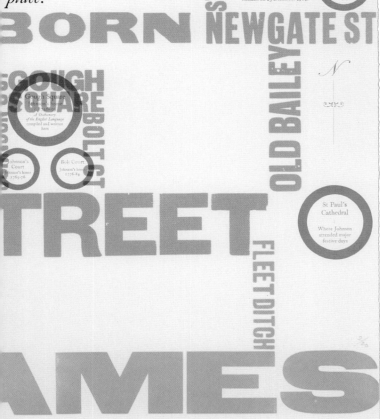

As digital typography has come to dominate graphic design, Alan Kitching has continued pushing letterpress to its limits. His first typographic map was of Brighton, following a project with students at the then Brighton Polytechnic. Instead of outlining streets and landmarks, Kitching indicated their importance and relationships by the size and weight of type.

The series has continued with themed maps of London. As well as the chunky wood type street names that have been a feature of the series, *Dr Johnson's London* includes text and quotes from the great lexicographer set in an antique cut of Caslon. Its swashes and ligatures delight, and the changes of scale lend emphasis and a change of pace to key passages of text.

Kitching's 2011 map of the historic Borough area of London, south of London Bridge, features his selection of landmarks picked out with bold rings of ink, including pubs, restaurants, print-related businesses and the Shard. The names of London Underground stations overlap their red rings in homage to the LU roundel.

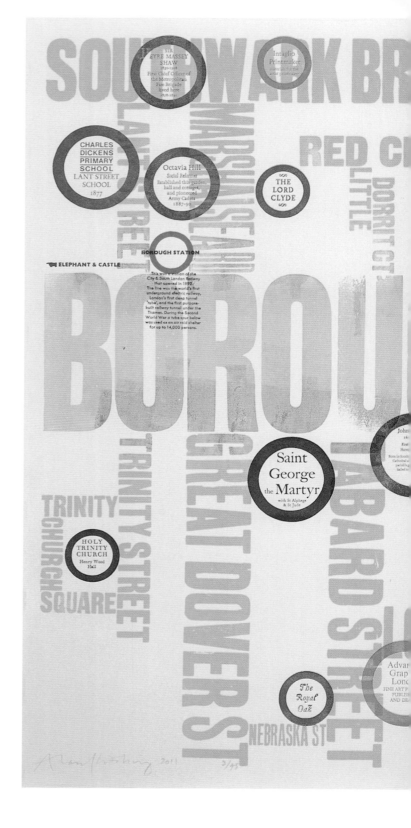

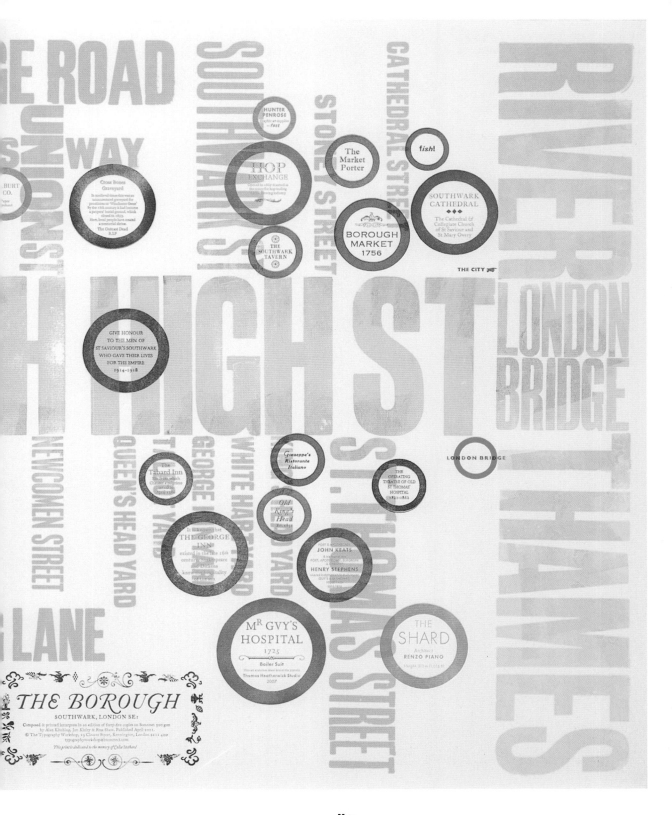

Map
Alan Kitching
2011

Type
Letterpress

THE
CULTURE

032c

00025

4 197236 712008

25th Issue Berlin Winter 2013/14
D€12 EU€12 US$19.90 www.032c.com

Inez & Vinoodh

RIHANNA wears GUCCI

032c magazine (issue 25)
Joerg Koch, Mike Meiré
2013

Type
Helvetica, Futura and Times New Roman Condensed

196 Joerg Koch

Writer ANDREAS ROSENFELDER peers out over Mali's Bandiagara Escarpment, a sandstone cliff where the Dogon people, who worship ancient snake and crocodile gods, carved their homes directly into the rock.

Rosenfelder first traveled to the UNESCO World Heritage Site in 2011, when the threat of Al-Qaeda kidnappings prompted severe travel restrictions in the area. "Our guide drove us through the desert in silence," recalls Rosenfelder, who went to West Africa to write a story for the German newspaper *Die Welt*, where he's an editor. "He was playing Bob Marley tapes over and over again." A year later Islamist radicals took over half the country, until the French Army forced them from power in January this year.

Mali's artisans produce a range of crafts. While the Tuaregs specialize in the production of arms, they also make elegant silver jewelry. Bögölanfini is a traditional Malian cotton fabric dyed with the mashed and boiled leaves of *n'gallama* trees and painted with fermented mud. But political instability and military conflicts continue in Mali, making it a destination to be avoided. If you do find yourself there, however, the British global insurance company Bellwood Prestbury offers kidnap insurance, providing trained negotiators and ransom.

www.bellwoodprestbury.com/kidnap-insurance

36

Stylist EVE SAND and entrepreneur DANIEL NOAH SHEIKH are our lovebirds in Munich. Here Daniel tests the water resistance of *032c*. Call it extreme reading.

Photography: Max von Treu

Munich is more than 300 miles (500 kilometers) from the coast and 700 miles (1,100 kilometers) from surfable ocean break. Yet beginning in the 1970s an ingenious and loosely associated band of Bavarian surfers have transformed a run of the city's Eisbach river into a surfing mecca. At the southern edge of the Englischer Garten, where the fast-flowing Eisbach ploughs into a deeper section of the river that barely moves at all, Müncheners have nurtured a dangerously consistent standing wave. Until 2010 river surfing there was illegal, obliging a countless many to retrieve their boards from the police station, after having escaped the fuzz through the forest. Today, however, there are more than 1,000 active surfers on the hydraulic jump, which offers no time to get up and let the wave approach and can only be jockeyed laterally.

Just a few feet over is the Haus der Kunst, where surfers use the toilets. You can head there as well, if not for the contemporary art then for a drink at the Goldene Bar. The Kunst Cocktail of champagne and gin is a favorite:

50 ml Tanqueray No. 10
50 ml fresh lime juice
2 tbsp powdered sugar
Perrier-Jouët Grand Brut champagne
Gin & tonic espuma*

Shake gin, lime, and sugar on solid ice
Strain into an icy tumbler
Top with champagne and espuma

*Place 60 ml gin, 100 ml tonic water, 30 ml lime juice,
2.5 egg whites into a cream siphon on 2 nitrogen capsules

www.goldenebar.de
www.meracl.com

37

Educated in Vienna and Berkeley, California, Hollein also designed a series of sunglasses for American Optical Corps in 1972. "The idea came very quickly," Hollein says, "while I was talking on the telephone." Here Hollein wears a pair layered with red transparent glass.

In 1964, at age 30, Austrian architect HANS HOLLEIN successfully landed a spacecraft onto a quiet shopping street in Vienna. A keyhole punched from its monolithic, anodized aluminum front sucks passersby into a compact, immersive interior. The Retti candle shop, Hollein's first executed project, forms a showroom and sales area out of two linked cubes, the first rotated 45 degrees, with corners chamfered and mirrored to infinity. Dramatically lit niches exhibit the shop's candles, bundled like compound Gothic piers, standing or hanging from their wicks. If the facade echoes the machinic fantasies of Hollein's paper architecture, then the quasi-devotional interior answers his earlier manifesto call for a "Return to Architecture" as sacral, pure, and functionless (except that the function of this *machine-for-selling* is of course clear). More than the postmodern pastiche of the Pritzker Prize winner's later work, Hollein should be remembered for his unique approach to display – a precursor to our economy of spectacular cultural experience.

Having won the American Institute of Architects' largest cash prize for his architectural debut, and a string of further retail commissions along with it, Hollein soon turned to the sale of another luxury good. Three years after the Retti shop, the eminent gallerist Richard L. Feigen asked Hollein to design an Upper East Side New York location for his gallery. Feigen had been assembling an exhibition of "visionary architecture" for his downtown gallery, with works by Buckminster Fuller, Frei Otto, Claes Oldenburg, and others. At the suggestion of his friend Armand Bartos – the art collector, philanthropist, and one-time architectural collaborator of Frederick Kiesler – Feigen included Hollein, and his photomontage of an aircraft-carrier-as-city imbedded in a rural landscape. When the two finally met, Feigen was surprised that he was "an architect who actually built." Never-

theless, he commissioned him on the spot to design a new uptown gallery.

Given the bottom two floors of an 1887 row house, and a white stucco facade of ornament-free regularity, Hollein pasted a shimmering, double-curve chromed-steel column, 18 feet tall (5.5 meters), over the structural brick pier in the two-storey entry. The enormous sheet of metal, Feigen recalls, took some wrangling to obtain, and was

> The quasi-devotional interior answers his earlier manifesto call for a "Return to Architecture" as sacral, pure, and functionless (except that the function of this machine-for-selling is of course clear).

eventually pulled from an order for Minoru Yamasaki's World Trade Center, then under construction. This and all interior fittings were hand-polished by an Austrian craftsman, flown in on an artist visa, working under cover of night to avoid union conflicts.

Passing through a grid of windows into the double-height main gallery, visitors could follow the sinuous line of a polished Art Deco handrail up a flight of stairs to the second floor, and around to a double-curved viewing balcony – evocative of a theater box, an ocean liner, a pair of breasts. This offered a view onto the salon-style hanging across the way, and more importantly, the society spectacle of a gallery opening below. Alternatively, following the choreography of the sale, one could pass to the rear of the ground floor, through two smaller galleries, and into a back room – as long and nearly as wide as the main gallery.

Anchored on one end by Feigen's office, with a prototype of Hollein's

The Schullin jewelry store in Vienna, begun in 1972, is an architecture of erosion rather than extrusion, drawing passersby into the basic shell of a 19th-century building. Hollein used materials with flagrant disregard for their real value: some are precious while others are common, but all tease the visitor with an impression of wealth and mystery.

127

032c magazine
Joerg Koch, Mike Meiré
2013

Type
Helvetica, Futura and Times New Roman Condensed

Joerg Koch 197

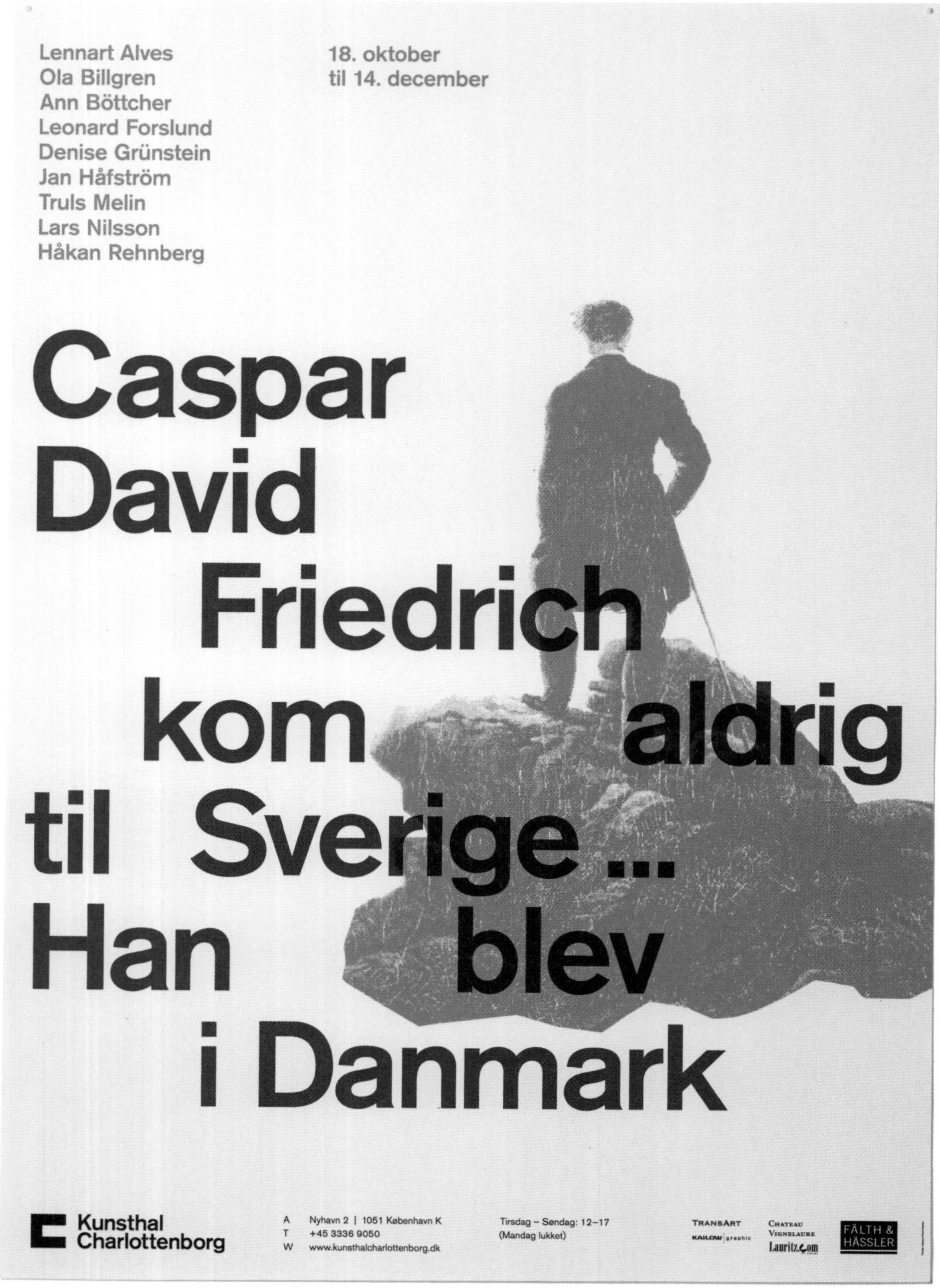

Lennart Alves
Ola Billgren
Ann Böttcher
Leonard Forslund
Denise Grünstein
Jan Håfström
Truls Melin
Lars Nilsson
Håkan Rehnberg

18. oktober
til 14. december

Caspar David Friedrich kom aldrig til Sverige ... Han blev i Danmark

Kunsthal Charlottenborg

A — Nyhavn 2 | 1051 København K
T — +45 3336 9050
W — www.kunsthalcharlottenborg.dk

Tirsdag – Søndag: 12–17
(Mandag lukket)

TransArt
KAILOW | graphic

Chateau
Vignelaure
Lauritz.com

FÄLTH &
HÄSSLER

Kunsthal Charlottenborg poster
Rasmus Koch Studio
2008

Type
Akzidenz-Grotesk

198 Rasmus Koch Studio

Kunsthal Charlottenborg poster
Rasmus Koch Studio
2007

Type
Akzidenz-Grotesk

Banotect Creme
100 ml
Kr 50.25
Pr liter 502,50 kr
220012

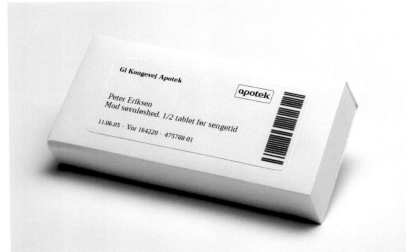

Thick verticals and thin horizontals: this font, developed by Kontrapunkt for Denmark's state pharmacy chain, reflects a typographic heritage in which text was handpainted on apothecary jars, and brushes were bolder on downstrokes than on strokes across the curved surface.

For simplicity and legibility many serifs were omitted. Those that remain are horizontal, balancing the otherwise strongly vertical orientation. 'Smooth curves combined with harsh vertical lines refer to the contradiction between health and disease,' say the designers.

Pharma font
Kontrapunkt
2006

Type
Pharma

bɅuhɅus-ɅRchiv museum für gestaltung
berlin   12.03.–10.06.2014
neue baukunst!
architektur   der   moderne   in
bild und buch

gestaltung L2M3.com

neue bɅukunst

täglich außer dienstag 10–17 uhr
www.bauhaus.de

bɅuhɅus-ɅRchiv museum für gestaltung
klingelhöferstr. 14, d-10785 berlin

Bauhaus-Archiv Berlin posters
L2M3 — Sascha Lobe, Marvin Boiko
2014

Type
Bayer Next

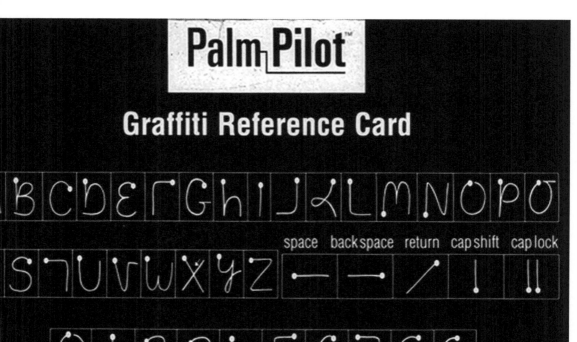

Hektor spray paint output device
Jürg Lehni
2002

Type
Custom made lettering

Hektor is a portable spray paint output device with its own inherently distinctive aesthetic. Its software is based on Scriptographer, a scripting plugin for Adobe Illustrator™ developed by Lehni, in collaboration with engineer Uli Franke as a diploma project at École Cantonale d'Art de Lausanne. By imposing the open-source philosophy on a 'closed' product, Lehni was issuing a call to creatives to break out of the limitations and predefined methods forced on them by the standards and conventions of design software.

'I wanted to create a machine that follows lines in a loose way, that adds certain characteristics to it and therefore has its own expression and style, which would directly be derived from how it was constructed. It should not draw on to something like paper but instead directly on to the floor or the walls and the line it draws should also be a bit imprecise, I thought. Therefore I soon decided to use spray cans and to search for a way of moving the can while pushing and releasing its nozzle automatically, all remotely controlled by a computer.'

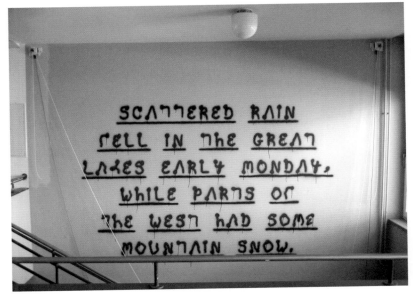

Hektor spray paint output device
Jürg Lehni
2002

Type
Custom made lettering

Principal Sponsor

HSBC Private Bank

Design Miami/ Basel
12/13/14/15/16 June 2007
Basel, Switzerland

The new forum for collecting,
exhibiting, discussing
and creating design

For more information
Call +1 305 572 0866
Email info@designmiami.com
www.designmiami.com

Design Miami identity
Made Thought
2007–08

Type
Akkurat

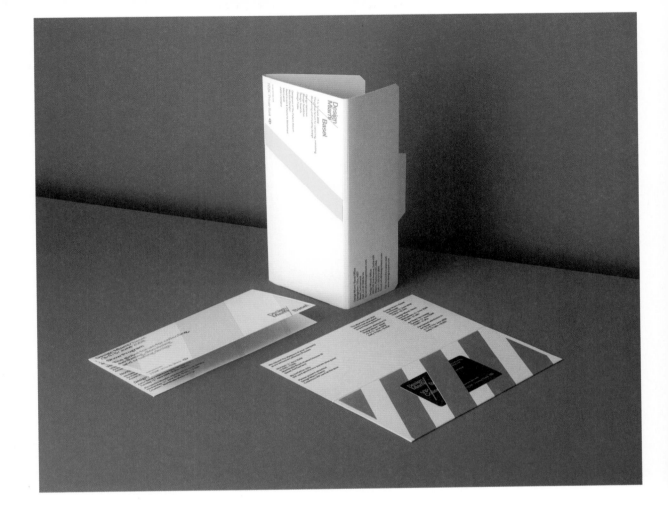

Design Miami identity
Made Thought
2007–08

Type
Akkurat

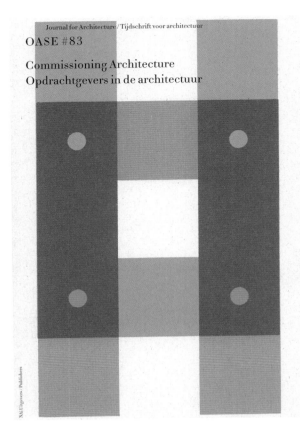

OASE #83

Commissioning Architecture
Opdrachtgevers in de architectuur

NAi Uitgevers · Publishers

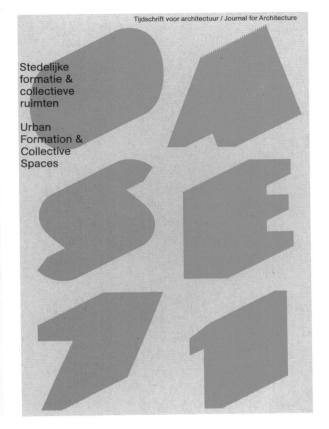

Stedelijke
formatie &
collectieve
ruimten

Urban
Formation &
Collective
Spaces

OASE is a Dutch architectural
journal, half-magazine,
half-book, published three
times a year. Karel Martens
started designing it in 1990,
juggling the constraints and
opportunities of print with
the journal's low budget to
produce a publication that
changes in personality with
every edition, from the cover
to the pages within.

He has compared the necessity
of this to that of preparing
a different meal every time
a certain set of guests come to
dinner. Each edition is a chance
to play with the grid, type and
margins, to reflect the theme
of the contents, which changes
with each issue.

OASE **magazines (issues 74, 83 and 71)**
Karel Martens
2007, 2010, 2006

Type
Various

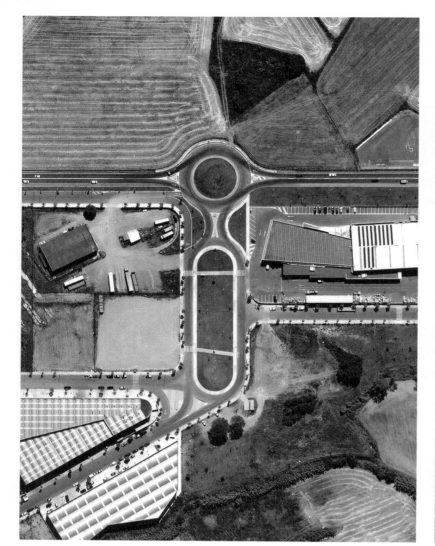

Catalunya satellite alphabet
Pablo Martin, Grafica
2011

Type
Catalunya Alphabet

In 2010, the Catalan National Council for Culture and the Arts (CoNCA) commissioned Grafica to design the identity of its National Cultural Awards. Grafica's proposal was for a catalogue that could incorporate each year's winners, with every year marked by the use of a different typeface. The cover of 2011's instalment featured an alphabet compiled from carefully selected satellite images of Catalonia, with letters composed of road junctions, buildings, waterways and an island.

Catalunya satellite alphabet
Pablo Martin, Grafica
2011

Type
Catalunya Alphabet

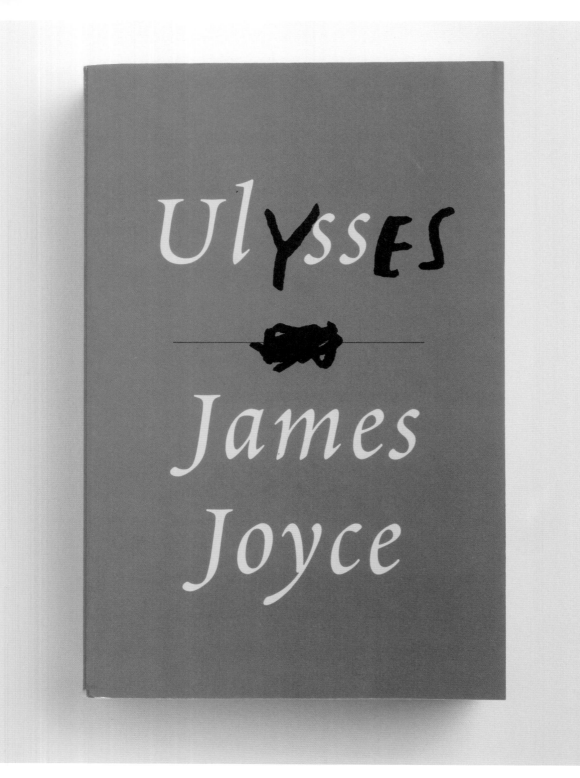

Ulysses by James Joyce
Peter Mendelsund
2013

Type
Poetica Chancery and handwritten

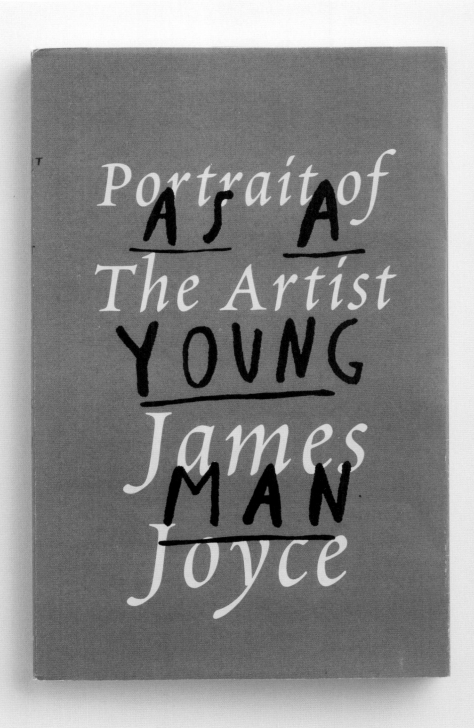

***Portrait of an Artist as a Young Man* by James Joyce**
Peter Mendelsund
2013

Type
Poetica Chancery and handwritten

Happy Crisis
Metahaven
2011

Type
Times New Roman and Helvetica

Radical Transparency
Metahaven
2011

Type
Times New Roman and Helvetica

Time Out
Amsterdam

THE CITY'S BEST
RESTAURANTS
THEATRES
CLUBS
BARS
SHOPS
AND MORE

Best of
Amsterdam
2011

GET MORE
OUT OF
AMSTERDAM
December 2011
timeoutamsterdam.nl

THE 50
WINNERS
REVEALED
24,367 PEOPLE VOTED
299,496 VOTES CAST

Time Out Amsterdam
Niels Shoe Meulman
2011

Type
Calligraffiti

Why waste your tears on someone who makes you cry mural
Niels Shoe Meulman
2011

Type
Calligraffiti

Cooper Union signage and environmental graphics
J. Abbott Miller, Pentagram
2009

Type
Foundry Gridnik

William Kentridge: *Five Themes* exhibition catalogue
J. Abbott Miller, Pentagram
2009

Type
News Gothic, Mercury

MONOCLE

A BRIEFING ON GLOBAL AFFAIRS, BUSINESS, CULTURE & DESIGN

issue 47 . volume 05
OCTOBER 2011

(A) AFFAIRS Algiers: A case study in rocking the casbah

(B) BUSINESS Pitts perfect: the steel town reinvention

(C) CULTURE Frieze frame: five art fair players to know

(D) DESIGN Letters play: the first high-street font store

(E) EDITS Cosy autumn recipes from Helsinki and a 'hood on the rise in Sydney

EXPO Press ahead: inside Brazil's most powerful newspaper

And, finally, here's the good news

Newspapers booming, book sales up, record shops opening: Monocle charts the media trend that's e-free, profitable and going global

01 MUSIC
•••
Just in: your local record store is back in business (and the manager has put a few nice things aside for you)

02 BOOKS
•••
In a surprise move (small) book shops are opening around the globe

03 RADIO
•••
We bring you the stories of the stations making waves

News Flash
•••
Look smarter with our 56-page Style Directory

BREAKING NEWS

THE NEW MEDIA MODEL?

Reports from São Paulo to Stockholm: confirmation that old-school media models are fit and healthy, and how the American media stuffed itself

Monocle
News Network   (M)(N)(N)

04 PRINT
•••
We also have a report on an old-fashioned press baron doing good

05 MAGAZINES
•••
We meet the investigative reporters taking Asia by storm

06 TV
•••
Also stay tuned for our report on why quality news channels are a Nordic success story

And finally, real anchors never wear purple

SEK 95
10 > UK £5   JPY ¥2,310
USD $10   AUD $12.95
EUR 12 (GER) SGD $19.90 (w/gst)
EUR 10 (ITA)   CDN $10.00
DKK 122

9 771753 243006

Monocle magazine (issue 46)
Monocle
2011

Type
Plantin, Helvetica

E

MY LAST MEAL
Jens Risom

The ultimate table
New Canaan

Preface
The Danish designer chooses a
historic restaurant, full of personal
memories, in his adopted US
hometown as the venue for his
hypothetical 'farewell banquet'.

Writer
Aisha Speirs

Photographer
Elizabeth Weinberg

01

"When I moved to New Canaan, Connecticut, in 1950, there weren't many creative people here. But it was becoming a
hub for architecture. A group of five architects, which included Marcel Breuer and
Philip Johnson, came from Harvard. I
knew most of them, and I worked on some
of their projects. They happened to come
here, and they stayed because there was
work to be done. People didn't move here
simply to design new houses; they moved
because they liked it, and it's an easy distance to New York. It didn't change the
culture of the entire town. Some residents
built contemporary houses, but there was
always an important sense of tradition. It
did mean that people were paying more
attention to architects and art exhibits.

This inn has been here forever, and is
well known in the area. They have a wonderful Sunday brunch with eggs benedict.
They also have wonderful lobster, and the
gravlax is very good. I eat a lot of fish; it's
very Scandinavian. My favourite foods are
lobsters, crabs, mussels and other fish. As
a child in Denmark in the twenties and
thirties, I remember eating with my par-
ents. We didn't eat too much meat, but the
meat we ate was mostly Danish meat. That
meant a lot of pork – what Denmark is
famous for. We ate a lot of freshly caught
fish. The fruits and vegetables that we ate
back then were seasonal, but at that time
we did get things like oranges and lemons
from Spain. When I moved to America, I
didn't notice much difference with the

02 03

food there. I ate pretty much the same as I
had in Denmark. It's been easy enough for
me to eat Danish food as I've been married to two Danish girls!

I have a large family – four children,
and 11 grandchildren. When we celebrate
things, like my 95th birthday earlier this
year, we like to have them all around. It's
rather morbid to think about my last meal,
but I'm sure they would be here for it.

My wife Henny moved here to New
Canaan from London in 1978, and we
were married in 1979. In fact, we had our
wedding lunch here at the Roger Sherman
Inn back then, over 30 years ago. We used
to do a lot of entertaining, both here in
New Canaan, and at our summer home
on Block Island, where my children and
their families still holiday.

We had great parties, cooked up by
Henny, but cleared up by us both. I tried

04

Profile

As one of the first Danish
furniture designers to move to
the United States during the
1930s, Jens Risom was a key
figure behind the development
of mid-century modern design
in America.

1916: Born in Copenhagen.
1939: Risom moves to New
York after meeting the
American ambassador to
Denmark the year before.
1941: Risom collaborates with
Hans Knoll to develop a line
of furniture.
1946 – 1972: After returning
from the Second World War,
Risom founds Jens Risom
Design (JRD). Initially
focusing on residential
furniture, JRD starts
producing non-residential
pieces in the late 1950s.
1973: Risom founds Design
Control in New Canaan
and creates products for
companies like Do-More and
the Howe Furniture Company.
2005: Ralph Pucci introduces a
new line of Risom-designed
furniture, including older
designs and new pieces.

05

Venue

An important Connecticut
landmark, the picturesque
white clapboard building of
the Roger Sherman Inn was
constructed in the 18th century
as a private home and is
named after the state's first
US senator. The inn's 17 rooms,
large restaurant and private
dining rooms make it popular
with local residents.

*195 Oenoke Ridge,
New Canaan, CT,
rogershermaninn.com*

Menu

Traditional chilled vichyssoise;
pan-roasted king salmon with
ratatouille, black olives, capers
and oven-dried tomato dressing;
white chocolate and pistachio
crème brûlée

216 — ISSUE 47

Monocle magazine (issue 46)
Monocle
2011

Type
Plantin, Helvetica

Rock & Roll
Julian Morey with technical assistance from François Lefranc
2003

Type
Neue Helvetica

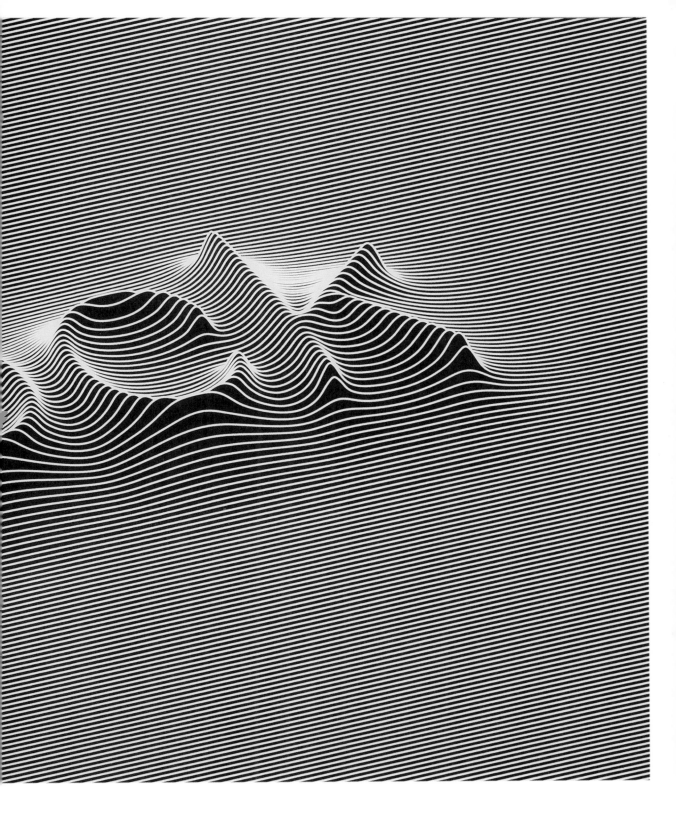

Four Corners Books' *Familiars* series invites artists to respond to classic, out-of-copyright novels and short stories of their choice. John Morgan Studio worked with the artists on the concept and format of each book, which differs according to the needs of the text and the artwork within.

Oscar Wilde's *The Picture of Dorian Gray*, for example, is re-imagined by Morgan and Gareth Jones as a large-format magazine-style publication—echoing its original physical form in *Lippincott's Monthly Magazine*—with a key phrase from the book's opening chapter excerpted on the cover in large, bold type.

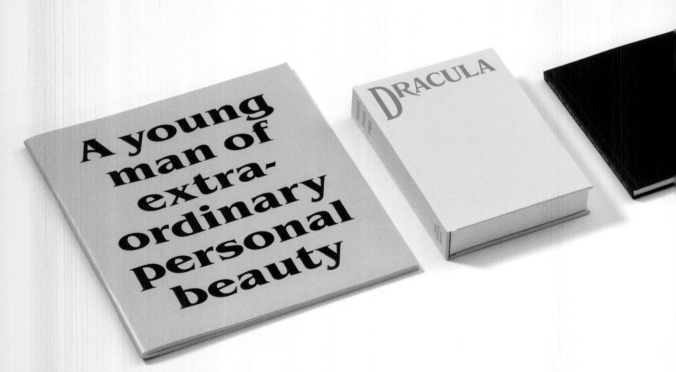

Four Corners _Familiars_
John Morgan Studio
2008–ongoing

Type
Various

Norm is the Zürich-based type/graphic design duo, Manuel Krebs and Dimitri Bruni. In their meticulously designed manual documenting the design of their font LL Replica, the pair use their own conversation as the commentary on the long, drawn-out process.

Much more than a standard specimen book, the manual displays the font's versatility in all seven weights and at eight different type sizes, in headlines, body copy and tables. It also offers a showcase of Norm's consummate talents as typographers and designers.

Their catalogue for a travelling exhibition of the works of conceptual artist Simon Starling presents photographs of Starling's installations, objects and place-specific events with clinical clarity and objectivity, like a manual or technical handbook.

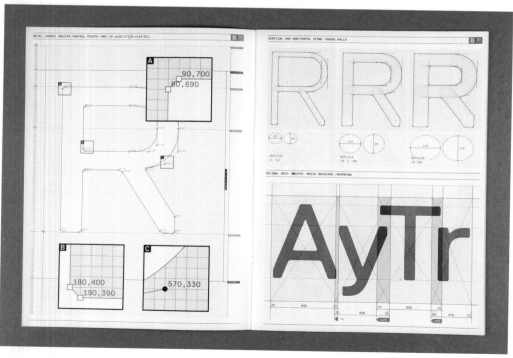

Replica specimen book
Norm
2009

Type
Replica

Works (Selection)
A–Z

Werke (Auswahl)
A–Z

New Projects
2005

Neue Projekte
2005

C 1

Textbeiträge

Texts

Simon Starling

Cuttings

Kunstmuseum Basel, Museum für Gegenwartskunst
The Power Plant, Toronto

New Projects
[A 1–32]

Neue Projekte
[A 1–32]

Works 1994–2004 (Selection)
[B 1–88]

Werke 1994–2004 (Auswahl)
[B 1–88]

Texts
[C 1–88]

Textbeiträge
[C 1–88]

Simon Starling, *Cuttings* **exhibition catalogue**
Norm
2005

Type
LT Univers Regular

Norm 227

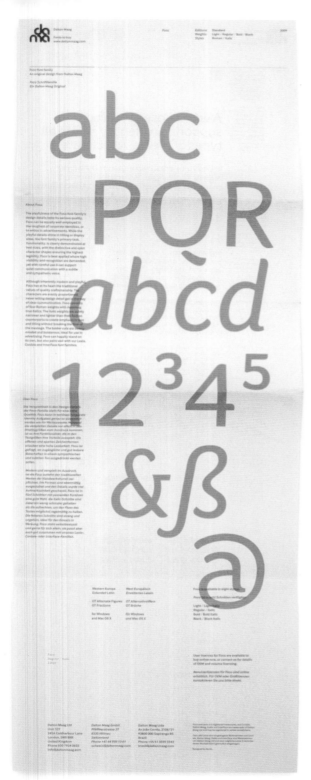

Dalton Maag type specimens
North
2008—ongoing

Type
Various

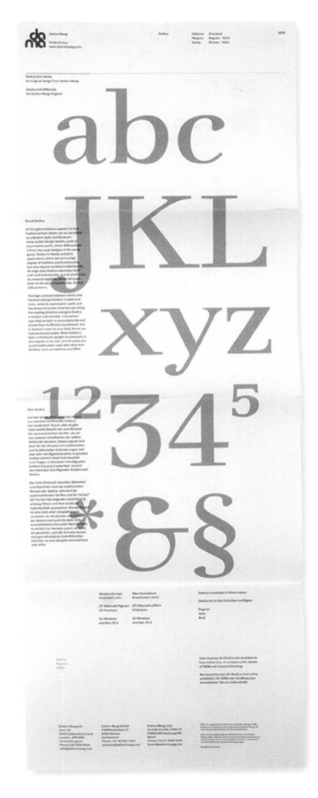

North has enjoyed a close working relationship with London type foundry Dalton Maag, co-designing custom fonts on numerous identity projects. Many of these are marketed to designers through the foundry's fold-out type specimens, also designed by North, which use the luxury of a large-format print piece to show off each font to its fullest.

Dalton Maag type specimens
North
2008—ongoing

Type
Various

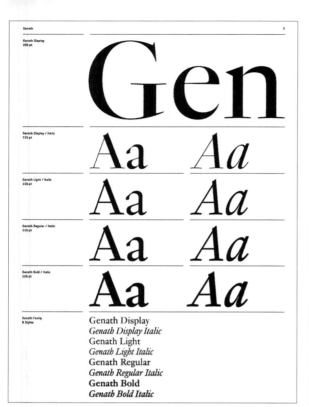
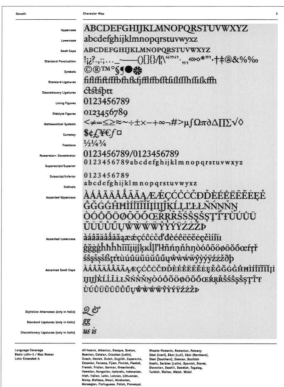
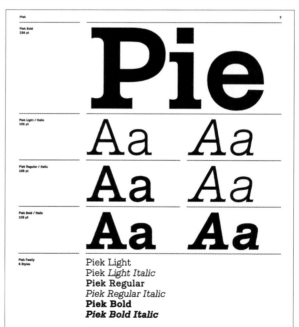

Genath, Didot Elder and Piek type specimens
Optimo, François Rappo (Genath, 2011 and Didot Elder, 2007) and Philipp Herrmann (Piek, 2007)

Hermes Regular
105 pt

Hermes Light / Italic
105 pt

Aa *Aa* Aa *Aa*

Hermes Regular / Italic
105 pt

Aa *Aa* Aa *Aa*

Hermes Bold / Italic
105 pt

Aa *Aa* **Aa** *Aa*

Hermes Family
6 Styles

Hermes Light
Hermes Light Italic
Hermes Regular
Hermes Regular Italic
Hermes Bold
Hermes Bold Italic

Hermes type specimen
Optimo, Gavillet & Rust
2003

Type
Hermes

Optimo 231

A TYPEFACE DESIGNED BY PETER MOHR. SPECIMEN #6 FAYON. ©2011 OURTYPE

Fayon

OurType SALES

www.ourtype.com
Baron de Gieylaan 41 B-9840 De Pinte Belgium
telephone +32 (0) 9 220 26 20 fax +32 (0) 9 220 34 45

we make fine type

Fayon specimen sheet
OurType, Peter Mohr
2011

Type
Fayon

Invitation cards for exhibition of stencil type
OurType
2012

Type
Ludwig, Couteau, Bery Tuscan, Puncho, Standing Type

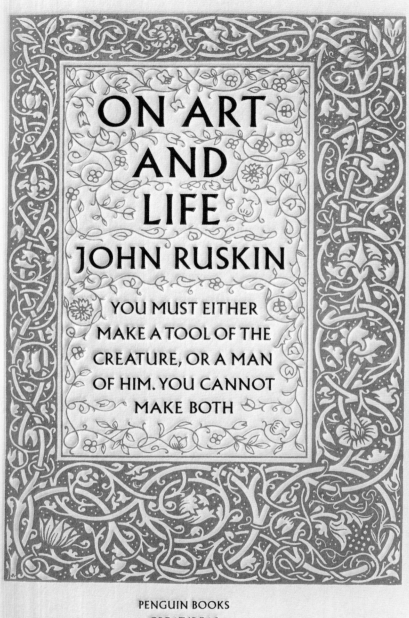

ON ART
AND
LIFE
JOHN RUSKIN

YOU MUST EITHER
MAKE A TOOL OF THE
CREATURE, OR A MAN
OF HIM. YOU CANNOT
MAKE BOTH

PENGUIN BOOKS
GREAT IDEAS

On Art and Life **by John Ruskin**
David Pearson (based on an original by William Morris)
2004

Type
Albertus

NO ONE CAN BE SAID TO HAVE A HAPPY LIFE WHEN ITS VIOLENT TERMINATION BRINGS HIS SLAYERS NOT MERELY IMPUNITY BUT THE HEIGHT OF GLORY

C

AN ATTACK

I

ON AN ENEMY

C

OF FREEDOM

E

PENGUIN BOOKS

R

GREAT IDEAS

O

VIOLENT TERMINATION BRINGS HIS SLAYERS NOT MERELY IMPUNITY BUT THE HEIGHT OF GLORY

NO ONE CAN BE SAID TO HAVE A HAPPY LIFE WHEN ITS

VIOLENT TERMINATION BRINGS HIS SLAYERS NOT MERELY IMPUNITY BUT THE HEIGHT OF GLORY

An Attack on an Enemy of Freedom by Cicero
David Pearson (art direction) and Phil Baines (design)
2005

Type
Johnston

Arnold Bloch Leibler
Lawyers and Advisers

ABL *Solutions* cover
David Pidgeon
2009

Type
Custom made lettering

Playtype Type Foundry and Concept Store
Playtype/e-Types
2011

Type
Custom made lettering

Playtype is an experiment in bringing type design to non-designers and typographers—one that goes beyond publishing, film (such as *Helvetica)* and the retailing of type-led products in more generalist shops. Playtype is a store focused completely on type, in the centre of Copenhagen, created by Danish design studio e-Types as a physical manifestation of their type foundry, playtype.com —a street-level introduction to typography.

Oversized letters are printed on the glazed storefront; inside, fonts feature on mugs, T-shirts, wine labels and in pictures frames. The designers call it 'the physical experience of typography—a new dialogue with a wider audience about the significance of typography as an element of lifestyle.'

Playtype Type Foundry and Concept Store
Playtype/e-Types
2011

Type
Various

Mark Porter's 2005 redesign of *The Guardian* newspaper and all its associated sections is a landmark of editorial design. The new blueprint introduced a new modular grid that allowed more fluidity in the length of stories, greater flexibility in the display of photography and infographics, and more varied, engaging pages as a result.

Porter commissioned Paul Barnes and Christian Schwartz (Commercial Type) to develop a comprehensive family of fonts that would establish a distinctive identity for the newspaper, much as David Hillman's radical redesign had done in 1988.

Schwartz recalls what was an unorthodox process: 'Paul decided to see what would happen if he drew an Egyptian (slab serif), then trimmed the serifs off to get the sans—the same evolutionary path that the very first sans serifs had taken —because he had an idea that this would be the best way to get something both interesting and compatible with the serif face. The Egyptian was planned as a "missing link"— an evolutionary step that would help us get from serif to sans, but would not be used in the paper—but it quickly emerged as a clear favourite for both headlines and text.'

The Guardian redesign—International section
Mark Porter
2005

Type
Guardian Egyptian

David Bailey's Naked people

Exclusive preview
of his latest project
in the new
Weekend magazine

Christian O'Connell
Crying over sport
Sport, page 16

The way we live now
New today
8-page
Family section

Free Inside
56-page
fashion handbook

Inside Weekend

£1.20
Saturday 17.09.05
Published
in London and
Manchester
guardian.co.uk

theguardian

Radical plan to stop Muslim extremism

Under this picture, a master. But who?

Column five
Life through
a rolled-up
fiver

Emma Brockes

Vikram Dodd

A royal commission to investigate how and why the London bombings happened and a media unit to rebut negative stories about Muslims and counter propaganda from Islamist extremists should be set up, according to proposals to be sent to Tony Blair by government-appointed taskforces on tackling Islamist extremism.

The Guardian has obtained details of the plans drawn up by the taskforces, set up after the July bombings. They were asked to come up with ideas to help prevent British Muslims turning to terrorism, and which would also counter a sense of alienation some Muslims feel from British society and institutions. Their proposals will go to the prime minister and home secretary next week.

Coverage of Islam in the media has long irritated many British Muslims. The proposed media unit would counter press articles considered to be inaccurate or malicious attacks on Islam, and rebut statements by extremist groups. The taskforces consist of seven groups of Muslim MPs, peers, academics and community leaders.

One of their proposals is the setting up of a royal commission. Senior Home Office officials discussed the proposal with Muslim groups on Wednesday and are expected to give a formal answer in a week.

If agreed, the royal commission would be held in two parts: an initial examination of the bombings, followed by an exploration of wider issues, such as the role of foreign policy in radicalising the terrorists, and whether victims of the bombings received speedy and adequate financial compensation and support. The government has so far resisted the idea.

The groups all feel that British foreign policy, especially Mr Blair's support for the Iraq war, has fuelled resentment. One proposal is that Islamic schools, or madrasas should teach "citizenship" in an attempt to tackle the conflict some youngsters feel between being British and Muslim.

Under the plans, suspected extremists would be tracked by a monitoring centre. A website would be created to allow young Muslims to discover mainstream Islamic views on issues. Public forums for debating issues such as foreign policy and politics would also be set up.

11 »

Restoration of this canvas has uncovered a painting valued at £5m. See page 9

Is that a zit or a freckle?" It was hard, from the photo, to tell. There were faint streaks around the left eye that could have been crows' feet or bleed from her mascara. Either way, the most compelling thing about pictures of Kate Moss apparently snorting cocaine through a rolled-up fiver, published in the Mirror last week, was that however hard you looked you still couldn't find evidence to confirm that she was actually human.

The 31-year-old model was secretly filmed taking drugs with her boyfriend, Pete Doherty, in a recording studio in west London, which as exclusives go might only have been equalled if Liberace had ever, officially come out. There should be a word for it: when a common assumption, long withheld from the public for lack of evidence, is finally stood up and which despite its obviousness a newspaper feels obliged to release like a scream.

There is still a lot more to come out. Everyone is wondering who took the 40-minute video, not least inside the Babyshambles camp, where a lot of finger-pointing is now rumoured to be going on. The model herself is variously reported to be "terrified" about the safety of her modelling contracts and "laughing her head off" at the triviality of it all. Neither of these positions does much to substantiate the possibility that she exists in the third dimension.

The Mirror, meanwhile, has finally got all that pent-up frustration out of its system. "Cocaine Kate, supermodel snorts line after line" it yelled last Thursday, with the promise of "more amazing pic-

Continued on page 2 »

BBC money may go to C4

The government is considering breaking the BBC's historic monopoly over the licence fee by handing some of the money to Channel 4 to help pay for the switch to digital television.

Details of the plan emerged in a draft speech by the culture secretary, Tessa Jowell, seen by the Guardian. A key passage, which was cut from the final version delivered to TV executives in Cambridge on Thursday night, suggested that some of the BBC's revenue could be transferred to its rival. Ms Jowell also planned to float the idea of giving some of the digital television spectrum to Channel 4 for nothing, in order to help it launch new channels

and compete in a multichannel world. Although the payment would be a one-off, it would mark the first time in the corporation's 82-year history that it would have to share its income.

Ms Jowell is believed to have removed the passage from her eventual speech for fear of tying herself down to specific solutions at this stage.

She planned to suggest "one-off support from the BBC to help Channel 4 bear the capital cost of the conversion to digital, and the allocation of more capacity to help their offer on the DTT [digital terrestrial television] platform." **Owen Gibson**

4 »

National	**International**	**Financial**	**News**	**Sport**
Eight jailed for airport theft bid	**China to be biggest exporter by 2010**	**British Gas tells staff to sell or face sack**		**Prince William next FA president**

The Guardian **redesign—cover**
Mark Porter
2005

Type
Guardian Egyptian

Mark Porter 241

Orange in yellow peril
Van Basten cuts his
cloth for Argentina

World Cup, page 10 »

The rogue returns
Jimmy Connors goes
back to grass roots

Tennis, page 15 »

Simon Hattenstone
I have turned into a
World Cup addict

Page 20 »

sport

Ragged England stumble after Owen collapses

Group B
Kevin McCarra Cologne

Sweden 2 (0)
Allback 51, Larsson 90

England 2 (1)
J Cole 34, Gerrard 85

England have won Group B and go on to a last-16 tie with Ecuador in Stuttgart on Sunday, but they has got there through a forced march rather than a regal progress. Michael Owen has fallen by the wayside, damaging his right knee in the opening seconds. His World Cup is probably over and, before today's scan in Baden-Baden, Sven-Goran Eriksson admitted that "it looks bad".

His team was also an eyesore by the end, despite a confident first half in which the outstanding Joe Cole scored an intoxicating goal. That was a heady time, but the players again wound down after the interval and Sweden not only equalised but could have built an unassailable lead. With four minutes remaining, the substitute Steven Gerrard did put Eriksson's side in front once more with an irresistible header after Joe Cole crossed from the right.

The injustice of it was to be righted. The back four could not deal with Erik Edman's long throw in the 90th minute and Henrik Larsson dabbed in the goal that preserved Sweden's 38-year unbeaten record against England. Eriksson's players will not care too much about that when there has to be an inquest into the weaknesses they revealed to their rivals.

Corners and throw-ins were tantamount to weapons of mass destruction for the England defence. The goalkeeper Paul Robinson did not dominate and matters became even more alarming when Rio Ferdinand, who had a minor groin strain, went off and Sol Campbell, after a tormented season at Arsenal, took over.

Eriksson has more reasons to shudder.

> Swedish set pieces were tantamount to weapons of mass destruction for the England defence

The loss of Owen is aggravated by the fact that the manager was wilful in his choice of a small and idiosyncratic coterie of strikers. Only Wayne Rooney, Peter Crouch and Theo Walcott remain healthy. Eriksson, initially happy with his wager, is now just another punter leaving the bookies with fists bunched in his empty pockets.

No matter the longer term consequences, however, his fortunes were restored handsomely after 34th minutes in Cologne. Niclas Alexandersson cleared but Joe Cole controlled the ball on his chest and, from some 30 yards out on the left, sent a spinning volley off the outside of his right foot that went high into the far corner of the net.

It was a stirring, if truncated, reaffirmation of England's potential. The energetic and unflagging Owen Hargreaves showed how much he has to offer in the holding role and his relevance was undoubted, particularly as Frank Lampard was liberated by the tactical switch.

There had been five attempts by the Chelsea player before the interval. Any shortfall in devilment and individualism will be made good, too, as Rooney's match fitness is gradually replenished. All of his gusto was restored in the episode when he lobbed the ball over Olof Mellberg in the 25th minute and ran on before the other Sweden centre-half Teddy Lucic got himself in the way of the finish. The England striker was being partnered by Owen's replacement Peter Crouch.

Assuming that Owen is sidelined, Eriksson will need to decide whether he wants to keep faith in that combination. One obvious alternative exists. Gerrard, with the risk of suspension now removed, could come into the starting line-up as a quasi-forward.

England did well enough as they were up to half-time. It had been comfortably their best display of this World Cup, yet Sweden, as ever, was tenacious. The identity of the scorer of the equaliser summed up the durability his country has and its knack of collectively transcending individual reputations. Marcus Allback may have been derided at Aston Villa and he started here purely because of Zlatan Ibrahimovic's thigh injury, but that did not stop him from contributing an equaliser.

The forward met a corner from the former Everton midfielder Tobias Linderoth with an angled header after 51 minutes

Continued on page 2 »

Michael Owen lies on the touchline in agony after badly twisting his right knee in the first minute of last night's game against Sweden Alex Morton/Action Images

Knee injury will end World Cup and could ruin his season

Daniel Taylor Cologne

A tumultuous evening for Sven-Goran Eriksson ended with the England manager admitting he feared the worst about Michael Owen's knee injury. England's medical staff suspect serious ligament damage and a sombre Eriksson does not expect the striker to play any further part in the tournament.

"The doctors have their suspicions but the scans will tell us for certain," he said. "It is better to wait until we are certain before we make an announcement, but it doesn't look very good. I spoke to Michael at half-time and he was very unhappy, as you would expect. I feel very sorry for him as he has just come back from another injury and he was looking better and better."

Owen will travel to hospital this morning and there could be further implications for Newcastle United if, as expected, Eriksson's worst fears are confirmed. The 26-year-old has managed only 29 minutes of competitive club football since the turn of the year and, in the worst-case scenario, a ruptured cruciate ligament would rule him out for about nine months.

> **Sven-Goran Eriksson** said of Owen's injury last night: 'The doctors have their suspicions. It doesn't look good'

"What kind of knee injury it is we can only guess at the moment," Eriksson emphasised. "I wish I could tell you more but we have to wait until after his scan. All I can say is that I am sorry for Michael Owen." The striker limped off the pitch after only 53 seconds last night and then was taken away on a stretcher.

"It's a big blow for us and our thoughts are with Michael and his family," said Joe Cole, the man of the match. "It is a huge blow for him and we're all thinking of him. He's had a very difficult 12 months with injury and now he clearly has a real battle on his hands to get over this. But I'm sure that he will be back soon enough and scoring goals for England. Everyone feels terrible for him."

Gary Neville, the Manchester United right-back, was already scheduled to have a scan today on his calf strain and, with injuries threatening to undermine England's campaign, Rio Ferdinand will also need a check-up after leaving the game with a thigh problem.

"It was a precaution," reported a visibly downcast Eriksson. "He felt it went a bit stiff and it wouldn't loosen so he thought he should probably come off."

The Guardian redesign—Sport section
Mark Porter
2005

Type
Guardian Egyptian

242 Mark Porter

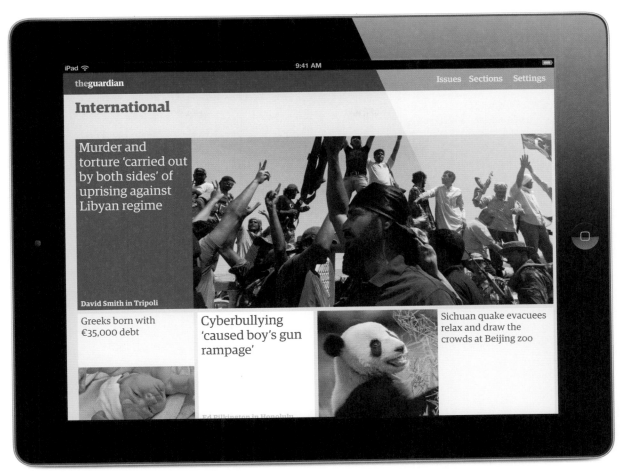

When *The Guardian* newspaper produced its first internet edition in 1997, it offered an experience that was designed specifically for online interaction; it made no attempt to replicate the printed publication.

Its iPad edition is the same: a creature that belongs to its medium and that medium's unique style of fingertip interaction. Stories are presented in a highly modular grid, occupying one, two, four or more units of area, allowing the creation of a clear news hierarchy.

The iPad edition extends the use of *The Guardian* collection of fonts, which now includes a range of headline fonts, a text font and an agate font, all in a number of weights.

The Guardian—iPad edition
Mark Porter
2011

Type
Guardian Egyptian

Opened in April 2011, SALT is a not-for-profit cultural institution in Istanbul that hosts exhibitions, conferences and public programmes, and carries out cultural research projects.

The institution's name has a unique position within the identity system. The letters S-A-L-T are not represented as a formal, stand-alone logotype; instead, they are embedded within a custom-designed typeface, Kraliçe, created by type designer Timo Gaessner for Project Projects.

There is another twist to the identity. Every four months, a new designer is invited to re-imagine the letters S-A-L-T and, in doing so, the Kraliçe font. The SALT identity itself thereby becomes subject to regular artistic intervention— a kind of distributed exhibition space.

SALT identity
Project Projects
2011

Type
Custom made lettering

Project Projects 245

Self-confidence Produces Fine Results
Sagmeister Inc.
2008

Type
Constructed from real life bananas

Self-confidence Produces Fine Results
Sagmeister Inc.
2008

Type
Constructed from real life bananas

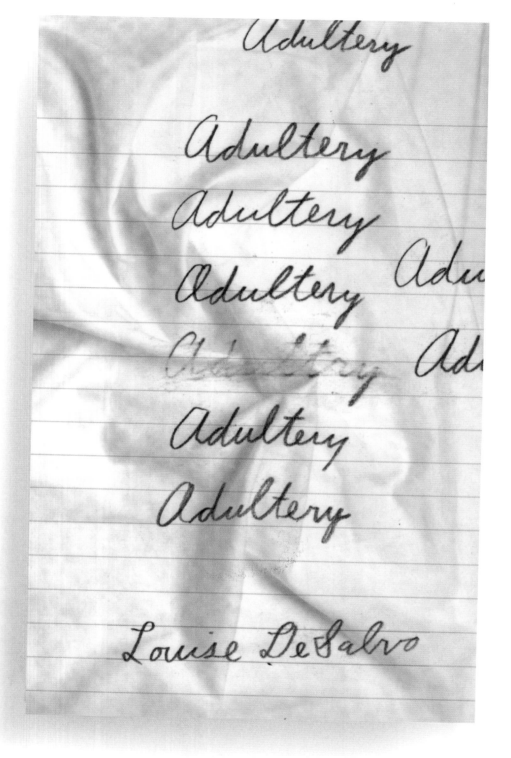

Adultery by Louise DeSalvo
Office of Paul Sahre
2000

Type
Custom made lettering

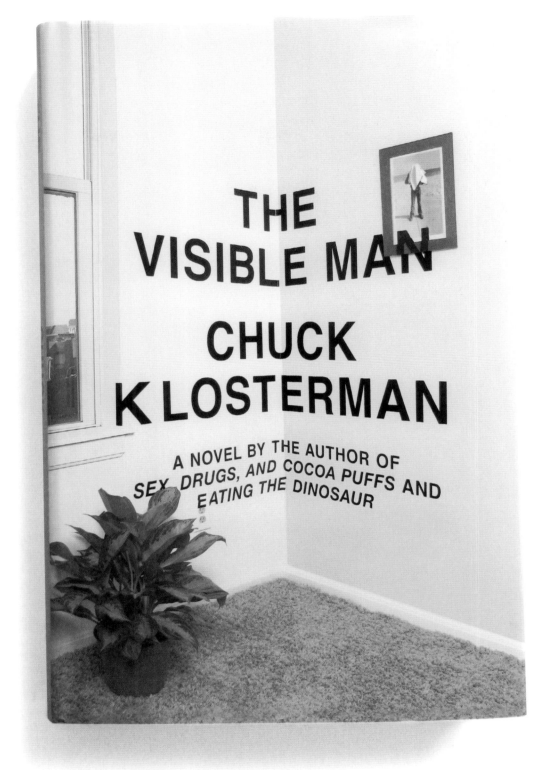

THE
VISIBLE MAN
CHUCK
K LOSTERMAN

A NOVEL BY THE AUTHOR OF
SEX, DRUGS, AND COCOA PUFFS AND
EATING THE DINOSAUR

The Visible Man by Chuck Klosterman
Office of Paul Sahre
2011

Type
Helvetica

For more than 30 years, starting with his classicist and neo-Futurist sleeves for Factory Records, Peter Saville's album art has appropriated the typography of the past as freely and as inventively as it has co-opted different forms of imagery and graphic convention.

His 2001 sleeve for Pulp's *We Love Life* reflects the title in the depiction of the band's own name: a well-nourished Victorian woodblock type embellished with leaves and flowers.

We Love Life **by Pulp**
Peter Saville with Jarvis Cocker
2001

Type
Louis John Pouchee c. 1820

A few years later, Saville was viewing the latest request for a New Order album cover as something like a siren's call. 'Selling stuff to people isn't something I want to be a part of,' he told *Creative Review* in 2005. 'Often, with packaging design, I'd like to just write across it, "Don't bother, you don't need it".' The 'No' was inspired by seeing the word in fluorescent letters on a truck door at Berlin Airport. An abbreviation of 'number' and New Order, it was no less a statement of Saville's own disillusionment.

Waiting for the Siren's Call **by New Order**
Peter Saville
2005

Type
Neue Helvetica

Paula Scher's murals at a new middle and high school campus in Forest Hills, Queens, bring together two areas of special interest for the designer: her very public superscale typographics, or 'supergraphics', which have featured in many of Scher's projects for corporate clients; and the typographic map paintings that were once a private passion, but which are now gaining her as much notoriety as her design work. In these two wall-to-wall, 225-sq-m (2,430-sq-ft) murals, students at the campus 'enter' the paintings, then look up and enter districts and neighbourhoods, and finally find a place or street name that is 'theirs'. Scher painted maquettes which were then enlarged by projecting sections on to panels and repainting them at a larger scale.

Map murals at Queens Metropolitan Campus
Paula Scher, Pentagram
2010

Type
Custom made lettering

Map murals at Queens Metropolitan Campus
Paula Scher, Pentagram
2010

Type
Custom made lettering

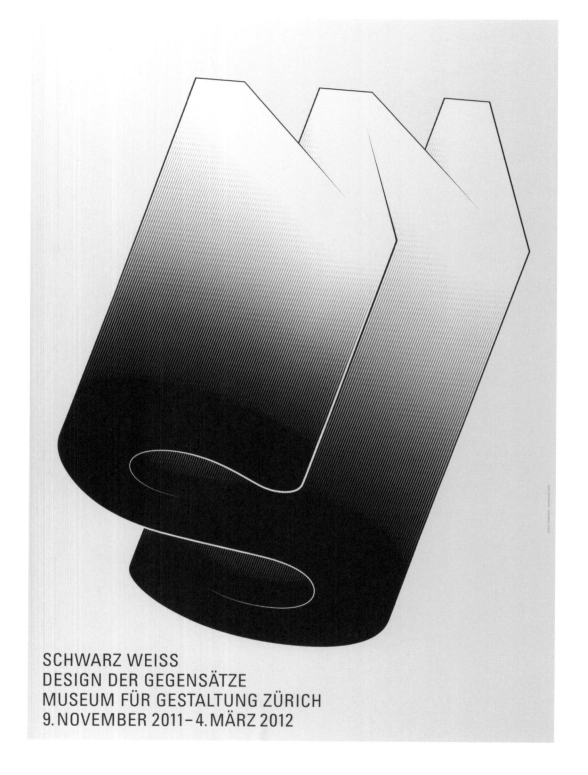

SCHWARZ WEISS
DESIGN DER GEGENSÄTZE
MUSEUM FÜR GESTALTUNG ZÜRICH
9. NOVEMBER 2011–4. MÄRZ 2012

Black White
Ralph Schraivogel
2011

Type
Custom made lettering

FILMPODIUM
JULI-AUG.02

Film Podium
Ralph Schraivogel
2002

Type
Custom made lettering

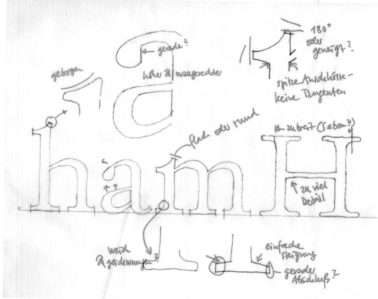

DB font
Erik Spiekermann, Christian Schwartz
2006

Type
DB Sans, DB Serif

A central element of Edenspiekermann's new corporate design system for Deutsche Bahn (the German national railway company), the DB font originated from experiments on a cut of Garamond by Christian Schwartz. These involved adding more pronounced corners to many of the font's soft forms, such as the ends of serifs and serif brackets.

A closely related sans was developed, only loosely based on the serif, and with more regular proportions. The family had to cover every application, from printed timetables to large-scale signs to DB's internal newsletter.

DB Serif
Bahnsteig

DB News
Bahnsteig

DB Serif
Bahnsteig

DB Serif Italic
Bahnsteig

DB Head Light
Bahnsteig

DB Head Black
Bahnsteig

DB Sans Compressed
Bahnsteig

DB font
Erik Spiekermann, Christian Schwartz
2006

Type
DB Sans, DB Serif

Fundacion Proa identity
Spin
2008–09

Type
Fundacion Proa font

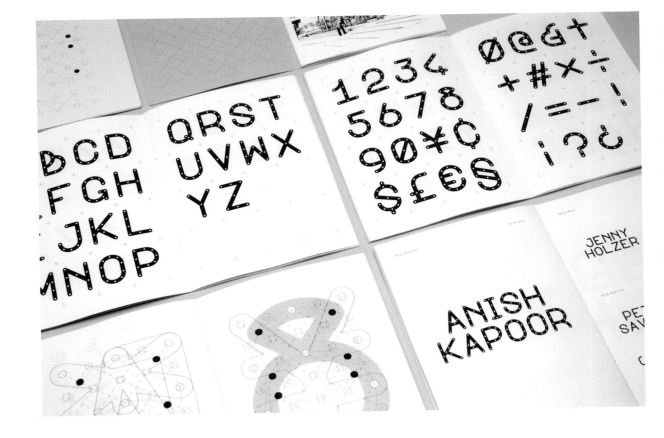

Fundacion Proa in La Boca, Buenos Aires, has a broad remit, exhibiting art from the ancient to the contemporary and cutting-edge. Spin's widely acclaimed identity for the Whitechapel Gallery helped secure the commission for a new image for Proa, which was developed to coincide with the gallery's expansion and refurbishment.

Spin took the inspiration for its Meccano-like Proa font from the criss-crossing steel truss structure of a Buenos Aires landmark overlooked by Proa: the Nicolás Avellaneda transporter bridge over the Riachuelo River.

According to Spin founder, Tony Brook, 'The bridge is such a powerful and evocative physical symbol of the area, and Proa has maintained a close relationship with the bridge over the years, reinforcing its cultural significance. It seemed a profound, unique and in many ways, natural choice.'

Fundacion Proa identity
Spin
2008–09

Type
Fundacion Proa font

Mercè Rodoreda: The Death of Innocence exhibition poster
Astrid Stavro
2008

Type
Caslon Graphique

Correspondencia
Carl Einstein
Daniel-Henry Kahnweiler
1921-1939

Edición a cargo de Liliane Meffre

EDICIONES DE LA CENTRAL   Museo Nacional Centro de Arte Reina Sofía

14 × 22 **collection**
Astrid Stavro
2008–09

Type
Courier, Monotype Grotesk, Clearface

Astrid Stavro 263

Moderna Museet, Sweden's state museum of contemporary art, greeted its refurbishment with a comprehensive identity programme that had at its centre a signature logotype, handwritten by Pop artist Robert Rauschenberg. Like a signature in the corner of a painting, or the signature-style branding on early packaging for Kellogg's Corn Flakes and Campbell's soup cans, the handwritten name indicates the authenticity of Moderna Museet as an international art institution.

Moderna Museet identity
Stockholm Design Lab
2004

Type
Gridnik MM

elegy for a rose

Candida Thompson,
leiding & viool

vrijdag 7 oktober 20.15 uur
Muziekgebouw aan 't IJ

James Gilchrist, tenor
Jasper de Waal, hoorn

reserveren 020 788 20 00
www.sinfonietta.nl

artistiek leider Candida Thompson

Amsterdam Sinfonietta

Liszt
Schnittke
Schulhoff
Strauss
Ysaÿe

viool

julian rachlin

do 5 & za 7 februari 20.30 uur
Muziekgebouw aan 't IJ

reserveren 020 788 20 00
www.sinfonietta.nl

randstad
hoofdsponsor

Ravel
Tsjaikovski
Beethoven

Natalia Gutman

Celloconcert
Saint-Saëns

Candida Thompson,
leiding & viool

vr 24 februari 20.15 uur
Muziekgebouw aan 't IJ

reserveren 020 788 20 00
www.sinfonietta.nl

de clown, de viking en de classicus

Candida Thompson,
leiding & viool

vr 7 & za 8 december 20.15 uur
Muziekgebouw aan 't IJ

Dejan Lazić, piano
Wim van Hasselt, trompet

reserveren 020 788 20 00
www.sinfonietta.nl

Amsterdam Sinfonietta promotional posters
Studio Dumbar
2009–13

Type
Helvetica bold

Michael Clark monograph
Studio Frith
2011

Type
Eureka, Eureka Sans, custom made display typeface

Michael Clark monograph
Studio Frith
2011

Type
Eureka, Eureka Sans, custom made display typeface

LOVE

FASHION AND FAME

ISSUE ONE

Icons of our Generation

Beth Ditto

Lily Allen
Iggy POP
Eva Mendes
Courtney Love Amy Winehouse
Sofia Coppola
Kate Moss
Anjelica Huston
Kelly Brook
Pixie Geldof

By Mert & Marcus

SPRING/SUMMER 2009 £5.00

LOVE magazine (issue 1)
Suburbia
2009

270 Suburbia

Type
Custom made lettering

LOVE

LARA
SUPER
NATURAL

432 PAGES OF
DISCIPLINE,
OBSESSION
& DESIRE

PHOTOGRAPHED BY
MERT ALAS AND
MARCUS PIGGOTT

LOVE magazine (issue 6)
Suburbia
2011

Type
Perpetua Titling MT

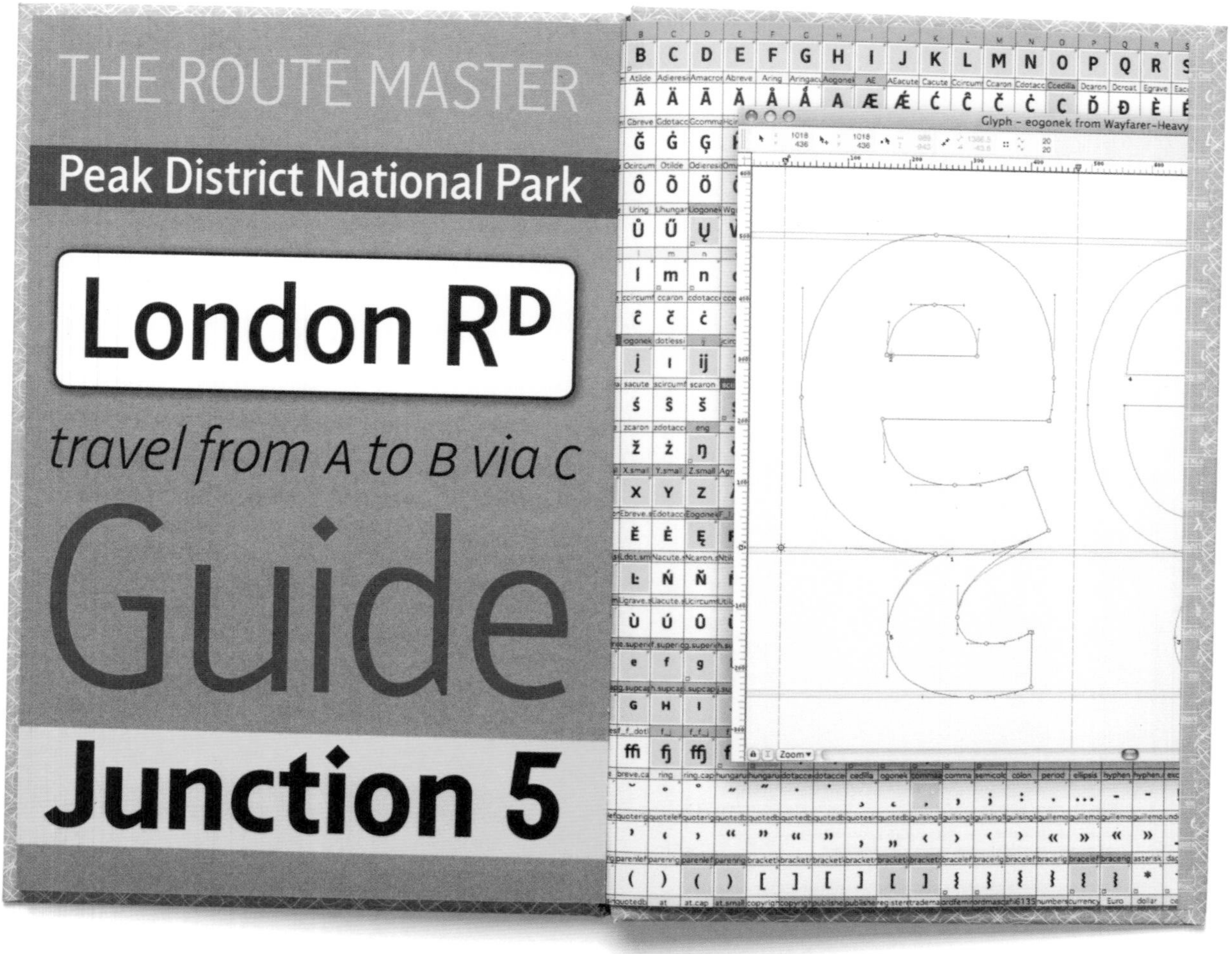

THE ROUTE MASTER

Peak District National Park

London R^D

travel from A to B via C

Guide

Junction 5

Wayfarer sketchbook
Jeremy Tankard
2006

Type
Wayfarer

random
oui
PALIGA!
go
NORTHWEST
takk

não
LINJEBUSSEN
BANNAÐ
Köln
ENLIGHTENMENT
Ei!

Inspiration for the basic forms of Jeremy Tankard's six Shire Types came from the Grotesque (sans serif) and Egyptian (slab serif) lettering styles of nineteenth-century England: lettering cast in iron, painted on locomotives and shop fascias. 'These things display the wealth of invention and diversity of lettering artists throughout Britain,' says Tankard. 'The vigour and robustness of these forms belie their beauty. Once common-place, many examples have now gone, these letterforms having fallen out of favour. The intent here was not to pastiche but to revitalize. Reinvigorated letterforms are combined with a series of visual interpretations of the Shires based upon position, industry, dialect, history and countryside.'

The Shire Types sketchbook
Jeremy Tankard
2012

Type
The Shire Types

Museum Boijmans Van Beuningen identity
Thonik
2006

Type
Custom made lettering

Thonik's house style for Rotterdam's premier museum of contemporary art and design builds on that previously established by Mevis & Van Deursen. M&VD had introduced versions of an inline font for use in headlines, signs and posters. Thonik took the inline aesthetic several stages further, heavily basing MBVB's new headline house style on the one developed by Lance Wyman for the 1968 Summer Olympics in Mexico, which itself was influenced by art traditional (ancient Mexican stone carvings) and modern (Op art of the 1960s). Small differences include the redesign of the 'E' to resemble a reversed '3'. What was previously a relatively restrained system now dominates the museum's communications and environments, from optically challenging poster titles to murals and exhibition walls humming with line and colour.

Museum Boijmans Van Beuningen identity
Thonik
2006

Type
Custom made lettering

Supermarket Series poster
Triboro (Stefanie Weigler, David Heasty)
2010

Type
Hand-painted custom typography

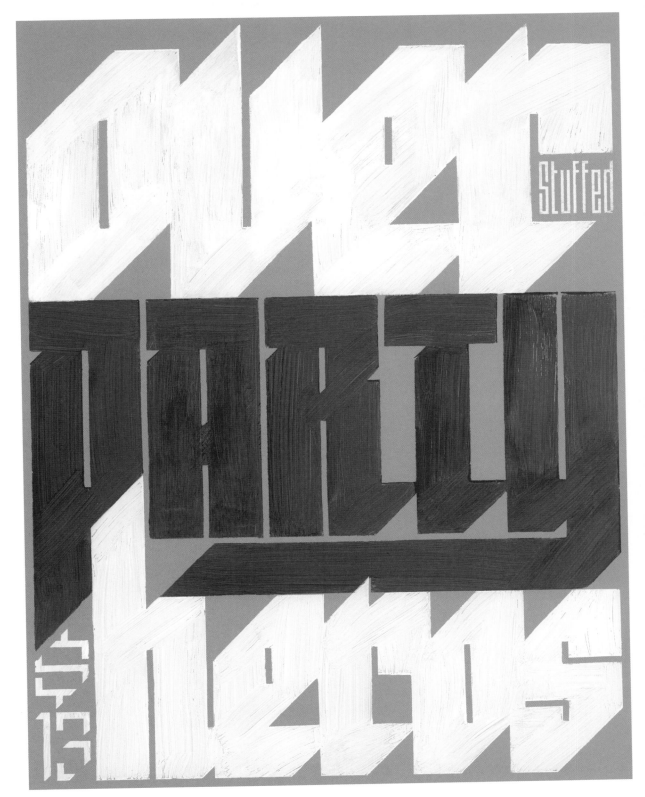

Supermarket Series poster
Triboro (Stefanie Weigler, David Heasty)
2014

Type
Hand-painted custom typography

Troika's three-dimensional, kinetic, typographic sign for the Victoria & Albert Museum references the simple beauty of Alan Fletcher and Quentin Newark's celebrated V&A identity.

With each half-turn of portions of the letterforms (and the ampersand), the monogram deconstructs and reconstructs itself, forming a palindrome readable from either side of the ceiling-mounted capsule.

Suspended from a lit casing, the bright blue letters are each 50cm (20in) high. The revolving motion is generated using only the three small mitre gears seen on the top of the ampersand. As the gears turn they produce a gentle ticking sound, reminiscent of a Victorian clockwork automaton.

Palindrome
Troika
2010

Type
V&A monogram, originally designed by Alan Fletcher

Palindrome
Troika
2010

Type
V&A monogram, originally designed by Alan Fletcher

Craig Taborn Piano Solo festival poster
Niklaus Troxler
2012

Type
Futura Bold

Mut zur Wut. Plakataktion Heidelberg 2010. Niklaus Troxler

***Mut zur Wut: Schluss mit der Schwarzmalerei* ('Enough of that Doom and Gloom') poster**
Niklaus Troxler
2010

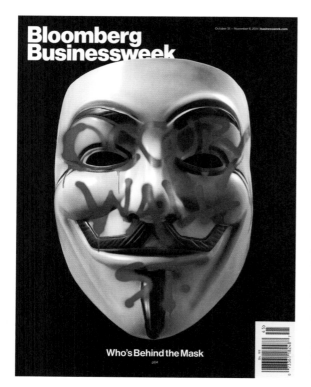

Bloomberg Businessweek
Richard Turley
2010–ongoing

Type
Various

Bloomberg
Businessweek

CAN THIS MAN SAVE

BANK OF AMERICA?

Exclusive:
Brian Moynihan holds the fate of the U.S.'s
largest bank—and the entire financial system—
in his unproven hands p60

$4.99

3 8>

Bloomberg Businessweek
Richard Turley
2010–ongoing

Type
Various

Richard Turley 283

University of Applied Sciences Osnabrück signage system
Andreas Uebele
2004

Type
FF DIN

University of Applied Sciences Osnabrück signage system
Andreas Uebele
2004

Type
FF DIN

The Economist Sculpture Space invitations
Value and Service
2004–06

Type
Neuzeit, Belwe

Commissioned by

The Economist Group

Presented by

Contemporary
Art
Society

Artist

Paul
Hosking

Exhibition Dates

08 March — 01 April 2005

Venue

**The Economist Plaza
25 St James's St.
London SW1**

You are invited
to the opening
reception

Private View

08 March 2005 6.30 — 8.30pm

The Economist Building provides the
only outdoor public exhibition space
in Central London committed to a
continuous programme of sculptural
works by contemporary artists.

The Economist **Sculpture Space invitation**
Value and Service
2004–06

Type
Neuzeit, Belwe

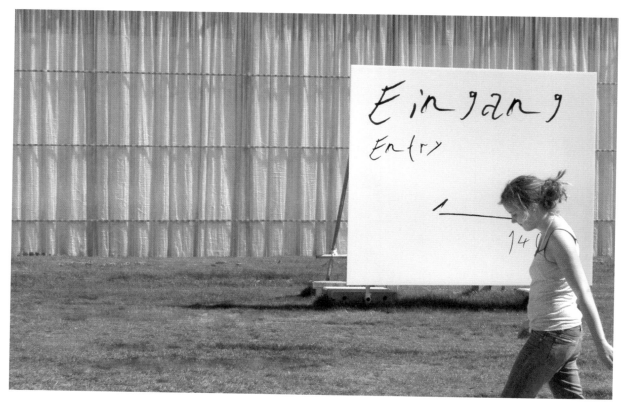

documenta 12 exhibition signage
Vier5
2010

Type
Custom made lettering

***documenta 12* exhibition signage**
Vier5
2010

Type
Custom made lettering

Time Out
London
LONDON'S WEEKLY LISTINGS BIBLE
JULY 13-20 2005
No.1821 £2.50
OUR
CITY
LONDON CARRIES ON

Time Out London
Micha Weidmann Studio
2005

Type
Franklin Gothic

Time Out London
Micha Weidmann Studio
2005

Type
Handmade

A GEAGULL FLYING, ACROSS MORECAMBE BAY, THOUGH "IT'S LO

Morecambe Bay, a seaside town in Lancashire, is a mecca for bird-watchers, as well as the migratory birds they come to observe. As part of a series of ornithological public artworks aimed at reviving interest in the resort, Andy Altman of Why Not Associates, with sculptors Gordon Young and Russell Coleman, created a 300m(984ft)-long path of bird-related poems, quotations, lyrics, nursery rhymes and sayings, from the new station, past two car parks to the Midland Hotel on the seafront.

The words are engraved, cut and cast into steel, stone, concrete, bronze and brass. All the lettering is in typefaces by Eric Gill, whose carvings adorn the refurbished Midland Hotel.

A Flock of Words
Why Not Associates
2003

Type
All fonts by Eric Gill

A Flock of Words
Why Not Associates
2003

Type
All fonts by Eric Gill

Museum für Gestaltung Zürich exhibition poster
Cornel Windlin
2004

Type
Custom made lettering

Visiting and Revisiting Art, etcetera
Issue 13 — Summer 2008
Brooks Adams *on Boetti, Polke, Clemente & Taaffe* [p32] / Briony Llewellyn *on British Orientalist Paintings* [p40] / Max Kozloff, David Goldblatt, Juergen Teller *and others on Street and Studio Photography* [p48] / Claire Daigle *on Cy Twombly* [p62] / Alfred Weidinger *&* Herbert Lachmayer *on Gustav Klimt* [p70] / Wilfried Dickhoff *on Marcel Broodthaers* [p84] / Eric Fernie *&* John Onians *on Neuroarthistory* [p86] / *In the Studio: John Baldessari* [p98] / David Lewis *on Ben Nicholson* [p102] — *Plus: MicroTate* [p106] / Hari Kunzru *on King Mob* [p110]

TATE ETC.

9 771743 885001

13 >

Price £5
Printed in the UK
www.tate.org.uk/tateetc

Ernst Klimt
Young Couple in the Garden (Paolo and Francesca) (c. 1890)
Oil on canvas
125 × 95 cm

Philip Taaffe
Untitled (2003)
Pigment on paper
28.5 × 37.5 cm

Richard Prince
Detail of *Untitled (couple)* (1977)
Ektacolour photograph
51 × 61 cm

TATE ETC. magazine (issue 13)
Cornel Windlin
2008

Type
Custom made lettering

VideoEx festival poster
Martin Woodtli
2003

Type
Custom made lettering

Index

Picture Credits

Items in bold refer to page numbers.

9, 12 The Beinecke Rare Book and Manuscript Library, Yale University; **11r** courtesy www.p22.com; **15** Monotype; **16** © DACS 2015; **17a** © 1935 Benno Schwabe & Co, Basel, used with permission. Image courtesy Felix Wiedler, www.wiedler.ch; **17b** reproduced with permission from Penguin Books Ltd; **18** Museum für Gestaltung Zürich, poster collection; **20** © 1957 Niggli Verlag, Teufen, used with permission. Image courtesy Felix Wiedler, www.wiedler.ch; **21l** © Niggli Verlag, Teufen, 1981. Image courtesy Niggli Verlag © DACS 2015; **21r** images Ralf Metzger via Flickr © DACS 2015; **22** Gift of Armin Hofmann. Digital image, The Museum of Modern Art, New York/Scala, Florence; **23** Gift of the Swiss Commercial Extension Office, Lausanne. Digital image, The Museum of Modern Art, New York/Scala, Florence; **24a** HfG Archiv, Ulm, courtesy Florian Aicher; **24b** courtesy and © Hyphen Press; **25a & b** photos courtesy the authors; **26a** this edition © 1956 Vintage/Random House, used with permission; **26b, 27, 28, 30** The Herb Lubalin Study Center; **29l** cover of *Common Worship: Services and Prayers for the Church of England* designed by Derek Birdsall RDI is reproduced by kind permission of Church House Publishing, Official Publisher of the Church of England, and is © The Archbishops' Council 2000; **29r** reproduced with permission from Penguin Books Ltd; **31a & b** Poster Museum at Wilanow, Division of the National Museum in Warsaw; **32** Milton Glaser Collection, Milton Glaser Design Study Center and Archives, Visual Arts Foundation; **33a** Gift of Keith Godard. Digital image, The Museum of Modern Art, New York/Scala, Florence; **33b** Alan Fletcher Archive; **34a** Albertina, Vienna; **34b** Nederlands Fotomuseum © Ed van der Elsken; **35a** Condé Nast; **35b** Stone Type Foundry; **36a** used with the permission of Brody Associates; **36b** *Fuse* is published by TASCHEN; **37a** 8vo; **37b** designed by 8vo, published by EightFiveZero. Editors M Burke, S Johnston, M Holt, H Muir. Photos courtesy Idea Magazine; **39** Emigre; **40** *Tibor Kalman: Perverse Optimist* © 1998 published by Booth-Clibborn Editions, used with permission; **43** Typothèque, photo by Peter Bil'ak; **45** 3D Systems; **46a & b** General Motors; **48** Julia UK; **49** reproduction by Commercial Type in collaboration with Dino Sanchez, New York, 2011, featuring Marian by Paul Barnes. Photograph by Paúl Rivera; **53** © 2010 Khatt Books, cover illustration by Naji El Mir; book design by Studio Carvalho Bernau; photograph by Edo Smithsuijzen; **55** courtesy of the artists and Greene Naftali, New York; **56** The Riklis Collection of McCrory Corporation. Digital image, The Museum of Modern Art, New York/Scala, Florence © DACS 2015; **57a** courtesy of the artists and Lisson Gallery, London; **57b** © David Shrigley. Courtesy David Shrigley and Stephen Friedman Gallery; **58** © Martin Creed. Courtesy of the artist and Hauser and Wirth, London, photo by Hugh Glendinning; **59** courtesy of the artist and Hauser and Wirth, London; **60** courtesy Benesse Art Site, Naoshima, photo Mitsumasa Fujitsuka © 2015 Bruce Nauman/Artists Rights Society (ARS), New York,

and DACS, London; **61** courtesy White Cube via deSingel, Antwerp; **62–3** courtesy of the artist and Greene Naftali, New York; **64** courtesy Moved Pictures Archive, New York City © 2015 Lawrence Weiner/ARS, New York and DACS, London; **65** courtesy of the artist, photo Christie's Images, London/Scala, Florence; **66** MBG#4057 © Barbara Kruger, courtesy Mary Boone Gallery, New York; **67** courtesy of the artist; **68** reproduction with permission of the Corita Art Center, Immaculate Heart Community, Los Angeles; photo by Joshua White; **69** courtesy of the artist and Simon Lee Gallery, London & Hong Kong.

Laurence King Publishing would like to thank all the designers and their studios, named in the main section of the book, who have kindly supplied examples of their work for inclusion in this book. Copyright for all material belongs to the designers and their studios. Additional credits are as follows.

75–77 © ADAGP, Paris and DACS, London 2015; **78–79** photos: Dominic Tschudin; **84–85** concept: Ludovic Balland Typography Cabinet. Book A designed in conjunction with Ivan Weiss; B with Jonas Oehrli; C with Toru Wada; **86** cover art direction by Kelsey Blackwell and Brian Morgan, The Walrus; **90–91** © 2002 Sony Music, courtesy of Risky Folio, cover photo: Markus Klinko; **92–93** graphic design: Nick Bell; curated by the Science Museum, London; lead consultant: Casson Mann (3D exhibition design); programming: Immersion Studios, Toronto; photos: Andreas Schmidt; **94–97** courtesy Top Publishers BV. **94** Photo of Raf Simons: Willy Vanderperre, stylist: Olivier Rizzo, **95a, 96a** photos: Daniel Riera, styling: Simon Foxton, Bernat Sobrebals; **95b, 96b** photos: Zoë Ghertner, styling: Sam Logan, Haidee Findlay-Levin; **97** photo of Phoebe Philo: David Sims, stylist: Camilla Nickerson; **98** © 2009 Dreck Records; **100** © ADAGP, Paris and DACS, London 2015; **104–105** courtesy Pentagram and Yale University School of Architecture; **106–107** courtesy Typothèque; **110–111** courtesy Wiels Contemporary Art Centre, Brussels; **112–113** published © 2010 University of Amsterdam Press BV; **114–115** courtesy Kulturrestaurant Parterre, Basel; **116** published by Concrete Hermit; **117** printed by Adams of Rye, East Sussex; **118–119** City ID and Cartlidge Levene; **122–123** art direction and design: Susana Carvalho and Kai Bernau, website implementation: Systemantics, courtesy De Zaak Nu; **124–125** design: José Albergaria & Rik Bas Backer; client: Lille 3000; architect: Franklin Azzi; photos © DR and Change is Good; **126** Austin designed by Paul Barnes with Berton Hasebe & Ilya Ruderman 2007–11; Dala Floda: Paul Barnes, 2010; Giorgio & Graphik: Christian Schwartz 2008-9; Guardian Egyptian: Paul Barnes & Christian Schwartz with Berton Hasebe 2009–1012; Lyon: Kai Bernau, 2009–10; Marian: Paul Barnes, 2012; Platform: Berton Hasebe, 2010; Publico: Paul Barnes & Christian Schwartz with Kai Bernau & Ross Milne 2010; Stag: Christian Schwartz with Berton Hasebe & Ross Milne, 2008-9; **128–129** design: Pepijn Zurburg, Richard van der Laken; **131ar** designed in conjunction with Will Holder; **131br** illustrations: Tamara Shopsin; **132** The Druid King by Norman Spinrad © 2003 and used by permission of Alfred A Knopf, a division of Random House, Inc; **134–135** © 2013 Spector Books, Leipzig; **136** © 2010 Phaidon Press; **137** © 2007 Phaidon Press; **138–139** with thanks to Eye magazine; **140–141** courtesy Danish Society for Patient Safety; **143** © Museum of Contemporary Art, Chicago; **144–145** commissioned by the Walker Art Center and the Cooper-Hewitt National Design Museum; **148–149** © 2009 Sony Music; **152-153** courtesy Sydney Dance Company; **154** 60th Anniversary Limited Edition © 2006 published by Penguin Classics; **155** © 2004–2008 published by Fuel; **156** © 2012 Granta; **157** © 2003 Phaidon Press; **158–159** © 2012

Spector Books, Leipzig; **160** published by JRP| Ringier; **163** © 2012 Yale University Press; **164–165** exhibition design by Casson Mann, courtesy Science Museum, London; **166–167** photos: Nigel Shafran; **168–169** courtesy and © 2002–2010 Phaidon Press; texts © Thomas Amman Fine Art AG, images of works by Andy Warhol © the Andy Warhol Foundation for the Visual Arts, Inc; **172–175** HORT, 2010, Bauhaus Dessau Foundation. Poster series includes images by Ola Kolehmainen; **178–179** images © 2007 Swiss Dots Ltd; **183** photos: Jim Goldberg; **184–185** design: Valerio di Lucente, Erwan Lhuissier, Hugo Timm; **186–187** design: Jan Wilker, Hjalti Karlsson; **188-189** © 2008-11 Sternberg Press; **190** words: Scott King & Earl Brutus; **191** photo: Jonathan de Villiers; **196** photo of Rihanna: Inez & Vinoodh/Trunk Archive; **197 top** photos: Max von Treu; **204–205** Hektor developed in collaboration with Uli Franke; **206–207** courtesy Design Miami; **208–209** Issue 74 in collaboration with Enrico Bravi; issues 71 and 83 with Aagje Martens. Published by NAi 010 Uitgevers (Publishers), Rotterdam © DACS 2015; **210–211** additional design: Rafa Roses & Pedro Ponciano at Studio Grafica; **212–213** © 2013 published by Vintage, a division of Alfred A Knopf; **216** courtesy Time Out Ltd; **219** © 2009 published by Yale University Press in association with the San Francisco Museum of Modern Art and the Norton Museum of Art ; **222–223** www.abc-xyz.co.uk; **224–5** courtesy Four Corners Books, photo Michael Harvey; **227** © 2005 Hatje Cantz Verlag; **234–235** reproduced with permission from Penguin Books Ltd; **240–243** © Guardian News & Media Ltd 2005. Design: Mark Leeds, Richard Turley, Michael Booth, Sarah Habershon; type design: Paul Barnes, Christian Schwartz; Guardian iPad design: Andy Brockie, Barry Ainslie; project manager Jonathon Moore; lead developer Martin Redington; **244–5** courtesy SALT, Istanbul; **246–249** design: Richard The & Joe Shouldice for Deitch Projects; **250** reprinted by permission of Beacon Press, Boston; **251** © 2012 Scribner, an imprint of Simon & Schuster; **252** © 2001 Polygram Records; **253** © 2005 London Records; **256, 257** Museum für Gestaltung Zürich, poster collection; **260–261** © Fundación Proa; **262** for Palau Robert; **263** design by Astrid Stavro & Ana Domínguez © 2008 Ediciones de la Central and Reina Sofía Museum, Madrid; **264–265** Moderna Museet, Stockholm. Project partners: Henrik Nygren Design, Greger Ulf Nilson, Thomas Eriksson Architects, Marge Arkitekter (MM Stockholm), Tham & Videgård Arketekter (MM Malmö); **268–269** © 2011 Violette Editions; **270** Mert Alas and Marcus Piggott/LOVE © The Conde Nast Publications Ltd; handwritten lettering by Stuart Spalding and Stefania Tomasello; **271** Mert Alas and Marcus Piggott/LOVE © The Conde Nast Publications Ltd; creative direction and design: Lee Swillingham and Stuart Spalding; **274–5** courtesy Museum Boijmans van Beuningen; **275b** photo Maurice Boyer; **278–279** design: Conny Freyer, Sebastien Noel, Eva Rucki; photos © Troika 2010, used courtesy Victoria and Albert Museum, London; **282–283** courtesy Bloomberg Business; **284–285** architect: Jockers Architekten bda; photos: Andreas Körner; client: Staatliches Baumanagement Osnabrück; **290–291** courtesy Time Out Ltd; **292–293** photos: Why Not Associates; **294** Museum für Gestaltung Zürich, poster collection; **295** courtesy and © Tate Etc, published by Tate Publishing, a division of Tate Enterprises; **296** www.woodt.li